A Practical Guide to X Window Programming

Developing Applications with the Xt Intrinsics and OSF/Motif™

A Practical Guide to X Window Programming

Developing Applications with the Xt Intrinsics and OSF/Motif™

Brian J. Keller

CRC Press
Boca Raton Ann Arbor Boston

Library of Congress Catalog Card Number 90-81308

Direct all inquiries to CRC Press, Inc., 2000 Corporate Blvd., N.W., Boca Raton, Florida, 33431

International Standard Book Number 0-8493-7406-5
Printed in the United States of America

Once in a lifetime a person comes along
and really makes a difference in another person's life.
This book is dedicated to the person who made
that difference in mine.

To Kim

Contents

Preface

Application development is the art of filling erratic requests for unusual system requirements in a "need it yesterday" mode from end users. Many who ". . . choose to accept this mission" are confronted with rapid technological changes that must be kept up with (if not for technological curiosity, then simply because "that's the way to go"). For many, the X Window System has become "the way to go."

When X was first introduced, the documentation was limited to manuals and "overview" documents. For those of us who started with X early on these were a blessing, but learning how to create X clients was not easy or straightforward. There were few examples and hardly any books that could explain the details of X Window programming. This lack of a text spawned the idea to create a book that would cover the details, with sufficient practical examples so that the army of application writers who wanted to develop applications could do so without too much pain.

To start, this book is not an Xlib book. Xlib is much too low-level for application writers. Instead, this book addresses the layer of development referred to as the *Xt Intrinsics*. This is a higher level of interaction with the X Window System than Xlib. It is based on a notion called *object-oriented programming*, and can greatly increase your productivity as you develop X Window clients. This book is a practical guide to Xt, and can be used as a source for application examples. It covers topics that are useful to the many application programmers who need education in developing with the Intrinsics.

The audience for this book is anyone who wants to develop Xt-based X Window clients. It is written with the end-user application writer in mind, so the style is straightforward and direct. No complicated, technically confusing, "beat around the bush" verbage! The assumption is that the reader is not creating four-dimensional cyberspace artifical-reality applications. Instead, the reader develops applications that are based on end-user requests (those erratic "need it yesterday" specifications). These people have little time to discuss "byte splitting" or the challenges involved in piping instructions to UNIX utilities. They need answers now.

As a practical guide, this book continually builds on knowledge as it is acquired. Chapter 1 begins with the history of X, so that you have an idea where it all started. Chapter 2 is a fundamentals section that covers some important points in the C language that you need to be comfortable with before starting Xt programming. This chapter also includes Window System basics, event-driven programming, and object-oriented programming concepts.

Chapter 3 is a basic introduction to Xt and the notion of widgets. Chapter 4 discusses several Xlib details that Xt application writers should be aware of, including graphic contexts, font handling and naming, color allocation, and textual display. Chapter 5 is the core part of the book. It uses several examples to discuss all of the major components of the Xt Intrinsics (resource gathering, command-line parsing, event handling, translations, etc.).

Chapter 6 is a detailed look at primitive widgets. This is accomplished through the construction of a useful "field editor" widget. This widget is integrated into a character-oriented application later in the book.

Chapter 7 is a basic overview of container widgets.

Chapter 8 looks into the details of designing Xt applications. It demonstrates the use of several widgets for constructing interface components including pop-up menus, pop-up option lists, command buttons, entry fields (using the widget from Chapter 6), and help facilities. There are also sections that cover keyboard traversal and ways to streamline development.

Chapter 9 introduces the commercial application environment called Motif provided by the Open Software Foundation (OSF). The chapter explores, at a high level, the various widgets and how to work with or customize the Motif Window Manager (mwm). Some clients are developed to demonstrate the use of the Motif widgets, including a client that demonstrates the mixing of widget sets (Athena and Motif).

Chapter 10 shows how to port the application developed in Chapter 8, making it a Motif-compliant application. This chapter demonstrates pop-up help, pull-down menus, push buttons, text widget, field editing, keyboard traversal, and two kinds of help mechanisms.

Finally, Chapter 11 discusses some of the advanced topics in the Intrinsics. These topics include interclient communication, selection mechanisms in Xt, and controlling multiple displays with the same client.

Technical books for the most part are not much fun. The style is often esoteric, dry, and sometimes boring. From the beginning, I intended this project to be different. I think the reader should enjoy the time spent reading. After all, you're taking the time out of a busy schedule to read this book. Why not enjoy yourself and learn at the same time? If I've done my job right, you'll have a few laughs and learn quite a bit.

Acknowledgments

As we go through life, we seldom get a chance to publicly acknowledge those who have had some influence on what we do. This book could not have been possible if it weren't for a few individuals whose actions in one way or another made the dream of writing into a reality.

Vincent G. Alonzi has been a friend and colleague for quite some time. As a friend, he has made many a day very entertaining (*I believe you still owe me two dozen bagels?*), and as a colleague, every new job an adventure (*Who could forget Trevose, PA?*). It was his "Psst, gotta job for you at . . ." that triggered the idea for this book. His thoughtful review and suggestions have greatly helped me in this effort. (*Can you actually believe it's done?*)

Bennie Larrier has helped me in ways neither he nor I can understand. I don't know many who would put themselves on the line to get someone an opportunity like he did for me.

Paul Kavanaugh acted as the "network node" that brought this book to a real publisher. His "It's good . . . . A bit too folksy for a Brit" made me realize that I actually did hit the mark.

Alan Rose is the man behind the scenes. He gave me a chance, bought me some lunch, got me the loaned computer, and gave me all the time I needed. Alan, thanks!

Hal Remish made the IBM PS/2 Model 70 (the development platform for all clients in this book) available. I'm sure when he gave it to me he thought it would be back shortly. Thanks, Hal, for understanding the delays.

Thanks to all the folks who had anything to do with creating and maintaining the X Window System. If it weren't for their hard work and dedication to bringing their dreams to realities, mine would not exist. The world needs more of you.

Lastly, Kimberly A. Lanning provided me with my inspiration. From the day I met her I knew she was someone special. Her patience and understanding during this long process has made me realize just how special she really is, and how lucky I am to have her in my life. Thanks, Honey. I love you.

Brian J. Keller

1

Introduction

This chapter provides you with a brief history of the X Window System (also called just *X*), its architecture, a discussion of Xlib, and reasons why Xt is better suited than Xlib for most application development.

1.1. A Brief History of X

X started as a research project driven by the need to create a hardware-independent display mechanism for Project Athena. Project Athena is a major research project being conducted at the Massachusetts Institute of Technology (MIT) to advance the state of technology for distributed systems. This project is heavily financed by International Business Machines (IBM) and the Digital Equipment Corporation (DEC).

The original system was designed by Robert Scheifler, Ron Newman, and Jim Getty. It borrowed some design ideas from a window system created at Stanford University called W. The current release, X11, has been worked on by thousands, and is still being improved as we all start to use it.

X was developed to provide a distributed mechanism to run applications (referred to as *clients*) across a network on a variety of hardware platforms. The developers focused on providing highly portable code, so that the system could be implemented on micros (IBM PCs), minis (MicroVaxes), workstations (IBM Risc System 6000, Sun Sparc), and supercomputers (Cray). The system had to be able to run under several operating environments and provide high performance. And, in keeping with open systems concepts, X had to be free from user interface policy.

The ability of X to run on and across different platforms makes it perhaps one of the most innovative technologies to be developed in computing in recent years. And for this very reason, major vendors (IBM, AT&T, DEC, HP, and Sun) have embraced X as their display standard for advanced workstations.

1.2. The X Window System Architecture

1.2.1. Client-Server

The X architecture is based on a *client-server relationship*. The server (called the *X server*) is responsible for the display. A display is considered an *X station* (a computer that runs the X server) with one or more CRT, keyboard, and mouse (or other pointing device). A single instance of an X server is called a *display*; therefore, a display (CRT) may have multiple displays by running multiple X servers, as shown in Figure 1-1.

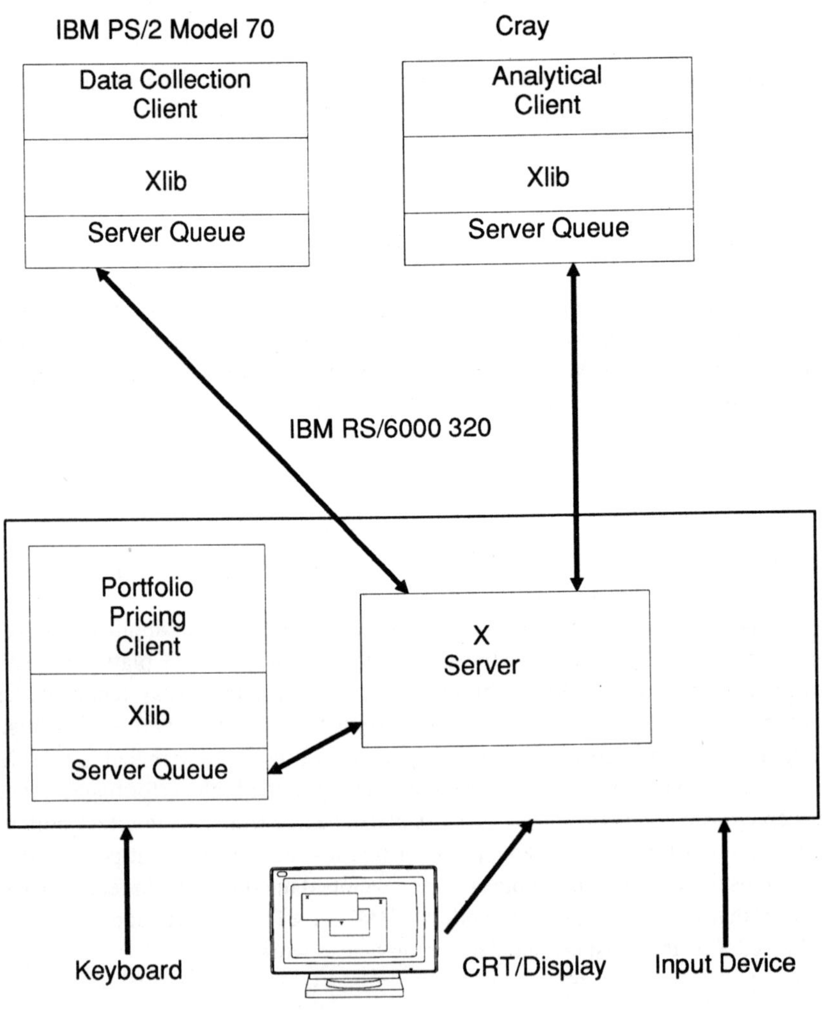

Figure 1-1 Client-server model.

X is a network windowing system that allows a client to run on either the server host or any other host on the network. The server sends and receives display information (i.e., screen-writing commands, keyboard hits, or mouse movements). This capability implies that a single display station could have numerous clients from all over the network sending messages to it. An IBM PS/2 could have a client running on a Cray, another running on an IBM Risc System 6000, and still another locally. This is truly a distributed processing capability.

1.2.2. X Server Responsibilities

The server is responsible for five tasks:

1. Providing multi-client access.
2. Receiving and understanding client messages.
3. Sending user responses in the form of messages to the clients.
4. Performing all drawing.
5. Storing and maintaining data structures for limited resources (color maps, cursors, fonts, and graphic information known as "graphics context").

As we mentioned before, the X server can handle client requests over a network. This provides for the distributed nature of network computing. It is now feasible to connect several processor classes in your network to handle specific applications. What this really means is that additional computing power can be added incrementally, allowing for a more controlled increase in a site's computing power.

When clients make requests to the server, the server must be able to decipher what is being requested. The X server acts like a dispatcher directing traffic in a city, who receives a request and must determine what the request is for. Based on the requirements of the request, he must decide which type of vehicle to use: a cab, a van, or a bus? The X server acts in a similar fashion. It must figure out what drawing or action it should take based on the request received, and then take action accordingly.

One of the primary tasks that the X server provides is the control of input and output functions. Whenever a key is pressed, the server must determine which client should be informed of it, if any. Similarly, when the mouse is moved the server must inform one or more clients.

As a way of improving performance, the X server has the responsibility of performing all drawing that the clients request. So, when a client intends to draw a line or a character of text, it makes a request to the server, and the server performs all the necessary steps for generating the graphics. This greatly improves performance since the client need not be concerned about the "how" of drawing. Additionally, the X server maintains the resources required for generating the graphics.

Fonts, colors, window coordinates, and other graphical pieces of information are the kinds of resources stored by the server. These data items are given identification codes by the server so that clients may refer to them. This makes more sense than sending an entire graphics structure with large amounts of information over a network. By doing it this way, X reduces the network traffic and leaves bandwidth for other messages.

1.2.3. Window Management

X was developed as a generic mechanism for providing display capabilities in a network environment. MIT did not enforce a particular style for user presentation; rather, they provided a way of creating such display policies. One inclusion that is different from other window systems is the separation of window management (i.e., moving, iconifying, resizing) from the client.

The window manager is the "ruler" of the screen (see Figure 1-2). It is responsible for informing its windows about policy. The X Window System does not commit to any particular window manager. It was felt that the vendors who supported X would provide their own. This is demonstrated by the inclusion of a window manager for OSF/Motif as well as AT&T XWIN (Open Look) interface kits.

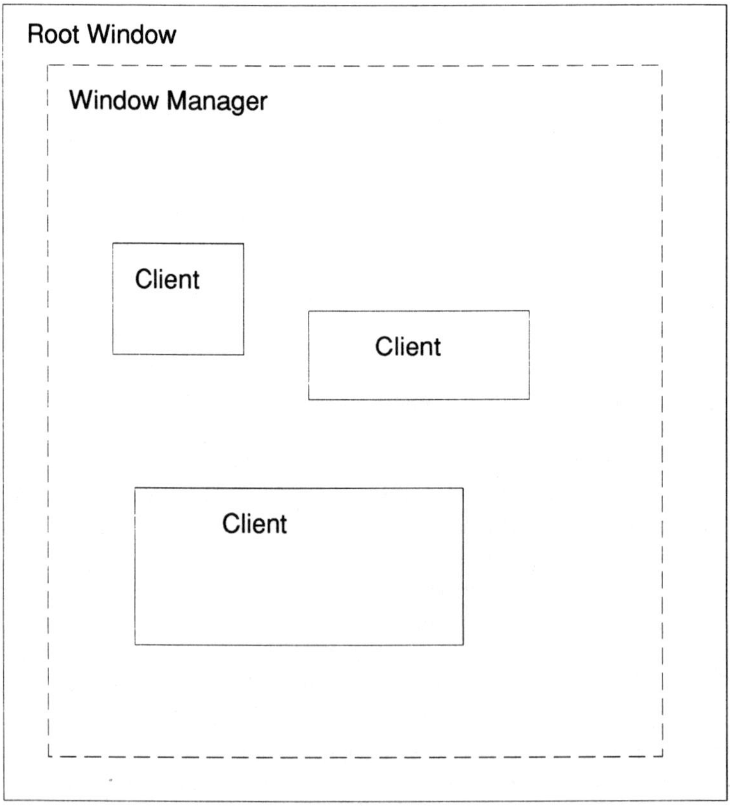

Figure 1-2 Window manager in X.

The window manager has the right to enforce anything it wants with respect to screen layout, overriding any and all client requests for space. It might elect to move windows to make room for others, or it might inform the client that it can only be a fraction of the size requested.

The notion that a requested window size may not be granted is significant to application writers. Take great care in designing applications so as to eliminate any dependency on a particular window manager's style. Your applications must be able to cooperate with any window manager, and also without one. Noting this early will save you a lot of time in the future.

1.2.4. X Protocol

I stated earlier that X has its own protocol. A *protocol* is nothing more than an agreed-upon form of communication. In the X world, this is accomplished via *network packets* (chunks of information). There are four kinds of packets that exist in X: events, replies, requests, and errors.

Events are things like a keyboard press, a mouse movement, or a screen update. Just like in the real world, events can happen at any time. Clients must be ready and able to cope with this. The client will never be able to know for sure if it has to respond to a keystroke or to repaint itself. In order to accommodate this, the client must inform the server of the events it cares about, and then provide processing for when the event is reported. (This is discussed in greater detail in a later section of this book.)

Requests are generated by a library function (Xlib) and sent to the server. A request packet might contain drawing information, or perhaps a question about a specific window. When the request is for locally stored information, it quite obviously does not have to go through the server. Otherwise, the request is passed to the server where it is acted on and a reply is sent.

Replies emanate from the server to Xlib only when a previous Xlib request was for server-based information. This situation is considered a round-trip, and as might be inferred, is quite costly. After all, the client pays the price for the request and must also pay for the reply. Considering the network framework, this could be quite substantial if the client makes many requests.

Errors are also sent by the server to Xlib. Xlib has two kinds of error-handlers: recoverable and fatal. The error is not sent to the client until the client-server connection is flushed (typically when an event is read). The reason for this latency in error reporting is due to a design consideration. Since X is network based, and it is more efficient to send chunks of data across a network, the designers chose to have the server queue up events and errors while the client queues up requests. The server gives the server queue to the client when the client initiates the transaction. At that time the client gives the server its queue.

1.3. The X Programming Interface — Xlib

All clients eventually will use Xlib. This is true if you write using straight Xlib or a higher level library like Xt. As stated earlier, Xlib translates the request into a network packet to be sent to the server.

As shown in Figure 1-3, Xlib is the lowest level that an application writer can use for creating X-based clients. The functions that make up Xlib perform everything that any client could possibly need. This includes things such as opening and closing the display, getting a particular font or color, drawing a line, drawing text, creating and destroying a window, getting user defaults, and parsing the command line.

The library is rich with functions and is currently being expanded to include extensions for 3-D drawing as well as Display PostScript. In any event, the technique for creating an X-based client is the same in all cases, and the process can be rather lengthy.

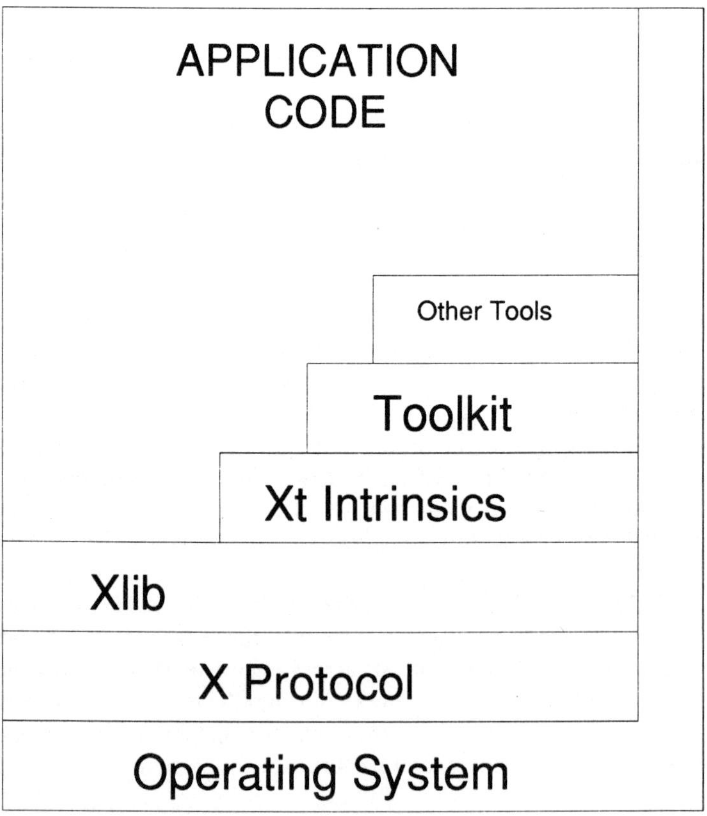

Figure 1-3 X programming layers.

1.4. Reasons for Using Xt Over Xlib

As any developer knows, a set of routines that perform the same task and are gathered into a library is invaluable. After all, who wants to write the same tired code all the time? If you were an Xlib developer, you would have to rewrite window-creation and resource-gathering routines for *every* client. Also, event-handling is not as intuitive in Xlib as it is in Xt. Lastly, the number of lines of code in an Xt client can be far less than the same one written using Xlib.

When X was first introduced, a basic toolkit was provided. It was a collection of routines that created display elements like scroll bars, command buttons, and text editing mechanisms. The writer simply had to invoke these convenience routines to create a window and add the functionality for a scroll bar. At this level, an application writer would find it easier to develop interfaces, and this would be the level most application writers prefer.

When the protocol changed from X10 to X11, the developers of X took the opportunity to re-create the toolkit. They did this by providing an objective approach to building interface components. This included the Intrinsics as mechanisms for using interface components and Athena widgets as samples of how to write them.

Xt is *not* a set of widgets, rather it is a style of programming. It defines how a widget must be written and how applications must use them, but it does not in itself provide a particular widget set. The Athena widget set (Xaw) has been provided as a model for application writers to get a feel for developing with and creating new widgets. Most vendors provide these widgets as samples, and for that reason they are used in many of the examples found in this book.

So why bother with widgets if you can create clients with Xlib? The reason is quite simple: widgets are easy to use (if documented correctly), and can eliminate many redundant steps that all X clients must perform. Also, Xt-based clients are easier to write, especially when the interface becomes complex. Lastly, the code savings is tremendous. This is due to the objective mechanisms that Xt employs (you'll see why as you read on).

1.5. Why a Practical Guide?

Anyone who has attempted to write applications without samples is a true pioneer, and deserves a tip of the cap. For the rest of us, an example goes a long way in aiding understanding. Most everyone I have ever developed with found that source code was the key to their success as developers. I must point out, though, that while having examples is great, they are simply a possible solution, not the only one. You are encouraged to use the techniques in this book, but you should also search for new and perhaps more efficient ways of doing things.

This book demonstrates the majority of topics that application writers need to address when they begin to write their own interfaces. Sure, you could do what I did to learn Xt. You would spend a lot of hours reading the pages of the Xt Intrinsics code along with the source from the widget sets (Athena and HP). You would attempt to use the MIT documents and search for examples over the network. You would go to lunch with one of the creators of the X11 Xt Intrinsics (Joel McCormack) and discuss the philosophy of the design of Xt. Finally, you would attend the X Technical Conference, purchase some Xlib books, and start to bang out code. In the end, you would finally be clear on how to write Xt-based clients.

I would recommend you save yourself some time and use this book. Believe me, you will get more out of this book than you realize. Enjoy!

2

Fundamentals: A Helpful Review for Understanding Xt

In order to get a foundation from which to build a better understanding of Xt, it is important to discuss a few concepts prior to diving in. This chapter is intended to get everyone on the same playing field.

2.1. Review of Structures and Pointers

If you haven't figured it out yet, let me tell you: C is the language used to program with Xt. For many an application programer this might cause a wince. After all, C can be a bit of a pain to deal with. It gives great flexibility to get at the low levels of the machine, but with that comes the ability to crash the system. (Has anybody ever crashed a system with a C program? Let's see a show of hands.)

Perhaps the most problematic part of the C language for many are these things called *pointers*. So, in an attempt to set you straight, let's discuss them for a bit.

A pointer is variable in the C language. Its sole purpose in life is to look at a place in the computer's memory. The thing a pointer holds is called an *address*. An address is simply a place in the computer's memory. You'll find the operating system, data, and programs loaded there.

In C there are a variety of data types. The usual are int (short and long), float, double, and char. Each of these can have an associated pointer type: int*, float*, double*, char*. For example, if you saw the following definition in a C program:

```
int x, *xp;
```

it would read "x is of type int and xp is of type pointer-to-int." This means that xp can contain the memory address of another variable that is of type int. The same holds true for float, double, and char.

To get a pointer to point at something, you must assign it the thing's memory address (see Figure 2-1). Recalling the earlier definition, you could have xp point to x by doing the following:

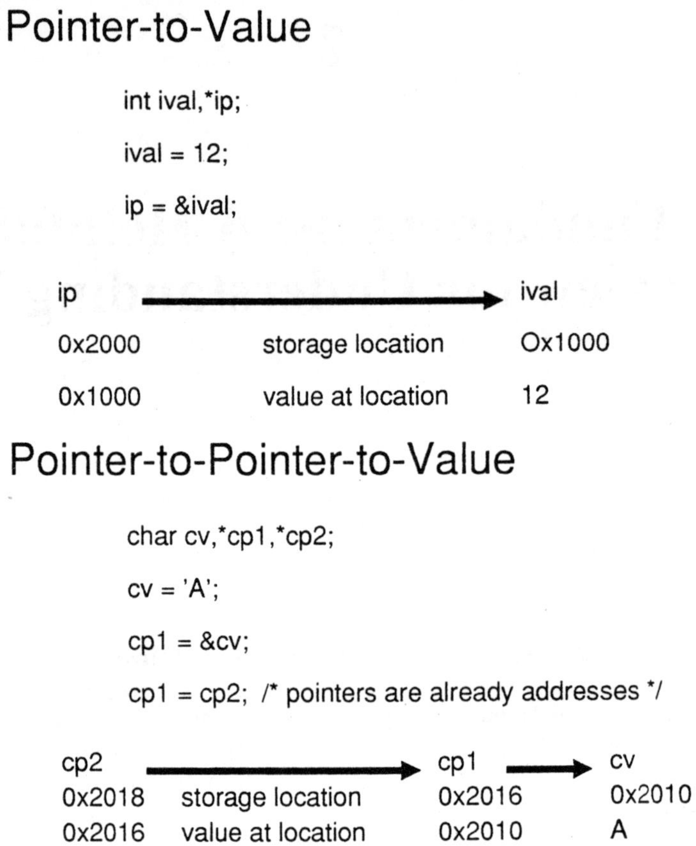

Figure 2-1 Pointer.

```
xp = &x;
```

This reads "assign the address of x to xp." Since xp is a pointer type, xp now looks at x.

Suppose you wanted to get the value that a pointer was looking at. How could you do that? It is pretty simple, actually. The C language provides the asterisk "*" as an operator for getting the value (not to be confused with multiplication or the definition of the pointer).

For example, suppose the code looked like the following:

```
int x = 2,*xp;
int q;
xp = &x;
```

and you wanted to assign the value in x to q. It would be easy to assign the value of x to q by simply saying

```
q = x;
```

but you are using pointers and would rather see how to do this using them. Therefore, to assign the value of x to q using the pointer xp, you write the following:

```
q = *xp;
```

This says "assign the value that xp is pointing at to q," so now q has the value 2. This really isn't so bad. Now that you think you feel good about pointers, just remember:

A Pointer is like 220 volts of electricity. If you don't ground it well, you could lose your life!

That is, pointers are fantastic when used with care, and very dangerous when they are not. Since they truly are memory addresses, you could be pointing to an area that is in the data space of another program — or anywhere else, for that matter. If you're not careful, eventually things will break and you'll either get that useful message, "Segmentation violation" (the OS cop is out to get you), or worse, your machine will start to reboot itself (the old pointer gremlin is at it again).

Now that you understand pointers better, let's look at another useful tool in C's arsenal: the structure. Just like the name implies, a structure gives you a way of placing data in a nice, neat, orderly manner.

If you have ever done database programming, you've come across structures when you defined records for the database. As an example, suppose you are interested in defining a structure for a trade (exchange of stocks or bonds) record. You know that the members would include security, trader id, buy/sell flag, quantity, and price. In C, this could look like the following:

```
struct {
     char       *security;
     char       *traderId;
     char       buy_or_sell;
     int        quantity;
     float      price;
} tradeRecord;
```

Another powerful feature of the C language is its ability to create new data types. This is accomplished using a *typedef* statement. Essentially, you can create a shorthand notation for a new storage class of your own. By far the most common use of the typedef statement is with a structure. For example, if you wanted to use the tradeRecord in other places in your program, you could create a typedef like this:

```
typedef struct _TradeRecord {
    char        *security;
    char        *traderId;
    char        buy_or_sell;
    int         quantity;
    float       price;
} TradeRecord;
```

You now have a new type called TradeRecord. With the new TradeRecord type you can go about defining some structures in your program.

```
TradeRecord Equity =
   {"IBM","BJK",'B',1000,100.25};

TradeRecord *PtrToIt;
PtrToIt = &Equity;
```

Now let's access some of the members:

```
printf("%s %c %d shares of %s at $ %f\n",
     Equity.trader,Equity.buy_or_sell,
     Equity.quantity, Equity.security,Equity.price);
```

This would print the following:

```
BJK B 1000 shares of IBM at $ 100.25
```

Notice that you used the "." (dot) operator to access the members. This is the way C gets to the members of structures when the structure variable is not a pointer type. Now let's use the pointer type PtrToIt to get the values:

```
printf("%s %c %d shares of %s at $ %f\n",
PtrToIt->trader,PtrToIt->buy_or_sell,
PtrToIt->quantity, PtrToIt->security,PtrToIt->price);
```

This would print the following:

```
BJK B 1000 shares of IBM at $ 100.25
```

Notice that you used the "->" (arrow) operator to access the members. This is the way C gets to the members of structures when the structure variable *is* a pointer type.

Since you are by now an expert at this, let's cover one last detail that is used heavily in Xt. This is the *opaque* pointer type. The opaque pointer type used in the Xt is "caddr_t" (changed to XtPointer in X11R4) and is defined as either "char *" or "void *" depending on the C compiler being used. The opaque pointer is allowed to assume the role of a pointer to int, pointer to float, or pointer to whatever, as in the following code fragment:

```
caddr_t     chameleon;
int          x = 2;
chameleon = &x;
printf("%d\n",*chameleon);
```

If this brief review of pointers and structures isn't enough, refer to one of the zillion books written on the C language. Or use the "default" book by Kerninghan and Richie (the second edition is quite good).

2.2. Window System Basics

In order to write applications for X, you should get a feel for some of the basic relationships that exist. X is built using a hierarchical window system termed a *window tree*. There will always be one *root* window. The root window always covers the entire display area, and all other windows are its descendants. Additionally, windows on the same level in the tree are called *siblings* while the parent of a child is called an *ancestor* to the child. This is shown in Figure 2-2.

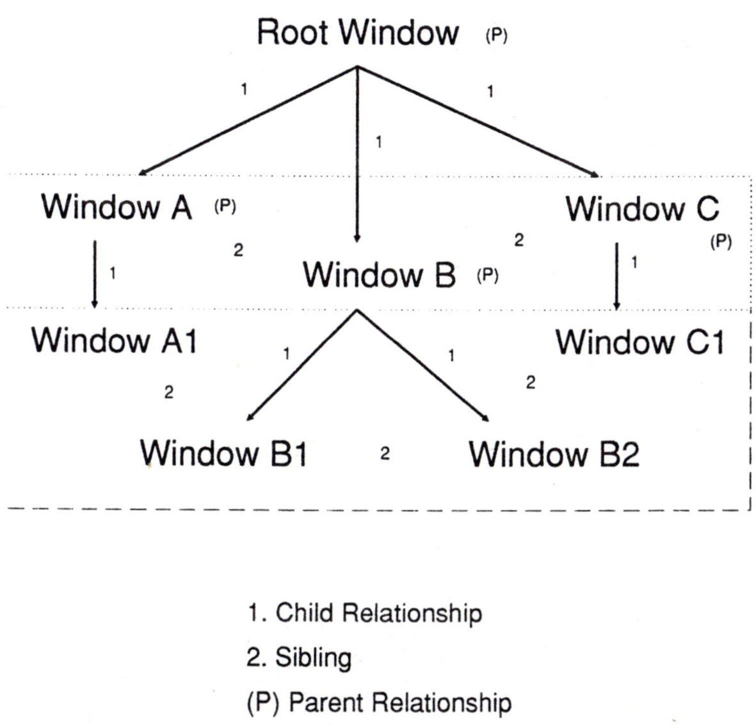

Figure 2-2 Parent/child/sibling.

An X window can be viewed as a "roundtangle" — usually, but not quite always, a rectangle. The reason for the new name is that for most of X's life all that programmers could get were rectangles. However, with X11R4, the folks at MIT incorporated a "shapes" extension, so windows need not be rectangular.

The upper-left corner of an X window is considered to be its origin (see Figure 2-3). The x-axis increases as you go left while the y-axis increases as you go down. All coordinates in X are relative, that is, from the window's point of view all things start at 0,0. If a window is created and is offset from the root window at 100,100 the root window's perspective of the child's origin is 100,100 while the child views it as 0,0.

The X server is where all windows live. Whenever a window is created, the application must ask the X server to do it. The server adds the newly created window to the window tree when the request is made. Once added, the client may request to be mapped and hence viewable by the user.

There are times when windows are mapped yet are not viewable. These situations occur for three reasons:

1. One of the ancestors is not mapped.
2. One window completely obscures another (as in window C of Figure 2-4).
3. When an ancestor completely clips a window.

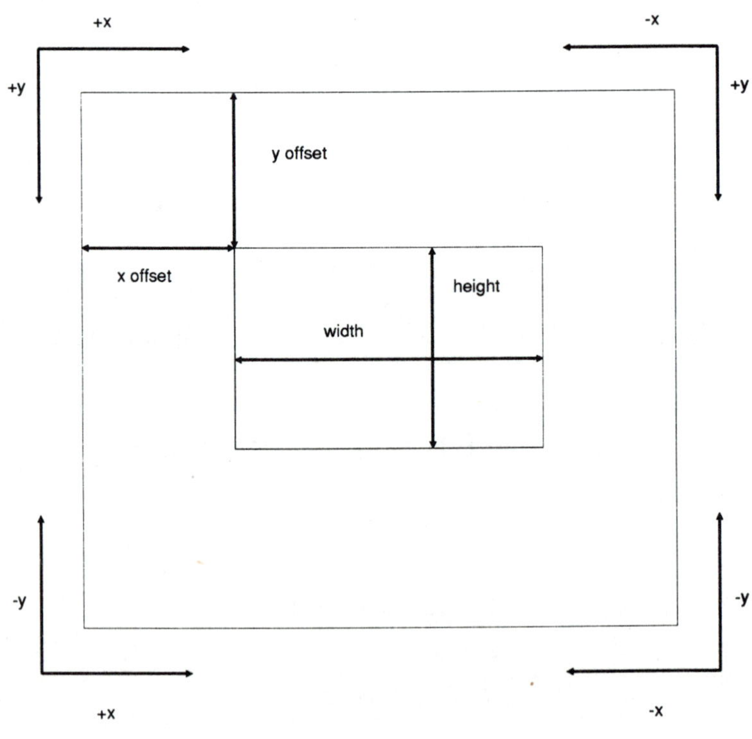

Figure 2-3 Window geometry.

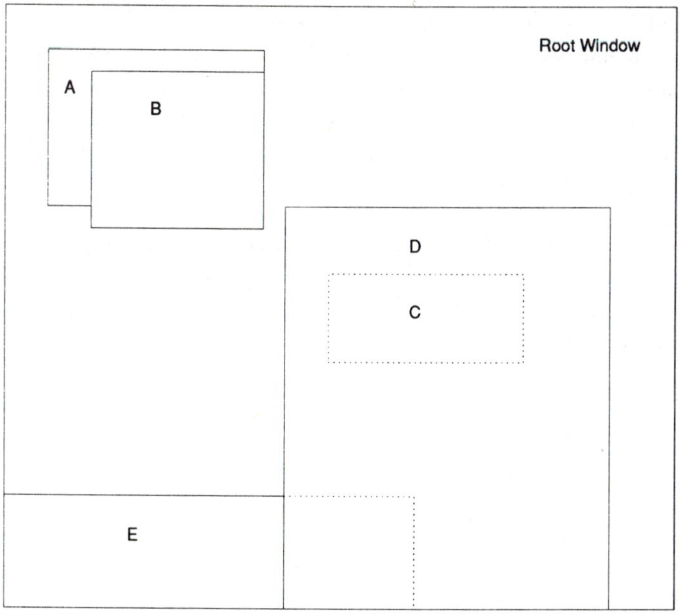

Figure 2-4 Window stacking/clipping.

If the ancestor isn't there, the child may be mapped, yet won't be visible. Only when all of its ancestors are mapped will the child have the chance to be visible.

When a larger window overshadows another, it makes sense that the user won't see the smaller one. This can be rectified by placing the smaller one higher in the stacking order. The *stacking order* is simply the way X views its windows. In this way, the little one gets recognized as being on top of the larger one, therefore obscuring a part of the larger (window B in Figure 2-4). You could view it as a deck of cards. If you wanted the card on the bottom of the deck, you would take it and move it to the top. The card that was on the top is now obscured (probably) by the one just placed on top.

If a child lies outside of its parents' boundaries, it will not be seen. As soon as the child comes back to the parents' boundaries, it will be viewable provided neither of the other two situations listed occurs.

2.3. Event-Driven Programming

X is an *asynchronous* system. This means that clients do not wait around for an answer from the server. Instead, the server and the client maintain queues of events that will be exchanged at various times (usually when the client "flushes" the queue).

This style is very different from earlier notions on developing applications. In the past, we would wait around for an activity to be complete (I can remember lots of loops waiting on keyboard entry). Not anymore! An application must be ready to address any event that its users care about. In order for the mouse to move, a keypress to register, or the window to be redrawn, the client must have asked and watched for any one or all of those events.

The mechanism we are talking about here is termed *event driven* and is a "don't call me, I'll call you" style of programming. Namely, you tell the server what you care about, and it will call you back when that thing you care about happens. In X, the clients tend to wait until the events they care about occur, then do something about them, then wait again. You will see this more when you start coding some examples.

2.4. Object-Oriented Programming

Xt is based on the notion of object-oriented programming (OOP). In the OOP world, there exist *objects* which are nothing more than data and ways of handling the data (called *methods*). These things called objects are self-contained. That

```
/* FILE:       sampleXt.c
 * PURPOSE: A very simple Xt base client.
 */

#include <X11/Intrinsic.h>
#include <X11/StringDefs.h>
main(argc,argv)
    int argc; char **argv;
{
    Arg arg[5]; int cnt;

    Widget top =
      XtInitialize(argv[0],"ThisClient",NULL,0,&argc,argv);

    cnt = 0;
    XtSetArg(arg[cnt],XtNlabel,"My Label"); cnt++;
    XtCreateWidget("label",labelWidgetClass,top,arg,cnt);

    XtRealizeWidget(top);
    XtMainLoop();

}
```

Figure 2-5 Sample Xt client.

means that if I had an editor object, it would contain all of the data needed to pull all of the editing, as well as all of the processing needed to deal with the data.

Objects are arranged in *classes* (types of objects). Classing allows objects to inherit things from superclasses. If you looked at it in a hierarchy, the superclass is the parent of the object. As the parent, it allows the child access to everything it owns (house, car). This leaves the child to concentrate on those things that the child cares about (going to school, listening to music). This implies that the child doesn't need to worry about too much (typical).

The idea behind OOP is to make life easier. By using objects, software is reusable, so you won't have to rewrite the same things over and over. The folks at MIT employed this concept with the introduction of X11 and called it Xt.

Xt implements the OOP style on top of X. It does this by using a C structure that contains both data and pointers to functions that operate on the data. Additionally, it provides for inheritance by having a class portion and defining procedures for dealing with the connections between structures (the Intrinsics). As we will shortly explore, the OOP style in Xt makes application development for X quite easy.

3

Xt Basics: An Introduction to Xt-based Widgets

This chapter covers the fundamentals of widgets based on the Xt Intrinsics. It discusses what a widget is, what makes up a widget, the basic widgets in the Xt Intrinsics, and a new concept called the windowless object (the OSF/Motif Gadget is an example of this).

3.1. What Is a Widget, Really?

For most of us, the term "widget" has been used to mean just about anything. In most college business textbooks you would find a case study on how many "widgets" the ACME Workstation Corporation could produce in one year in its Taiwan facility. And of course we all know what a "thing-a-ma-widget" is. In X, the phrase "widget" identifies a user-interface abstraction. Namely, a widget is a customizable X window that contains window attributes, operations, and window state data. Essentially, a widget encompasses all those things needed to create an X window of a specific type (such as a push button or scroll bar).

As you are probably aware, writing the same old code over and over again can get very tedious and quite boring. After all, we are application writers, and we should write application code. Well, widgets were created to rid you of that tedium and let you get to the business of developing applications.

Before we get into the structure of a widget, it is useful to point out the two types of programmers that exist in the Xt Intrinsic Domain: widget writers (WW) and client writers (CW). A widget writer cares how the widgets are structured. He or she is quite concerned about changes to the core elements of the widget. Client writers (in the ideal world) shouldn't really care about how a widget is written, they simply want to know how it behaves. This distinction is the way we would like to see things go, but Xt is yet to be an "ideal world," so it is fairly important for all Xt programmers to understand how widgets work.

If you're a client writer looking to skip to the next pages, stop for a moment. If you really want to write good clients, you should be very familiar with the way widgets are written. Case in point: When Xt first hit the street, it was "university grade." Some vendors snatched up the source for the Athena widgets and made "minor" changes. Those programmers who tried to write portable code would often find problems moving from machine to machine — especially when they had written new widgets that were subclasses of existing widgets.

3.2. Classes of Widgets

Xt is an object-oriented mechanism for creating X window clients. The architecture organizes its components (widgets) into classes as shown in Figure 3-1. Classes are nothing more than data and procedures (methods) that provide access to and enable you to operate on the data.

The fundamental or *meta-classes* defined by Xt are Core, Composite, and Constraint. Additionally, there exists a Shell class that has four public classes (Transient, Override, TopLevel, and Application). All widgets are subclasses of the CoreWidget.

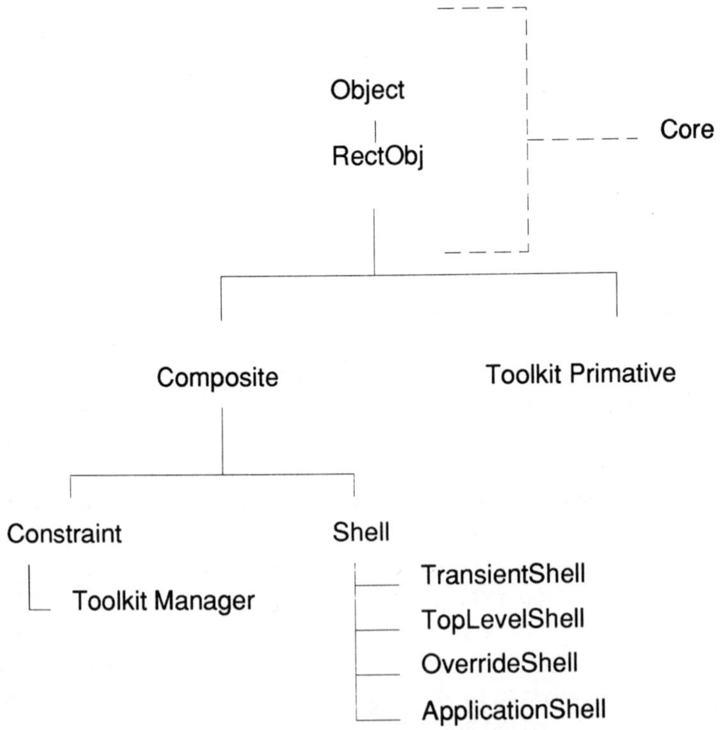

Figure 3-1 Xt widget classing.

This collection of widgets dictates the mechanism for the construction of subsequent widgets. Examples of widget sets that adhere to this protocol are the Athena, OSF/Motif, and AT&T XWIN (Open Look) widget sets. This book relies heavily on the Athena set because the source code is readily available. Additionally, the OSF/Motif set is used because it contains a rich set of widgets for developing applications.

Definitions of the protocol widgets are found in the three C header files CoreP.h, CompositeP.h, and ContraintP.h. They are explored in great detail later in this book.

3.3. The Components of a Widget

There are two parts to all widgets created using the Xt mechanism: the *instance* and the *class*. Each of these parts plays an important role in pulling off the magic of the Intrinsics. The class part defines those things that all widgets that are members of that class will use. Exposure handling, initialization, resizing, and resource setting are a few examples of methods or procedures that belong to the class part. In the instance part you find data specific to a particular widget's instance. The window id, the x and y offsets, and the border color are examples of instance resources.

3.3.1. The Class Part of a Widget

The class (ClassPart) is the thing that binds the mechanism together. It allows for inheritance of superclass methods and data via a pointer to the superclass's class record. Through this pointer, new widgets may use the superclass's code as if it were their own. This notion is quite powerful. It implies that writing new widgets can be simply a matter of adding a few things rather than rewriting the entire code.

In Chapter 2 you reviewed how pointers and structures work — a pointer is nothing more than a place in memory, an address. With this address you can peer into the actual locations to get and update the information stored there. Since a structure is nothing more than an organization of members in a contiguous block, if you have a pointer to a structure and the structure's definition, you can access each member. This is exactly what happens in the inheritance mechanism. The source of the Intrinsics and the well-defined approach insure that things work.

All widgets have at least the members in the ClassPart. If additional class information is required, the widget may add new fields by defining a "newWidgetClassPart" and chaining it to the end of the CoreClassPart (this is discussed in greater detail in Chapter 6). Note that there will be only one instance of the ClassPart for any number of created widgets. That is, if you had two buttons in your client that were of the same widget class, you would find a single occurrence (instance) of the class record, and multiple occurrences of the instance record. The reason is simple: the ClassPart is shared by all members of the class, while the instance record is specific to that occurrence of the widget. The following C code shows how the core ClassPart is defined. (Read on, it gets better.)

```
typedef struct _CoreClassPart {
     WidgetClass           superclass;
     String                class_name;
     Cardinal              widget_size;
     XtProc                class_initialize;
     XtWidgetClassProc     class_part_initialize;
     Boolean               class_inited; /* XtEnum in X11R4 */
     XtInitProc            initialize;
     XtArgsProc            initialize_hook;
     XtRealizeProc         realize;
     XtActionList          actions;
     Cardinal              num_actions;
     XtResourceList        resources;
     Cardinal              num_resources;
     XrmClass              xrm_class;
     Boolean               compress_motion;
     Boolean               compress_exposure; /* XtEnum in X11R4 */
     Boolean               compress_enterleave;
     Boolean               visible_interest;
     XtWidgetProc          destroy;
     XtWidgetProc          resize;
     XtExposeProc          expose;
     XtSetValuesFunc       set_values;
     XtArgsFunc            set_values_hook;
     XtAlmostProc          set_values_almost;
     XtArgsProc            get_values_hook;
     XtWidgetProc          accept_focus; /* XtAcceptFocusProc */
     XtVersionType         version;
     _XtOffsetList         *callback_private; /* XtPointer */
     String                tm_table;
     XtGeometryHandler     query_geometry;
     XtStringProc          display_accelerator;
     caddr_t               extension; /* XtPointer in X11R4 */
} CoreClassPart;
```

The second part of the widget is its instance record. For every occurrence of a widget there will be an instance record. Its structure contains information that is specific to this particular occurrence. Items such as the x,y coordinate or the window id is stored in this record. All widgets will have at least every member of the CorePart.

The instance record is the *thread* of the inheritance mechanism. This means that the record points to the widget's class record, which points to the superclass. As you can see, it's kind of like weaving. If the superclass had a superclass, its CorePart would point to it, and so on. The "how" of widgets is discussed in Chapter 6; for now, examine the following instance record:

```
typedef struct _CorePart {
     Widget          self;
     WidgetClass     widget_class;
     Widget          parent;
     XrmName         xrm_name;
     Boolean         being_destroyed;
     XtCallbackList  destroy_callbacks;
     caddr_t         constraints; /* XtPointer in X11R4 */
     Position        x,y;
     Dimension       width, height;
     Dimension       border_width;
     Boolean         managed;
     Boolean         sensitive;
     Boolean         ancestor_sensitive;
     XtEventTable    event_table;
     XtTMRec         tm;
     XtTranslations  accelerators;
     Pixel           border_pixel;
     Pixmap          border_pixmap;
     WidgetList      popup_list;
     Cardinal        num_popups;
     String          name;
     Screen          *screen;
     Colormap        colormap;
     Window          window;
     Cardinal        depth;
     Pixel           background_pixel;
     Pixmap          background_pixmap;
     Boolean         visible;
     Boolean         mapped_when_managed;
} CorePart;
```

3.4. A Windowless Object: The OSF/Motif Gadget

As of X11R4, the Core widget has been split into two components: Object and RectObj. Object contains the absolute minimum set of things that interface components would need (i.e., destruction methods). RectObj contains those things that all rectangular components would need (i.e., x,y coordinates and height). There is also a third part often referred to as WindowObj, which is used by many widget sets, although it is not defined by the X11R4 Intrinsics.

This separation of function is very important. In the OOP style that Xt offers, this separation allows for the creation of abstractions that do not need windows. In fact, the Motif Gadget is one such example. A windowless object is like a widget except it does not have event handlers, translations, pop-up children, or a window. Since it lacks a window id, it must rely on its parent to be informed of events.

From an application programmer's perspective, windowless objects should improve the performance of the client over the widget version by reducing the X protocol needed to inform windowed objects of what is going on. From the server's point of view, the demand on memory is decreased, since there is no window so the server need not store any information that it does for windowed things. These two arguments are the reasons that these new abstractions were created.

In the Motif widget set the following gadget classes are defined: XmLabelGadget, XmSeparatorGadget, XmArrowButtonGadget, XmPushButtonGadget, XmToggleButtonGadget, and XmCascadeButtonGadget. (Rumor has it that an XmTextEditGadget is in the works for Motif V1.1.) These are fairly simple, and are often used. They are the kind of components that fall into the realm of "probably good uses" for a windowless object. Some might say the work of OSF and AT&T influenced this change to the Intrinsics.

4

Basic X Graphics: Text, Fonts, Bitmaps, and Colors

Though most of the details of graphic operations are hidden from the application writer when using widget sets, it is important to have a general understanding of some of the basic topics. This chapter introduces you to how X handles text, fonts, bitmaps, and colors.

4.1. Text and X

X paints text to the display through bitmaps, which represent characters. A collection of bitmapped characters is called a *font*. The actual character bounded by a rectangle is called a *glyph*. The painting operation is performed using Xlib primitives that perform a graphic operation called *filling* using a font. Two such routines for drawing strings are:

```
XDrawString(dpy, drawable, gc, x, y, str, len)
```

and

```
XDrawImageString(dpy,drawable, gc, x, y, str, len)
```

The two routines differ in that the second one fills in the background region for each character.

The argument "dpy" is the display where the text is to be painted, "drawable" is either a window id or a pixmap (off-screen memory), "gc" refers to the graphics context to be used for the operation, "x,y" are the pixel offsets in the drawable, "str" is the string to be painted, and "len" is how long the string is.

A pixmap is created by the client to store images for later copying to the screen. They may be used for quick paints of screens to yield a smoother scrolling look. They are also used for creating icons (discussed later in this chapter).

4.2. Graphics Context

Graphics context refers to the information that Xlib primitives use to know how to perform a painting operation. Things such as foreground and background colors, line width, line style, fill style, font, and graphics function are a few items used in graphic operations.

The argument "gc" in the two routines XDrawString( ) and XDrawImage-String( ) is of type GC. It is created using either the Xlib primitive (XCreateGC( )) or Xt (XtGetGC( )). The Xt version creates a GC that is shareable and cannot be altered. The Xlib routine creates a GC that *is* alterable. It should be noted that GCs are stored by the server, and as such are a limited resource. Where possible, limit the number of GCs you create by using the Xt version when static (shareable) GCs are okay.

The routines for creating Xlib and Xt GCs are

```
XCreateGC(dpy, drawable, mask, &values)
```

and

```
XtGetGC(widget, mask, &values)
```

The structure for "values" is of type XGCValue and is defined as follows:

```
Structure Definition                Default Values

typedef struct {
        int function;                   GXCopy (we care)
        unsigned long plane_mask;       All
        unsigned long foreground;       0 (we care)
        unsigned long background;       1 (we care)
        int line_width;                 0
        int line_style;                 LineSolid
        int cap_style;                  CapButt
        int join_style;                 JoinMiter
        int fill_style;                 FillSolid
        int fill_rule;                  EvenOddRule
        int arc_mode;                   ArcPieSlice
        Pixmap tile;                    Foreground
        Pixmap stipple;                 1
        int ts_x_origin;                0
        int ts_y_origin;                0
        Font font;                      Implementation (we care)
        int subwindow_mode;             ClipByChildren
        Bool graphics_exposures;        True
```

```
    int clip_x_origin;              0
    int clip_y_origin;              0
    Pixmap clip_mask;               None
    int dash_offset;                0
    char dashes;                    4
} XGCValues;
```

It is a rather long structure; however, we need mostly be concerned about foreground, background, and font when discussing text. Function is also important, but it is often set to GXCopy.

4.3. Handling GCs

There are at least two ways of handling GCs. The first is to create one without passing any values (Xlib only), then set the elements using some Xlib primitives (such as XSetForeground( ), XSetFont( )) or pass the values when it is created, as shown here:

```
XGCValue values;
GC       gc;

unsigned long valuemask;

values.foreground = 2; /* Pixel value 2 will be some color */

values.background = 4; /* Ditto */

valuemask = GCForeground | GCBackground;

gc = XCreateGC(XtDisplay(widget),XtDisplay(widget),
               valuemask, &values);
```

or

```
gc = XtGetGC(widget, valuemask, &values);
```

When you are finished with a GC and would like to free it, you should use one of the following:

```
XFreeGC(XtDisplay(widget),gc); /* Xlib */
```

or

```
XtReleaseGC(widget,gc);
```

4.4. Multi-Font Text

Another interesting function provided by Xlib is XDrawText(). This function draws strings of text using multiple fonts in a single operation. Its use is shown here:

```
XDrawText(dpy, drawable, gc, x, y, items, num_items);
```

In this example, "items" is of type XTextItem and "num_items" is the number of items. The XTextItem structure is defined as follows:

```
typedef struct {
      char        *chars;
      int         nchars;
      int         delta;
      Font        font;
} XTextItem;
```

(The OSF/Motif Toolkit also provides a compound string notion. This topic is discussed in Chapter 9.) The discussion in this section was provided to yield some insight for application programmers to the workings of graphic contexts. Refer to the MIT documentation or any of the published works on Xlib if you need a more detailed discussion in this area.

4.5. Fonts

4.5.1. Font Metrics

Figure 4-1 displays the characteristics of a font. The two structures that are most important for fonts are XCharStruct and XFontStruct. The XFontStruct contains several members. The ones we care most about are fid, direction, min_bounds, max_bounds, ascent, descent, and per_char. The "fid" is the font id used to refer to the font, "direction" indicates which way the characters are defined, "min_bounds" is the bounding box of the smallest character, "max_bounds" is the bounding box of the largest character, "ascent" tells how far above the baseline the font is, "descent" tells how far below the baseline the font is, and "per_char" is the array of XCharStruct structures for each character in the font. The XCharStruct is

```
typedef {
      short              lbearing;
      short              rbearing;
      short              width;
      short              ascent;
      short              descent;
      unsigned short attributes;
} XCharStruct;
```

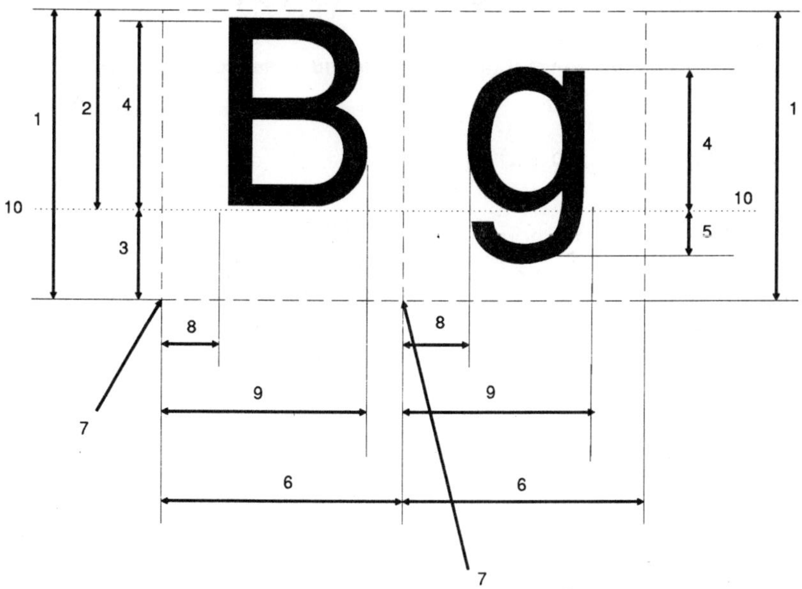

1. Font Height
2. Font Ascent
3. Font Descent
4. Character Ascent
5. Character Descent
6. Font Width
7. Origin
8. lbearing
9. rbearing
10. Baseline

Figure 4-1 Font metrics.

so if you wanted the maximum height for a font, you would use the font structure, go into the max_bounds member, and write the following:

```
font->max_bounds.ascent + font->max_bounds.descent
```

You will find support for both monospace (constant width) and proportionally spaced fonts in X. The next section talks about the XLFD (X Logical Font Description) conventions.

4.5.2. Font Naming Conventions

If there is one thing that X has, it's a slew of fonts. It seems as if everyone and his brother has "donated" fonts to MIT for incorporation with the release tapes. These names can be rather long. The following name, for instance, is one of several:

```
-adobe-courier-medium-i-normal--18-180-75-75-p-104-iso8859-1
```

Fortunately, a naming convention has arisen and is supported by the Xlib font functions. It goes as follows:

1-2-3-4-5-6-7-8-9-10-11-12-13-14-15

1	registry	X register name
2	foundry	adobe, dec, ibm, etc.
3	family	courier, helvetica, etc.
4	weight	normal, medium, bold
5	slant	r, o, i, ri, ro, ot
6	setwidth	normal, condensed, etc.
7	style	serif, sans serif, etc.
8	pixelsize	10, 14, 18, etc.
9	pointsize (in 10ths)	100, 140, 180, etc.
10	xres	75, etc.
11	yres	75, etc.
12	spacing	m, p, c
13	avgwidth	98, etc.
14	charsetregistry	iso8859, etc.
15	charsetencoding	1, etc.

The registry is an X registered name that tells you who owns the remaining part of the syntax and semantics that make up the remainder of the name; the foundry tells who provided it; family is the typeface; weight is the appearance; slant is either r (upright), o (oblique), i (italic), ri (reverse italic), ro (reverse oblique), or ot (other); pointsize tells how big it is, spacing is either m (mono), p (proportional), or c (charcell); avgwidth tells the average width of the characters; and charsetregistry tells what body the font is registered with. (You gotta love these standards.) You will find a complete discussion on font conventions in the X Consortium document, "X Logical Font Description Conventions" (available on the X11R4 tape).

4.5.3. Wildcards in Font Names

The new naming convention can be quite tedious, not to mention a real pain. Once again, though, the MIT folks did not forget you. Instead of having to type in 15 fields of font information, you can insert wildcards to allow for matching. This gets the first font in the font directory that matches; however, if you really care about a particular font, then you would still have to (ugh!) hardcode it.

The following is an example of these wildcards:

```
*-*-courier-bold-r-*-*-*-140-*-*-*-*-iso8859-1
```

This says "match a courier, bold, non-oblique, 14 point, latin-1 font." If you wanted the first 14 point latin-1 font available, you would use

```
*-140-*-iso8859-1.
```

4.5.4. Loading Fonts

Most of the Xt Intrinsics hide the details of many of the graphic elements, either through the resource management or via the built-in converters (see Chapter 6). Though these conveniences are nice, you should be aware of some of the routines for loading and unloading fonts.

To load a font, use one of the following:

```
XLoadFont(dpy,name);
```

or

```
XLoadQueryFont(dpy,name);
```

XLoadFont() returns a font id to be used. It will look for the font and have it loaded. XLoadQueryFont() does the same thing except that it will return an XFontStruct. The "name" argument is of the form described in the previous section.

To unload a font, use this:

```
XUnloadFont(dpy, font)
```

4.6. Bitmaps for Icons

It is often nice to provide a useful icon for when the application is dormant (or iconic). To do this you need to create a bitmap. A bitmap is a pixmap with a depth of one. The *depth* refers to the number of bits available to represent a color.

You can create a bitmap using the tool available on the MIT tape called "bitmap." This tool will create a file that looks like this:

```
#define xit_width 30
#define xit_height 30
#define xit_x_hot -1
#define xit_y_hot -1
static char xit_bits[] = {
0x00, 0x00, 0x00, 0x00, 0x00, 0x00, 0x00, 0x00, 0x00, 0x00, 0x00,
0x00, 0x00, 0x00, 0x00, 0x00, 0x00, 0x00, 0x00, 0x00, 0x07, 0x80,
0x00, 0x00, 0x1e, 0xc0, 0x00, 0x00, 0x3c, 0x60, 0x00, 0x00, 0x78,
0x30, 0x00, 0x00, 0x78, 0x18, 0x00, 0x00, 0xf0, 0x08, 0x00, 0x00,
```

```
0xe0, 0x0d, 0xee, 0x3f, 0xc0, 0x07, 0xee, 0x3f, 0x80, 0x03, 0x0e,
0x07, 0x80, 0x03, 0x0e, 0x07, 0xc0, 0x07, 0x0e, 0x07, 0x60, 0x0f,
0x0e, 0x07, 0x30, 0x0f, 0x0e, 0x07, 0x10, 0x1e, 0x0e, 0x07, 0x18,
0x3c, 0x0e, 0x07, 0x0c, 0x78, 0x0e, 0x07, 0x06, 0xf0, 0x0e, 0x07,
0x03, 0xe0, 0x0e, 0x07, 0x00, 0x00, 0x00, 0x00, 0x00, 0x00, 0x00,
0x00, 0x00, 0x00, 0x00, 0x00, 0x00, 0x00, 0x00, 0x00, 0x00, 0x00,
0x00, 0x00, 0x00, 0x00, 0x00, 0x00, 0x00, 0x00, 0x00, 0x00};
```

To make it usable as an icon, you use the Xlib primitive:

```
XCreatePixmapFromData(dpy,wdw,bits,width,height);
```

This makes it a pixmap that can be installed as an icon (see Chapter 5).

4.7. Foreground and Background

X was designed to allow clients to use a multitude of colors. The client issues a request to the server to allocate the colors it needs. If another client has already requested the same color, the server will give back a pointer to the color. Otherwise, the color is loaded and the pointer is returned.

The "palette" is a *colormap*. Think of a colormap as an array of colors (kind of like a look-up table). Some interesting things happen with colormaps and window managers. Clients can install their own colormaps that may be different than other clients', so when the client has the focus, the window manager installs the colormap. But, since it differs from the one being used by other clients, and the colormap indices do not change when new colormaps are installed, the other clients might not appear in their true colors.

There are several Xlib primitives for creating, installing, and removing colormaps. This area is beyond the scope of this book. Most application writers can rely on the Xt Intrinsics to provide a good colormap (although there is some disagreement with this statement).

Additionally, there are several routines for getting, allocating, and storing colors. Since the Intrinsics has internal converters, you need not be too concerned with doing this. One useful routine to be aware of, however, is:

```
XAllocNamedColor(dpy,cmap,name, &color, &exact);
```

This routine returns an XColor type that is suitable for using with the resource setting needs of applications (see Chapter 5).

Whenever you need a color for painting, you must first allocate it. In Xt programming, however, the toolkit and widgets tend to hide these details and do most of the work for you. The next chapter provides a client that demonstrates these areas, as well as the others addressed in this book.

5

Building Applications: Developing with Xt

With the knowledge acquired up to now, you can begin to explore the Xt Intrinsics. This chapter covers most of the topics that you will encounter when you start to develop your own Xt-based clients.

5.1. Conventions

As in most programming environments, Xt has its own set of conventions that client and widget writers should adhere to. With X11R3, the Xt Intrinsics have become an X Consortium Standard with defined programming conventions. These conventions are as follows:

1. Record components (members of structures) should use an underscore (_) to indicate compound words. Additionally, they should be written in all lowercase:

```
struct record {
      int component_one;
      int component_two;
};
```

2. Names of types and procedures start with uppercase letters and use uppercase and lowercase for compound words:

```
XtSetArg            (procedure/macro)
XrmOptionDescRec    (type)
```

3. Resource name fields are identical in spelling to the field name they refer to, with exception of compound words which use uppercase and lowercase. Each resource name should have a macro (#define) that starts with XtN (Motif uses XmN):

```
XtNwidth                "width"
XmNwidth   (Motif)      "width"
```

4. Resource class strings begin with XtC, and are written exactly like resource names with the exception of the first character, which should be capitalized:

```
XtNforeground        "foreground"   (resource)
XtCForeground        "Foreground"   (class string)
```

5. Resource representations are written exactly like resource class strings except for their prefix, which is XtR:

```
FwProc     "FwProc"(type)
XtRFwProc "FwProc"(representation string)
```

6. Use a capital letter as the first character of a new widget class and for compound strings:

```
FieldEdWidgetClass
```

7. Action procedures should follow the same convention as procedures (start with uppercase and use uppercase and lowercase for compound words):

```
MoveInsert
```

These conventions are fairly easy to live with, and go a long way in enabling future users of your code to understand exactly what you have done.

5.2. Application Structure

One of the first things to notice when you begin coding with Xt is that almost every client looks the same on the inside. That is, application structure is fairly well defined, and each client shares the same basic foundation.

As in all C programs, you start by including those header files necessary for the application. In Xt you always include the following:

```
#include <X11/Intrinsic.h>
#include <X11/StringDefs.h>.
```

The Intrinsic.h header file holds the definitions of all the functions (XtCreateWidget()) and all the macros (XtWindow( )) that are used by Xt-based clients. The StringDefs.h header file has standard resource names (XtN), resource class names (XtC), and representation type names (XtR) that are used in the Intrinsics.

In addition to those two headers, there are two additional header files that often are used in Xt applications:

```
#include <X11/Xatom.h>
#include <X11/Shell.h>
```

Xatom.h contains the predefined X atoms used for inter-client communication and selections (discussed in the last chapter of the book). Shell.h contains those definitions for application shells, which are the outer windows that all clients have.

After the X headers, add the "public" headers for the widgets that are used in the client. The term "public" refers to the header that client writers* use. For instance, the following header:

```
#include <X11/Xaw/Command.h>
```

would get the X11R4 Athena CommandWidget. For Motif, the following header would get the OSF/Motif version of a command button:

```
#include <X11/Xm/PushB.h>
```

The next section of the C program is for forward declarations, global variables, and any static definitions that are needed. The use of forward declarations is consistent with the ANSI standard. Global variables help pass information to subordinate functions. Static definitions provide useful mechanisms for your code (i.e., look-up tables).

Now you are ready for the main program. Figure 5-1 shows its structure. The steps for writing it are as follows:

1. Initialize the toolkit (XtInitialize()/XtAppInitialize()).
2. Create the widgets (XtCreateWidget( )/XtCreateManagedWidget()).
3. Realize the widgets (XtRealizeWidget()).
4. Wait on events (XtMainLoop()).

---

* Widgets are supposed to be written such that the client writer will use standard Xt mechanisms to get and set data in the widget, or use "convenience" functions provided by the widget writer. Sometimes widget writers leave out things that client writers need. In this instance a client writer *might* use the "private" header of the widget. **Warning:** If you do this, you accept responsibility for keeping track of changes to the widget so your client won't break. In this book we create a set of utilities for the Athena TextWidget (TextUtil.h, TextUtil.c) to overcome some of the X11R3 shortcomings. In there you will see the use of TextP.h which is the private header of the TextWidget.

```
#include <stdio.h>

#include <X11/Intrinsic.h>
#include <X11/StringDefs.h>

#include "WidgetsUsed.h"

Forward Declarations

Global Variables

static definitions
  - fallback resources (R4)
  - XrmOptionDescRec
  - New Action Procs
  - New Translation Tables

main(argc,argv)

  Initialize Toolkit
    - XtInitialize
    - XtAppInitialize

  Build Interface
    - XtCreateWidget/XtCreateManagedWidget

  XtRealizeWidget

  XtManageChildren/XtManageChild

  XtMainLoop/XtAppMainLoop
```

Figure 5-1 Application structure.

To demonstrate these components, you will build the ever-so-popular "This is NOT 'Hello World'!" client. The first thing to do is create your own "utility" header file. This will be used for every client created in the book. It contains the standard Xt headers that you need as well as some handy macros. Here is its code:

```
/* FILE:    XbkUtil.h
 * PURPOSE: Provide header for the utilities developed for the book
 *          applications.
 *
 */
/* This is a "trick" that will insure that this include file is
```

```
 * included only once.  If you look through the X header files you
 * will see this mechanism commonly used.
 */
#ifndef _XbkUtil_h
#define _XbkUtil_h

#include <stdio.h>
#include <ctype.h>

/* Xt header files that we will need */
#include <X11/IntrinsicP.h
/* Some may shudder at the inclusion of the private Intrinsic
 * header file, however, since we need some information out of the
 * structures and they are defined in the private, not the public
 * header, we have no choice.
 */
#include <X11/StringDefs.h>
#include <X11/Xatom.h>
#include <X11/Shell.h>

/* This is a symbolic constant that we will use when we define
 * our Arg array.
 */
#define MAXARGS 30

/* Whenever we need to use the bell to alert the user, we
 * will use BEEP.  BEEP is a way of passing the widget
 * id and using the Xlib primitive XBell.
 */
#define BEEP(w)          XBell(XtDisplay(w),50)

/* Sometimes we will need the default values for things such as
 * the black pixel value or the white pixel value.  Since
 * BlackPixelOfScreen is an Xlib macro, we want to provide an
 * Xt interface.  That's why we have created these macros.
 */
#define BP(w) BlackPixelOfScreen(XtScreen(w))
#define WP(w) WhitePixelOfScreen(XtScreen(w))
/* When we work with Graphic Contexts, we will often need the
 * colormap that is installed.  Since every widget has the
 * colormap stored as a member in the Core structure, we can get
 * the colormap from the structure.  We create a macro that
 * "hides" the details and make it look like a function.
 */
```

```
 #define XbkGetColormap(w) ((w)->core.colormap)
/* When we work with text, we often need the height of the font
 * that we are working with.  Since we know that the max_bounds
 * member of an XFontStruct has the information, we create a macro
 * that will do the work for us.
 */
#define XbkFontHeight(f)\
 (f->max_bounds.ascent + f->max_bounds.descent)

#endif
```

Now you can write the program:

```
/* FILE:       nothw.c
 */

#include "XbkUtil.h"

/* Widget headers to be used in this client */
#include <X11/Label.h>
```

In this client you simply create a label to display some text. In the Athena Widget Set, the LabelWidget is used to do this, so you need to include its public header.

The next two macros provide some names to give to the initialization mechanism of the Intrinsics. You will often find argv[0] being used as the name of the application shell, but I have chosen to use a #define in its place. You are free to use argv[0] and your own class name. You should, however, use the X conventions for class names. The code is as follows:

```
#define XbkShellName    "nothw"
#define XbkApplClass    "Nothw"
main(argc,argv)
     int argc;
     char **argv;
{
     Widget top,tag;         /* Widgets in this client */
     Arg[MAXARGS];           /* args to pass to Widget objects */
     int cnt;                /* counter for message setting
                                method 1 */

     top = XtInitialize(XbkShellName,XbkApplClass,
                    NULL,0,&argc, argv);
/*
 * Tell the widget some values we want stored.
```

```
 * Then create it.
 */
    cnt = 0;
    XtSetArg(arg[cnt],XtNx,0);          cnt++;
    XtSetArg(arg[cnt],XtNy,0);          cnt++;
    tag = XtCreateManagedWidget("tag", labelWidgetClass,
                top, arg, cnt);
/*
 * Now realize the top widget which will manage the child tag.
 */
XtRealizeWidget(top);
/*
 * Now just sit around waiting and doing things about events.
 */
    XtMainLoop();
}
```

The first thing Xt clients do is initialize. In this example, you are using an initialization procedure that is left over from the X11R2 days. It is supported in both X11R3 and X11R4. This procedure essentially starts the Intrinsics environment. It has the job of invoking the toolkit initialization procedure, opening a connection with the server, creating an application context (we'll discuss this soon), and creating a top-level shell. The R4 version of this, XtAppInitialize, performs essentially the same things with the exception of using explicit application contexts (discussed in Chapter 11).

There are six arguments for XtInitialize():

1. Application shell name, which is given to the window manager and used by the resource manager.
2. Application class name, used by the resource manager.
3. Application command-line parsing description, used to inform the command line parser of how to read and interpret the command line.
4. The number of records in the description.
5. The Address of argc.
6. argv.

In this client you do not add any parsing rules. Therefore, argument 3 is null and argument 4 is 0.

After initialization comes widget creation. You have two creation choices: managed or unmanaged. A managed widget lets the parent do the work of window mapping for it, and informs the parent of its geometry. An unmanaged widget is one that will eventually ask to be managed. As an unmanaged widget, the parent does not know what geometry the widget wants to be. This is important, since widgets negotiate geometry with parents, and it can be a rather time-consuming process.

When you create several widgets with one parent, it is often more efficient to create them as unmanaged, then manage them as a set. In this way, the parent conducts geometry negotiations with all of the children at one time instead of doing it for each separately. The functions for widget creation are

```
widget = XtCreateWidget("name",widgetClass,parent,arg,numArgs);
widget = XtCreateManagedWidget("name,widgetClass,parent,
         arg,numArgs);
```

The five arguments are

1. Instance name.
2. Widget class.
3. Parent widget.
4. Argument list.
5. Number of arguments in the list.

The *instance name* is used for getting resources from the resource database. An example of an instance name is "tag." In the resource database, you could set resources for this widget using "tag" in the specification. The *widget class* refers to the widget that is being created. For instance, the Athena Label widget's class is defined as labelWidgetClass and the Motif Form widget's class is xmFormWidgetClass. The *parent* is the "container" that this widget will belong to. The *argument list* is a list of resources, and the values desired for those resources. Lastly, the *number of arguments* tells the creation mechanism how many arguments in the list to worry about.

Arguments can be set for widgets by either resource specifications in the resource database (discussed in the next section) or through argument passing. There are a few argument-passing mechanisms that are commonly used in Xt. The first is shown here:

```
Arg arg[MAXARGS];int cnt;
cnt = 0;
XtSetArg(arg[cnt],XtNresource,value); cnt++;
XtCreateManagedWidget(widget,widgetClass,parent,arg,cnt);
```

This is the preferred development method because you can count the arguments after each setting, then provide the variable as an argument to the Create function. This minimizes the things that can go wrong. For instance, suppose you add a resource, then recompile your code. If the "number of arguments in list" argument is not incremented to take your new resource into account, the creation mechanism will not use it. You could spend significant time tracking down this bug. The other mechanisms force you to do the increment, but this way lets the computer do it.

The second argument-setting method is as follows:

```
Arg arg[] = {
     {XtNresource, NULL},
};
arg[0].value = something;
XtCreateManagedWidget(widget,widgetClass,parent,
 arg,XtNumber(arg));
```

This is the preferred production way as opposed to the previous method in which the computer does the work, meaning that CPU cycles are consumed just to add one to a counter. With this second approach, the work is done at compile time, not run time, thus saving CPU cycles.

Comparing the two methods, it is evident that you save an instruction for each argument set. It is not hard to see that this will add up to quite a savings, especially if there are many widgets created.

The last common method is shown here:

```
Arg arg[MAXARG];
XtSetArg(arg[0],XtNresource,something);
XtCreateManagedWidget(widget,widgetClass,parent,arg,1);
```

As you can see, this is extremely manual and can lead to some interesting bugs. Notice, too, that it is not as slow as the first technique and not as fast as the second one. Even so, you will see this method used.

When you have unmanaged widgets, you need to manage them using one of two routines: XtManageChild() or XtManageChildren(). XtManageChild(widget) accepts the widget you want managed as the argument and informs the parent that you want it to be managed. XtManageChildren(list,numInList) accepts a list of widgets that represent the children to be managed, and the number of children in that list.

Once all the widgets are created, you must "realize" them. Essentially, this instructs each of the widgets (by invoking their realize method) that they should map their windows and do anything else they might want to do before being displayed. The function to use is

```
XtRealizeWidget(node)
```

where node is the top of a widget tree to be managed. If all widgets are children of the top shell and are all managed, then invoking XtRealizeWidget(top) will cause all widgets to be realized. If one or more widgets is not managed, then you would have to realize them manually.

The last step in the event-driven style of programming is to "hang out" and wait for things to happen (XtMainLoop). This occurs in XtMainLoop(), a convenience routine that calls XtNextEvent() to get the event off of the queue, and then calls XtDispatchEvent() to tell the widgets about the event. XtMainLoop() looks like this:

```
for(;;) {
      XtNextEvent(&event);
      XtDispatchEvent(&event);
};
```

5.3. Providing Application Resources

One of the most powerful features of Xt is the *resource manager*, a collection of mechanisms for getting resources from a variety of places and converting a resource to the correct representation for the client. For example, if you would like to set the font for the Athena Label widget, you simply need to set a resource (XtNfont) for the widget (Label), and the resource manager will perform some magic that makes the string representation of a font become the actual font structure. This in itself is a good reason to use Xt. In fact, many Xlib programmers like this so much that they "fudge" and make hybrid clients just to set application resources. (You will soon explore the magic that goes on with the resource manager.)

5.3.1. Where Does Xt Get the Resources?

The client shown in Figure 5-2 ("nothw") doesn't look like it would do much. In fact, a label widget has been created without a label! Looking at the picture of this client, notice the text "This is NOT 'Hello World'!" in the window. Where did it come from? The answer is the resource manager.

When you initialize the toolkit with XtInitialize(), you invoke the resource manager. This is followed by a search through the file system and the command line for resource settings. There are nine possible places for resources:

1. /usr/lib/X11/$LANGapp-defaults/class, which is the "application" class defaults. In this case the class would be NothwCmd.
2. If step 1 resulted in a problem, then Xt uses /usr/lib/X11/app-defaults/class.

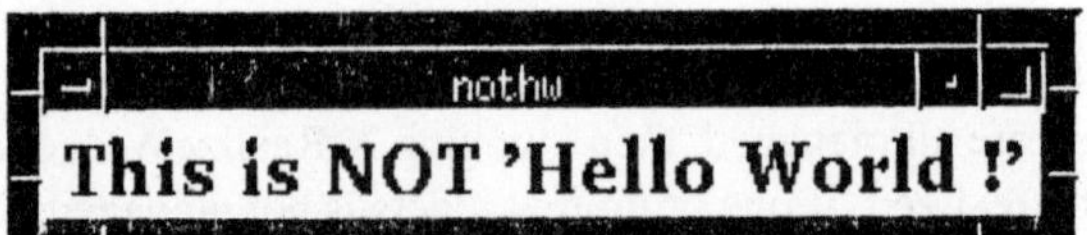

Figure 5-2 The nothw client.

3. Next it loads the file $XAPPRESLANGPATHclass.
4. If Step 3 fails, it goes after $XAPPRESDIRclass.
5. Now it loads the resources specified in the server's RESOURCE_MANAGER property.
6. If that wasn't there, then it goes after $HOME/.Xdefaults.
7. Now load the stuff in $XENVIRONMENT.
8. Guess what? If Step 7 didn't work, it tries $HOME/.Xdefaults-host ("host" is the machine name).
9. And last but not least, it uses the command line.

This procedure might seem like a lot of work, but it isn't that bad. You will find that most people stuff everything in their $HOME/.Xdefaults file. This isn't such a great idea. For one thing, it makes .Xdefaults pretty large, and for another, it makes things unorganized. You will usually have something in /usr/lib/X11/app-defaults/class and additional resources in your own .Xdefaults.

Another important point to note is that each step overrides the previous one. That is, if you have some nice defaults established in /usr/lib/X11/app-defaults/YourClass, the user may override them in their $HOME/.Xdefaults. For example, if you know the application writer set up the background to be magenta, yet it displays pink, it probably is not the color monitor. It's most likely the user's $HOME/.Xdefaults. **Remember:** When in doubt, check the $HOME/.Xdefaults.

5.3.2. Setting Up Resources in the Resource Files

Now that you know where to get the resources, how are they set? We made a point of talking about conventions in Chapter 3. During that brief discussion, items called resources, resource classes, and representation strings were pointed out. Well, the resources and resources classes are used in the resource databases, and the representation strings are for "kicking in" the converters.

In nothw, you have the application shell name, the application class name, and the widget instance name. Additionally, hiding in the label widget are resource names for the various resources that it uses. A quick look at the Athena Widget manual or a stroll through the code uncovers the resource name "XtNlabel," which has an actual string representation as "label" (this is found in StringDefs.h).

Suppose you would like to have "nothw" display the string "This is not 'Hello World'." How do you do that? First, note the application shell name "nothw," then the widget's instance name "tag." With these two, you can set the "XtNlabel" resource as follows:

```
nothw.tag.label:    This is not 'Hello World'
```

This says "set the application whose name is "nothw," that has a widget instance "tag" with a resource "label" to "This is not 'Hello World'."

You could have caused the same result a few other ways, such as the seven shown here:

1. `Nothhw*label:            This is not 'Hello World'`
2. `Nothw*Label*label:       This is not 'Hello World'`
3. `nothw*label:             This is not 'Hello World'`
4. `nothw*tag*label:         This is not 'Hello World'`
5. `nothw*tag.label:         This is not 'Hello World'`
6. `nothw*Label:             This is not 'Hello World'`
7. `nothw*Label.Label:       This is not 'Hello World'`

Had enough? Before you scratch your head, let me explain. The first line says all clients in the Nothw class (you know this is a class by convention, since all class names start with uppercase and use upper/lowercase for compound words) that have a resource with the name "label" should have it set to the value. Line 2 says all clients in the Nothw class, with any Label widget in the client, set its label to the value. This would make a client with 10 labels say the same thing. Line 3 says the client whose name is nothw should have all label resources set to the value. This would cause any widgets in nothw (if they existed) that have a resource using the name "label" to have the value stored in it. Line 4 singles out those widgets that are children of "tag" and have "label" as a string to set the value. Line 5 says just set tag's label to the values. In line 6, all widget resources that have a resource class name of "Label" are set to the values. And line 7 says only the Label widgets should have their labels set to the value.

As you can see there is a great degree of flexibility. There is also the chance for confusion. To keep things straight, you need to know how the resource manager handles conflicts. It does it using the following rules:

1. The class name or resource name of every component in the specification must match the requested item in the database. So, the resource specification that is created for the label in our client is as follows:

   ```
   nothw.tag.label
   Nothw.Label.Label
   ```

   Therefore the first line below matches, while the second does not:

   ```
   nothw.tag.label:     "Hello World"
   nothw.tag.string:    "Hello World"
   ```

2. Those entries with the "." (dot) are more specific than those with the "*" (asterisk). The asterisk is more for shorthand, so the first line below loses to the second:

```
nothw.tag*label:      "Hello World"
nothw.tag.label:      "Not Hello World"
```

3. Resource names always overrule class names, so the second line overrules the first:

```
Nothw.tag.label:      "Hello World"
nothw.tag.label:      "I won !!"
```

4. Resource names and class names will overrule an asterisk, so the first line below overrules the second:

```
Nothw*Label*label:     "I Win"
Nothw*label:           "I lost"
```

5. The specifications are scanned left to right, so the first entries below overruling the third:

```
Nothw*label:          "I win"
Nothw*width:          100
Nothw*label:          "I lose"
```

Now that you are comfortable with resource setting, it is easy to see how the client "nothw" can assume different appearances. At one time the label resource could be set "This is not 'Hello World'" while at another time it could be set to "Hello World," as shown in Figure 5-3. As you might imagine, this client is very simple, yet it demonstrates how you can change client behavior without recompiling — that's not such a bad thing.

5.3.3. Getting Application-Specific Resources

Now that you know about widgets and resources, how about the client? After all, it might be necessary to provide some command line options that get resources, and it would be useful to use the resource manager to do this.

The first thing you need to do is create a structure to warehouse your application-specific resources. Once that is done, an XtResource table is defined to inform the resource manager how to fill in our application resources.

Figure 5-3 Nothw with "Hello World."

The XtResource table has seven members, which are defined as follows:

1. Resource name (usually XtN).
2. Resource class name (usually XtC).
3. Representation type for the result.
4. Sizeof for the size of the type.
5. Address of the variable for the result.
6. Representation type you are coming from.
7. Any default value, in case it isn't found in the database.

The resource manager uses the resource name and resource class name for matching in the resource database. The representation type tells the resource manager what type the resource needs to be. When using the resource databases, the resource manager uses XtRwhatever to search a list of "from-to" representation strings that has an associated converter connected with it. So, if you wanted the resource to be of type int, you would specify XtRInt as the representation type. The resource manager would convert the string it reads from the database to an integer using one of the several converters that are supplied with the Intrinsics. It would place the result at the address specified for the result. The converters use the sizeof type to assist in the conversion. (Converters are discussed in greater detail in an example in Chapter 6.) If the resource did not exist in the database, then the default value would be used with the "from" representation string, which starts the correct converter and then fills in the address.

The first of the following two tables lists the representation types that are predefined in Xt. The second table lists the associated "to-from" converters.

Table 5-1
Predefined Representation Types
(From X11R4 StringDefs.h)

XtRAcceleratorTable	XtRAtom	XtRBitmap
XtRBool	XtRBoolean	XtRCallback
XtRCallProc	XtRCardinal	XtRColor
XtRColormap	XtRCursor	XtRDimension
XtRDisplay	XtREditMode	XtREnum
XtRFile	XtRFloat	XtRFont
XtRFontStruct	XtRFunction	XtRGeometry
XtRImmediate	XtRInitialState	XtRInt
XtRJustify	XtRLongBoolean	XtRObject
XtROrientation	XtRPixel	XtRPixmap
XtRPointer	XtRPosition	XtRScreen
XtRShort	XtRString	XtRStringArray
XtRStringTable	XtRUnsignedChar	XtRTranslationTable
XtRVisual	XtRWidget	XtRWidgetClass
XtRWidgetList	XtRWindow	

Table 5-2
Predefined Converters

To	Type	From
XtRAcceleratorTable	(XtAccelerators)	XtRString
XtRBoolean	(Boolean)	XtRString, XtRInt
XtRBool	(Bool)	XtRString, XtRInt
XtRCallback	(XtCallbackList)	XtRFunction
XtRColor	(XColor)	XtRInt
XtRCursor	(Cursor)	XtRString
XtRDimension	(Dimension)	XtRString, XtRInt
XtRDisplay	(Display *)	XtRString
XtRFile	(FILE *)	XtRString
XtRFloat	(float)	XtRString
XtRFont	(Font)	XtRString,XtRInt
XtRFontStruct	(XFontStruct *)	XtRString
XtRFunction	((*)())	
XtRInt	(int)	XtRString,XtRImmediate
XtRImmediate	(caddr_t)	
XtRPixel	(Pixel)	XtRString, XtRInt, XtRColor
XtRPixmap	(Pixmap)	XtRInt
XtRPointer	(caddr_t)	
XtRPosition	(Position)	XtRString, XtRInt
XtRShort	(short)	XtRString, XtRInt
XtRString	(char *)	XtRString
XtRTranslationTable	(XtTranslations)	XtRString
XtRUnsignedChar	(unsigned char)	XtRString, XtRInt
XtRWidget	(Widget)	
XtRWindow	(Window)	

The "to-from" table reads: "the representation in the 'to' column is of the type in the 'type' column, and may be converted using the representations in the 'from' column." Therefore, an XtRDimension may be converted using XtRString or XtRInt as follows:

```
static XtResource myAppResOpts[] = {
{XtNx, XtCX, XtRDimension, sizeof(Dimension), &ival, XtRString,
"1"},
{XtNx, XtCX, XtRDimension, sizeof(Dimension), &ival, XtRInt, 1},
};
```

Now you can create a client to get your own application-specific resources. This new client, called "nothwCmd" builds upon the previous client "nothw":

```
/* FILE:    nothwCmd.h
 */

/* Our utility header file */
#include "XbkUtil.h"

/* Widget headers to be used in this client */
#include <X11/Box.h>
#include <X11/Label.h>

#define XbkShellName       "nothwCmd"
#define XbkApplClass       "NothhwCmd"

/* We set up a structure that will have this applications default.
*/
struct _myAppRes {
        int num_labels;
} myAppRes;

/* Now, to pull off the resource manager "magic," we set up a
 * resource option table.  It will inform the resource manager of
 * the information needed for where to put the info, what form to
 * put it in, and some default value for a fallback.
 */

#define OFFSET(field)  XtOffset(struct _myAppRes*, field)
static XtResource myAppResOpts[] = {
   {"numLabels", "NumLabels", XtRInt, sizeof(int),
       OFFSET(num_labels),XtRImmediate, (caddr_t)NULL},
};
#undef OFFSET

#define   LIMIT     10
main(argc,argv)
     int argc;
     char **argv;
{
     Widget top,container,tag[LIMIT];

     Arg arg[MAXARGS];
     int cnt;

     top = XtInitialize(XbkShellName,XbkApplClass,
             NULL,0,&argv,argc);
```

```
/*
 * This function call invokes the resource manager using
 * the application resource table, and the structure that houses
 * the results.
 */
     XtGetApplicationResources(top, &myAppRes, myAppResOpts,
                     XtNumber(myAppResOpts),NULL, 0);
     if (myAppRes.num_labels > LIMIT) {
          printf("Sorry ... limit exceeded !!\n");
          exit(-1);
}
/* To avoid having to establish offsets for each widget created, we
 * may choose to use a container widget.  The Athena set has the
 * BoxWidget and the FormWidget.
 */
     container = XtCreateManagedWidget("container",boxWidgetClass,
             top,NULL,0);

/* Now instead of being a child of the top, we are children of the
 * container.  In this way the container can manage our layout.
 */
     for(cnt = 0; cnt = myAppRes.num_labels; cnt++)
          tag[cnt] = XtCreateWidget("tag", labelWidgetClass,
                    container, arg, 0);
/* We manage all the children at once.
 */
     XtManageChildren(tag,cnt);
     XtRealizeWidget(top);
     XtMainLoop();
}
```

Three new items have been added in this client: the resource gathering mechanism (XtGetApplicationResources()), a container widget (boxWidgetClass), and the use of XtManageChildren().

The function XtGetApplicationResources() has the following arguments:

1. Widget.
2. Base for results.
3. Resources looking for.
4. Number of resources.
5. Argument list.
6. Number of arguments in list.

The widget is used to instruct the resource manager of the resource databases to use. It is not used for searching for resources for that widget; rather, it is for the overall application. The base is the address of the application resource structure (myAppRes in this case). The resources argument is the list of resources being requested. The number of resources is the total number of resources in the resource list. The argument list is for overriding resources extracted from the database.

The boxWidgetClass is one of the "container" widgets provided in the Athena Widget Set, and is of the "composite" class (these are discussed in Chapter 7). It is responsible for managing the layout of its children. This widget places the children in a column format.

All widget sets include a few container widgets which assist in laying out children. The following is a table of the Athena and OSF/Motif container widgets:

Table 5-3
Athena and OSF/Motif Container Widgets

Athena	OSF/Motif	Similar
boxWidgetClass	xmBulletinBoardWidgetClass	yes
formWidgetClass	xmFormWidgetClass	yes
panedWidgetClass	xmPanedWindowWidgetClass	yes
viewPortWidgetClass	xmScrolledWindowWidgetClass	yes
	xmRowColumnWidgetClass	no

XtManageChildren() is used to manage a gang of kids after they have all been created. As stated earlier, doing this after all children have been created saves time when the manager (container) has to perform the geometry-negotiation process.

To set the application resource you add a specification into the application's class resource file. The resource file looks like this:

```
! Application Defaults for nothwCmd
*geometry: +0+0
*NumLabels:      1
*container.tag.label:   This could be 'Hello World !
*container.tag.font:    *-helvetica-*-r-*-180-*
```

The exclamation mark is used for commenting in your resource files. The result of this file is shown in Figure 5-4.

Figure 5-4 NothwCmd.

5.3.4. Building a Command-Line Options Table

A final level of option setting can be done through the command line. To do this, you simply create an XrmOptionDescRec table. This tells the command-line parser how to get things from the command line (argv). Next, the command-line options and the number of XrmOptionDescRecs are passed to the XtInitialize() procedure. There are four fields for XrmOptionDescRec:

1. Command line option to look for.
2. Resource specifier to use when creating the filling in the resource denoted by the option.
3. The option style, which is one of the following:

```
XrmoptionNoArg      means use the value in field 4.
XrmoptionIsArg      means use the value in field 1.
XrmoptionStickyArg means no white space after option.
XrmoptionSepArg     means use the next argv value.
XrmoptionResArg     means use the resource and value from the
                    next argv.
XrmoptionSkipArg    means ignore me and the next one.
XrmoptionSkipLine   means stop now; don't go any further.
XrmoptionNarg       means skip "n" args from this arg.
```

4. The value when 3 is XrmOptionNoArg.

To demonstrate the use of this table, let's add the command-line parsing mechanism to the previous client ("nothwCmd"). First, you must define the option that you are looking for. In this case, you would like to have the number of labels to create passed on the command line. Therefore, the XrmOptionDescRec table looks as follows:

```
XrmOptionDescRec myCmdOpts[] = {
{ "-numLabels", "*numLabels", XrmoptionSepArg, NULL,
};
```

It is "fed" into XtInitialize():

```
top = XtInitialize(XbkShellName,XbkApplClass,
             myCmdOpts,XtNumber(myCmdOpts),
             &argc, argv);
```

Now, specify the command line as follows:

```
nothwCmd -numLabels 10
```

This results in ten labels being displayed, as shown in Figure 5-5.

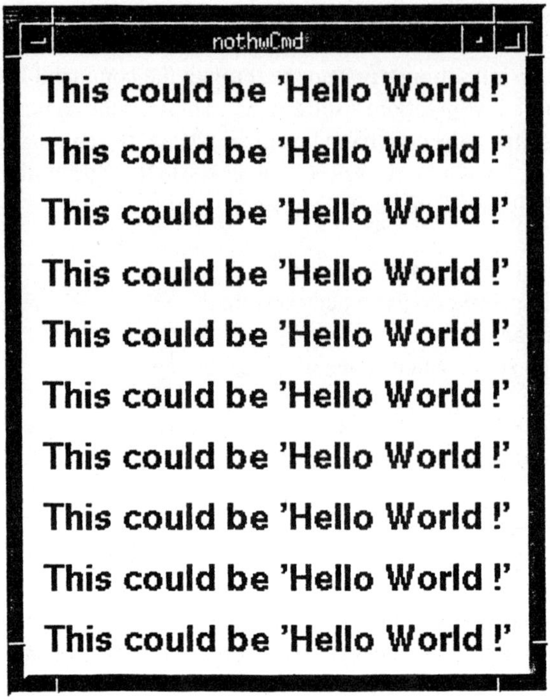

Figure 5-5 Ten labels.

5.4. Handling Events

As you know, X is an event-driven mechanism. Clients let the server know what events they want to be informed of, and the server lets the client know when those events occur. It is important to remember that the client has to tell the server of the events that it wants to be informed of. Otherwise, the client will not receive notification that anything has happened. There are 33 events that clients can be informed of. The following table lists the events and the masks used for each one.

Table 5-4
X Event Types and Masks

Event Type	Event Mask(s)
ButtonPress	ButtonPressMask
ButtonRelease	ButtonReleaseMask
MotionNotify	ButtonMotionMask,Button[1,2,3,4,5]Mask
MapNotify	StructureNotifyMask,SubstructureNotifyMask
EnterNotify	EnterWindowMask
LeaveNotify	LeaveWindowMask

Event Type	Event Mask(s)
FocusIn	FocusChangedMask
FocusOut	FocusChangedMask
Expose	ExposureMask
GraphicsExpose	GCGraphicsExposureMask
NoExpose	GCGraphicsExposureMask
VisiblityNotify	VisibilityChangeMask
KeyPress	KeyPressMask
KeyRelease	KeyReleaseMask
DestroyNotify	StructureNotifyMask,SubstructureNotifyMask
UnmapNotify	StructureNotifyMask,SubstructureNotifyMask
MapRequest	SubstructureRedirectMask
ReparentNotify	StructureNotifyMask,SubstructureNotifyMask
ResizeRequest	ResizeRequestMask
ConfigureNotify	StructureNotifyMask,SubstructureNotifyMask
GravityNotify	StructureNotifyMask,SubstructureNotifyMask
CirculateNotify	StructureNotifyMask,SubstructureNotifyMask
CirculateRequest	SubstructureRedirectMask
PropertyNotify	PropertyChangeMask
SelectionClear	Not Applicable
SelectionRequest	Not Applicable
SelectionNotify	Not Applicable
KeymapNotify	KeymapStateMask
ColormapNotify	ColormapChangeMask
ClientMessage	NoEventMask
MappingNotify	Not Applicable
ConfigureRequest	SubstructureRedirectMask
CreateNotify	StructureNotifyMask,SubstructureNotifyMask
None Applicable	OwnerGrabButtonMask
None Applicable	PointerMotionHintMask

5.4.1. A Brief Overview of Events

Events emanate from the server. For each of the 33 events, there is a corresponding structure that the server fills in. The structure has members that constitute the details of the specific event. Every event structure starts with the following five core fields:

1. type — the event type (found in the table).
2. display — the server the event occurred on.
3. window — the window the event occurred in.
4. serial — a tag used by the server for sequencing.
5. send_event — a flag that is set to "false" if the server sent the event, or "true" if a client did.

To define an event structure in code, you write the following:

```
XEvent event;
```

To access the members you write this:

```
event.type
```

So, if you wanted to check the event type of any event, you would do the following:

```
XtNextEvent(&event);    /* this takes an event off the
                           queue */
if (event.send_event)
     printf("A client told us that ...);
else
     printf("The server told us that ...);
switch(event.type) {
case KeyPress:
     printf("A key was pressed !!!\n"); break;
case KeyRelease:
     printf("A key was released !!!\n"); break;
}
```

This is all well and good, but with 33 events, which ones do you really care about? The answer depends on the client you are writing, but the next few sections explore how some common events are reported.

5.4.2. Keyboard Events

The server uses the XKeyEvent structure to report KeyPress and KeyRelease events to clients that register for them. Events may be registered for by using the Xlib primitive XSelectInput( ) or through one of the Intrinsic mechanisms (discussed in a moment). The additional members of the XKeyEvent structure are as follows:

```
Window     root;
Window     subwindow;
Time       time;
int        x,y,x_root,y_root;
unsigned   state,keycode;
Bool       same_screen;
```

The most important members of this structure (for many applications) are state and keycode. The "state" member indicates if one of the modifier keys (Ctrl, Alt, or Shift) are pressed. "Keycode" is the actual keyboard key that was pressed. To find out the symbol (referred to as a *keysym*) of the keycode, you need to use an Xlib primitive called XLookupString(). This is done as follows:

```
char keySymbol[80];       /* buffer to hold string */
KeySym *retKeySym;     /* X key symbol          */
XComposeStatus compStatus; /* results */
XLookupString(&event,keySymbol,80,&retKeySym,&compStatus);
```

where

- event is the XKeyStruct.
- keySymbol will have the string contents for the key stored.
- retKeySym is the X key symbol (see keysymdef.h), i.e., XK_F9, XK_a.
- compStatus holds some state information (you won't use this).

5.4.3. Focus Events

Key events are sent to the window that currently has the "focus." In most cases, application writers can rely on manager widgets (such as the OSF/Motif variety) to handle focus management. These events can be rather complex, especially when widgets (windows) are not accepting the focus. Chapter 9 provides an example of setting the input focus.

5.4.4. Pointer (Sprite) Events

The most commonly used device is the mouse. You might say X was created with the mouse in mind. This is one of the reasons that "traversing" with the keyboard is so complex.

Pointer events occur when either of the mouse buttons are pressed or released, or when the critter moves. The report of pointer events goes to the window that currently has the sprite (another name for the pointer) or to the window that has "grabbed" the pointer. Grabbing refers to telling the server, "I own the pointer and I want to know everything it does, so tell me." This is not necessarily the same as telling the place where the pointer (or sprite) is. Pop-ups are good examples of using grabs, since you want the user to deal with the pop-up before continuing to anything else. (You'll see this in Chapter 9.)

5.4.5. Enter/Leave Events

Whenever the sprite moves into a window, an EnterNotify event is generated. When the sprite leaves a window, a LeaveNotify event is generated. The top-level shells of most clients like to adjust their borders when such events occur. Some widgets can grab or lose the focus using these events.

Enter and leave events are termed *crossing events* and could be quite tricky if you were an Xlib client writer. To see why, suppose you were setting your top-level window's border on and off with enter and leave events, and you had some children. Well, if you blindly do the setting of the border, you would inadvertently set it off when the sprite moved to a child, because you are informed that the sprite has left your window when it goes to the child. There is some information in the details of the XCrossingEvent structure that are helpful to Xt client writers, but the "Intrinsics" manage this stuff for you. Another fine reason for using the Toolkit!

5.4.6. Exposure Events

There are three varieties of exposures: Expose (the most common), GraphicsExpose, and NoExpose. Expose occurs whenever part of a window (a region) is destroyed. This can happen if your window was overlapped by another and you are brought to the top. The GraphicsExpose event is sent by the server whenever the client uses XCopyArea(). NoExpose occurs when the client uses XCopyArea() and no region was exposed as a result of it.

The XExposeEvent structure contains the x,y location relative to the upper-left corner of the window (refer to Chapter 2), the height and width of the exposed region, and a count of the remaining Expose events. Widgets may instruct the Intrinsics to compress the Expose events into one prior to reporting an event. In this way, the Expose method in the widget deals with the single event rather than with each one separately.

5.4.7. Communication, State, and Colormap Events

Communication events are provided as a means of sharing information between applications. Clients cannot turn this off. The server will always write the event to the client's queue, but the client has to be looking for such events. This kind of an event is called *nonmaskable* because you cannot block it. (Interclient communication is discussed in Chapter 11.)

State events are generated whenever something regarding your configuration occurs. Things like GravityNotify, MapNotify, ReparentNotify, UnmapNotify, VisibilityNotify, ConfigureNotify, CreateNotify, and CirculateNotify are state events.

As discussed in Chapter 4, colormaps are your application's palette of colors to use. If you need to, you can be informed when the colormap changes. As a result of a change, you might choose to be "nasty" and quickly reinstall your previous colormap, or simply change your colors to some safe values.

5.4.8. Event Handlers

Now that you have a better understanding of what events are, where they come from, and the several that occur, you should see how to handle them. The Intrinsics provides two mechanisms for this: the event handler and translation management.

To understand the use of an event handler, let's examine a simple client that demonstrates it. This client uses an Expose event to draw text to the screen using various graphics contexts, set with different colors and fonts. This client also demonstrates the handling of GCs introduced in Chapter 4.

The EventHandler mechanism is a low-level mechanism for event handling. It is closely related to the Xlib primitive, XSelectInput( ), because they share common event mask names. Essentially, clients register an event handler with the Xt EventDispatch mechanism (XtDispatchEvent( )) informing it of which event(s) the client is interested in by using the appropriate event masks. This is done as follows:

```
XtAddEventHandler(drawing_area,ExposureMask,
    FALSE,Expose_Handler,NULL);
```

This says "install the event handler named 'Expose_Handler' for the widget 'drawing_area' and call it when an 'Expose' event type occurs on the widget (actually the widget's window) and don't pass it anything." The arguments are:

1. Widget.
2. Event mask(s).
3. Call-on-nonmaskable-events flag.
4. Event handler.
5. Data for the handler.

The "widget" corresponds to the widget with which the event handler is to be associated. "Event mask(s)" are the events you are interested in. You may provide more than one by "ORing" two masks together, using the format ExposureMask | KeyPressMask. The third argument indicates whether the event handler should be called when nonmaskable events are received. Nonmaskable events are things like ClientMessages (discussed in Chapter 11) or MappingNotify (when another client changes the keyboard mapping). The fourth argument is the name of the event handler to invoke. The final argument is the data the Intrinsics should give to the handler.

Event handlers are written as defined by the Xt Intrinsics manual. Each Intrinsic-specific function has its own mechanics for writing it that you must adhere to. Whenever you see a new routine introduced, assume that the Xt Intrinsics manual has defined the way it is to be written unless you are told otherwise.

The following is the client "XtandGC," which demonstrates the event handler. This client includes the standard Xt stuff in the Utilities header. As you go along, you will learn to add additional goodies that make your programming life easier. The results of this client are shown in Figure 5-6. The code is as follows:

```
/* FILE:    XtandGC.c
 */
#include "XbkUtil.h"
```

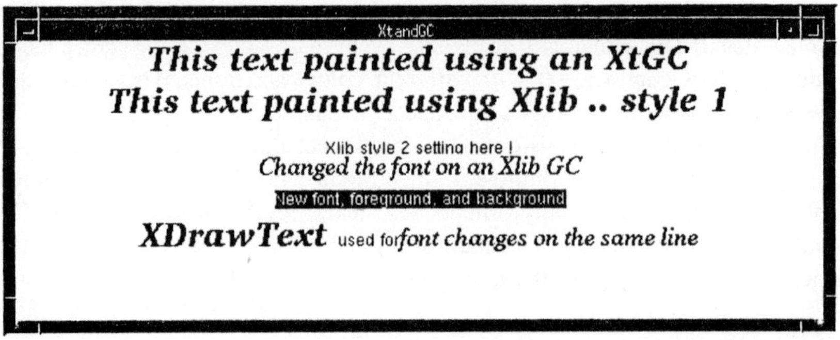

Figure 5-6 XtandGC.

```
/* Widget headers to be used in this client */
#include <X11/Simple.h>

#define XbkShellName        "xtandGC"
#define XbkApplClass        "XtandGC"

/* We set up some text for use in XDrawString, XDrawImageString,
 * and XDrawText.  We also will get some fonts and colors to use.
 */
static char     *some_text[]={
     "This text painted using an XtGC",
     "This text painted using Xlib .. style 1",
     "Xlib style 2 setting here !",
     "Changed the font on an Xlib GC",
     "New font, foreground, and background"};
static char     *some_strings[] = {"XDrawText ","used for",
                "font changes on the same line"};
/*
 * Here are some fonts.  Notice the naming convention and
 * use of wildcards (refer to Chapter 4)
 */
static char     *some_fonts[] = {
     "*-bitstream-charter-bold-i-*-240-*",
     "*-helvetica-medium-r-*-120-*",
     "*-times-medium-i-*-180-*"};
/*
 * Some colors to allocate.
 */
static char     *some_colors[] = {"red","white","blue","green"};
/*
```

```
 * These are variables required for the Xlib primitives.
 */
Colormap  cMap;
XGCValues gcVals;
GC        xtGC,
          xlibGC_style1,
          xlibGC_style2;
XFontStruct    *fonts[3];
XColor         goodColors[4],notNeeded;
int       valMask;
XTextItem txtItms[3];
Position  x,y;
Dimension wth,daWth;
/*
 * Here are some forward declarations
 */
XtEventHandler      Expose_Handler();
/*
 * Trust me on the callback for now.  We will discuss
 * these things very soon.  For now, this will get
 * called when the widget it is associated with is
 * destroyed.
 */
XtCallbackProc DestroyCB();
/*
 * This is a utility routine needed in the client.
 */
void      paint_text();
main(argc,argv)
     int argc; char **argv;
{
     Widget    top, drawing_area;
     int      cnt;
     top = XtInitialize(XbkShellName,XbkApplClass,
     NULL,0,&argc,argv);
/*
 * We can use the Athena SimpleWidget to get just a window.
 * Simple is supposed to be a Meta widget (Non-instanciated);
 * however, it has all of the basic functions we need from a
 * window, so we use it.
 */
     drawing_area = XtCreateManagedWidget("drawingArea",
                    simpleWidgetClass,top,  NULL, 0);
     XtAddCallback(drawing_area,XtNdestroyCallback,DestroyCB,NULL);
```

```
/*
 * Now install an event handler on drawing_area for exposures
 */
    XtAddEventHandler(drawing_area,ExposureMask,
            FALSE,Expose_Handler,NULL);
    XtRealizeWidget(top);
/* Now we can load the fonts and colors so we may use them */
    for (cnt = 0; cnt < XtNumber(some_fonts) ; cnt++)
        fonts[cnt] =
            XLoadQueryFont(XtDisplay(top),some_fonts[cnt]);
    cMap = XbkGetColormap(drawing_area);
    for (cnt = 0; cnt < XtNumber(some_colors) ; cnt++)
        XAllocNamedColor(XtDisplay(top),cMap,
            some_colors[cnt],&goodColors[cnt],&notNeeded);
/*
 * Notice one style of getting gcs.
 */
    gcVals.foreground = goodColors[1].pixel;
    gcVals.background = goodColors[2].pixel;
    gcVals.font      = fonts[0]-fid;
    valMask          = GCForeground | GCBackground | GCFont;
/*
 * This is an Xt gc. It is not alterable !
 */
    xtGC = XtGetGC(drawing_area, valMask, &gcVals);
    XtMainLoop();
}
/*
 * When we die, give back the resources we took
 */
XtCallbackProc     DestroyCB(w,callData,clientData)
    Widget w;
    caddr_t callData,clientData;
{
    XtReleaseGC(xtGC);
    XFreeGC(xlibGC_style1);
    XFreeGC(xlibGC_style2);
/*
 * Take the event handler away
 */
    XtRemoveEventHandler(w,ExposureMask,
        FALSE,Expose_Handler,NULL);
}
/*
```

```
 * Now, the event handler for Exposure Events
 */
XtEventHandler Expose_Handler(w,clientData,event)
     Widget    w;
     caddr_t   clientData;
     XEvent    *event;
{
     paint_text(w);
}
```

This really isn't such a bad client. The event handler in this case simply calls the support routine paint_text(). This is where all of the GC and different text-drawing things occur. In this function, you are introduced to another mechanism called XtGetValues(). This is the way you get things out of widgets.

Warning: The widget must cooperate with you. If it isn't written to give you the resource, you won't get it. This is discussed in more detail in Chapter 6.

To get the value from a widget, you write the following lines:

```
n = 0;
XtSetArg(arg[n],XtNwidth,&width); n ++ ;
XtGetValues(w,arg,n);
```

You tell the widget in the XtSetArg where to put the result. Notice that you need the address of the spot where you want things. If you had just said "width," you would have provided the value in "width," not the address (refer to Chapter 2).

The widget will have its get_values method invoked and the result will wind up in width:

```
void paint_text(w)
     Widget w;
{
     Arg arg[MAXARGS];
     int cnt;
/* We need to re-initialize the Xlib GCs each time since we
 * mess around with them later on.  Since this is the
 * "expose" procedure we need to do it every time.  Notice
 * that the xtGC is done in the "main."  The reason is
 * that that gc never changes so there is no need to
 * re-do it.
 */
     gcVals.foreground = goodColors[1].pixel;
     gcVals.background = goodColors[2].pixel;
     gcVals.font       = fonts[0]-fid;
     valMask           = GCForeground | GCBackground | GCFont;
```

```
    xlibGC_style1 = XCreateGC(XtDisplay(w),
                      XtWindow(w),
                      valMask, &gcVals);

    xlibGC_style2 = XCreateGC(XtDisplay(w),
                      XtWindow(w),
                         0,0);
    XSetForeground(XtDisplay(w),
             xlibGC_style2,goodColors[3].pixel);
    XSetBackground(XtDisplay(w),
             xlibGC_style2,goodColors[2].pixel);
    XSetFont(XtDisplay(w),xlibGC_style2,fonts[1]-fid);

/* Get the widgets width so we can center our text in the area */
    XtSetArg(arg[0],XtNwidth,&daWth);
    XtGetValues(w,arg,(Cardinal)1);

/* Draw the first string using xtGC */
    wth = XTextWidth(fonts[0],some_text[0],strlen(some_text[0]));
    x = (daWth - wth)/2;
    y = 20;
    XDrawImageString(XtDisplay(w),XtWindow(w),
        xtGC,x,y,
        some_text[0],strlen(some_text[0]));
/* Offset y by the previous font height using our tool, center
 * the text, draw the string using the xlibGC_style1.
 */
    y = y + XbkFontHeight(fonts[0]);
    wth = XTextWidth(fonts[0],some_text[1],strlen(some_text[1]));
    x = (daWth - wth)/2;
    XDrawImageString(XtDisplay(w),XtWindow(w),
        xlibGC_style1,x,y,
        some_text[1],strlen(some_text[1]));

/* Repeat same except use xlibGC_style2. */
    y = y + XbkFontHeight(fonts[0]);
    wth = XTextWidth(fonts[1],some_text[2],strlen(some_text[2]));
    x = (daWth - wth)/2;
    XDrawImageString(XtDisplay(w),XtWindow(w),
        xlibGC_style2,x,y,
        some_text[2],strlen(some_text[2]));

/* Do the offset, now change the font.  Notice, we can only do it
 * to the Xlib-created GC.
 */
```

```
    y = y + XbkFontHeight(fonts[1]);
    XSetFont(XtDisplay(w),
        xlibGC_style2,fonts[2]-fid);
    wth = XTextWidth(fonts[2],some_text[3],strlen(some_text[3]));
    x = (daWth - wth)/2;
    XDrawImageString(XtDisplay(w),XtWindow(w),
        xlibGC_style2,x,y,
        some_text[3],strlen(some_text[3]));

/* Now change the foreground and the background using the Xlib
 * functions provided to do that.
 */
    y = y + XbkFontHeight(fonts[2]);
    XSetForeground(XtDisplay(w),
        xlibGC_style1,goodColors[0].pixel);
    XSetBackground(XtDisplay(w),
        xlibGC_style1,goodColors[1].pixel);
    XSetFont(XtDisplay(w),
        xlibGC_style1,fonts[1]-fid);
    wth = XTextWidth(fonts[1],some_text[4],strlen(some_text[4]));
    x = (daWth - wth)/2;
    XDrawImageString(XtDisplay(w),XtWindow(w),
        xlibGC_style1,x,y,
        some_text[4],strlen(some_text[4]));

/* Finally, set up the "compound" text, center it, then draw it. */

    XSetForeground(XtDisplay(w),
        xlibGC_style1,goodColors[1].pixel);
    y = y + XbkFontHeight(fonts[0]);
    wth = 0;
    for(cnt = 0;cnt < XtNumber(some_strings); cnt++) {
            txtItms[cnt].chars  = some_strings[cnt];
            txtItms[cnt].nchars = strlen(some_strings[cnt]);
            txtItms[cnt].delta  = 0;
            txtItms[cnt].font   = fonts[cnt]->fid;
            wth = wth + XTextWidth(fonts[cnt],
                some_strings[cnt],strlen(some_strings[cnt]));
    }
    x = (daWth - wth)/2;
    XDrawText(XtDisplay(w),XtWindow(w),
        xlibGC_style1,x,y,txtItms,XtNumber(some_strings));
}
```

That was rather long, but it killed several birds with one stone. For the most part, the use of GCs will be taken care of by the widgets you are using. If you are like most application writers, you've just learned more about GCs than you probably need to know.

Note that the resource manager could have been used to avoid using the Xlib primitives for loading the fonts and colors. If you want some practice, rewrite this client using the resource manager in place of the primitives.

5.4.9. Translations, Actions, and Callbacks

Using event handlers has its place. In the preceding example, it wasn't such a bad idea to use an event handler for dealing with exposures, but the Intrinsics were created to give application writers quite a bit of flexibility, and event handlers are not very flexible.

Fortunately, there is another way of handling events. This mechanism uses three components: callbacks, action procedures, and the translation manager.

5.4.9.1. Callbacks Every widget has defined at least two sets of callback lists: standard (XtNcallback) and destroy (XtNdestroyCallback). I say at least these two, because some widgets add more. The OSF/Motif set is a good example. It uses callbacks for several kinds of activities, such as focus-in and -out events. Consider the phrase "callback list." It is just that, a list of procedures to call back. In many cases, the callback list contains a single procedure, but there could be several. One thing to be aware of is that the Intrinsics do not guarantee the sequence in which the procedures in the list are called, so don't rely on it.

In the "XtandGC" client, you installed a destroy callback on one of the widgets. This installed a procedure for the Intrinsics to invoke when the widget was being destroyed. Destroy Callbacks are used mainly to do some clean-up chores such as freeing GCs or releasing dynamically allocated memory. The callback is installed as follows:

```
XtAddCallback(drawing_area,XtNdestroyCallback,DestroyCB,NULL);
```

The four arguments are

1. Widget.
2. Callback list.
3. Callback procedure name.
4. Data to give to the callback.

The "widget" represents the one whose callback list is to have the callback procedure installed on it. "Callback list" is the resource name of the list that will be added to. "Callback procedure name" is the Intrinsics-specific callback procedure. The last argument is the data that you want to give to the callback when it is invoked.

To demonstrate the use of the standard callback (XtNcallback), let's create a client that uses this mechanism. This client displays a list of items, and when you click the mouse button on an item, a callback will be invoked and the selected item displayed in a label. The client is shown in Figure 5-7. The code for it is as follows:

```
/*    FILE:          xawlist.c
 */
#include "XbkUtil.h"
#define XbkShellName      "xawlist"
#define XbkApplClass      "Xawlist"
/* We will use three widgets: the Athena Form widget as a
 * container, the list widget, and the label widget.
 */
#include <X11/Form.h>
```

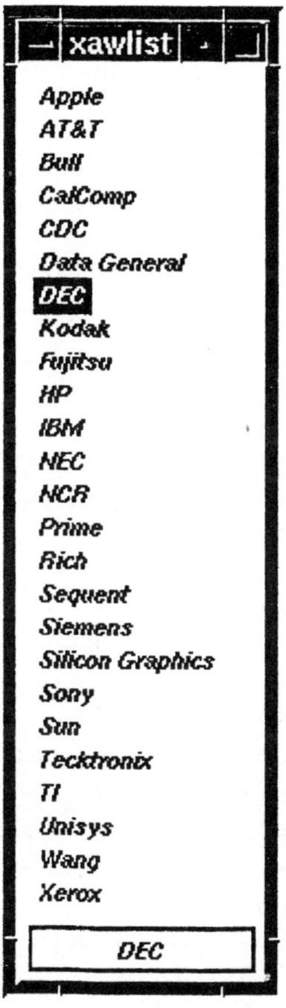

Figure 5-7 Xawlist.

```
#include <X11/List.h>
#include <X11/Label.h>
/*
 * This is the forward declaration of our callback
 */
static void selection_callback();
/*
 * We use a static initialization for our list elements.
 */
static String str[] = {
     "Apple","AT&T","Bull","CalComp","CDC",
     "Data General","DEC","Kodak","Fujitsu",
     "HP","IBM","NEC","NCR","Prime","Rich",
     "Sequent","Siemens","Silicon Graphics",
     "Sony","Sun","Tecktronix","TI","Unisys",
     "Wang","Xerox"};
Widget lbl;    /* We need to make it global so the callback can
                * use it. */
main(argc,argv)
int argc; char *argv[];
{
     Widget      top,container,lst;
     int  i;
     Arg  args[2];
     top =
XtInitialize(XbkShellName,XbkApplClass,NULL,0,&argc,argv);
/* We introduce the FormWidget.  It is a member of the constraint
 * class.  Essentially, it provides additional layout items
 * for each of its children and then manages the children with
 * those items (constraints).
 */
     container = XtCreateManagedWidget("container",
               formWidgetClass,top,NULL,(Cardinal)0);

     XtSetArg(args[0],XtNlist,str);
     XtSetArg(args[1],XtNnumberStrings, XtNumber(str));
     lst = XtCreateManagedWidget("list",
               listWidgetClass,container,args,(Cardinal)2);
/*
 * To install a callback you simply can wait until the widget is
 * created and then add the callback proc to the list using
 * XtAddCallback()
 * If you prefer, you could create a callback list, then pass it as
 * an argument to the creation mechanism.  In most instances we
```

```
 * will have a single callback proc installed so the post-creation
 * method is acceptable.
 */
    XtAddCallback(lst,XtNcallback,selection_callback, NULL);
/*
 * Callbacks do not get called automatically.  Something needs to
 * invoke them using XtCallCallbacks().  We will discuss the magic
 * in the next client we write.  For now assume the Intrinsics
 * "wizard" does the trick.
 */

/* This argument is one of those constraints that the FormWidget
 * has given us.  I want the lbl widget to be placed below the
 * first widget. To do that, I simply attach the constraint
 * XtNfromVert to lbl and the FormWidget does the rest.
 */
    XtSetArg(args[0],XtNfromVert,lst);
    XtSetArg(args[1],XtNlabel,"No selection yet !!");
    lbl = XtCreateManagedWidget("lbl",
              labelWidgetClass,container,args,(Cardinal)2);
    XtRealizeWidget(top);
    XtMainLoop();
}
/*
 * This is our callback procedure.  All callbacks are written the
 * same exact way.  That is, there are three arguments:
 *       w           - the widget that invoked the callback
 *       client_data - an address of where to put data that
 *                     the callback will give to the client.
 *       call_data   - an address of where the client put data
 *                     for the callback.
 *
 * Both client_data and call_data are "opaque" pointers.  Recalling
 * from the review in Chapter 2, the opaque pointer can assume the
 * role of several things.  In the case of the callback for the
 * ListWidget, the widget writer has defined call_data as a
 * pointer to XtListReturnStruct.
 *
 * When the magic invokes the callback, it
 * places some information into the members of the structure, then
 * passes it to the callback.
 */
static void selection_callback(w,client_data,call_data)
    Widget w;
```

```
        caddr_t *client_data;
        XtListReturnStruct *call_data;
{
/*
 * We want the callback to fill in the 'lbl' widget with the
 * information in the selection.  Notice that 'lbl' is a global
 * variable.
 */
        Arg args[1];
        XtSetArg(args[0],XtNlabel,(XtArgVal)call_data-string);
        XtSetValues(lbl,args,(Cardinal)1);
}
```

The important points in this client are the installation of the callback, the writing of the callback (an Intrinsics-specific procedure), the use of the formWidgetClass, and the use of XtSetValues().

Whenever you need to update resources in a widget, you use the Intrinsics mechanism XtSetValues(). It is very easy to use; you simply set up an argument list just like the one for XtGetValues(), except you provide the *value* of the resource as opposed to the *address* of the resource. After filling out your list, you simply pass it to XtSetValues() and the Intrinsics do the rest.

Warning: Just as XtGetValues( ) had a "gotcha" so too does XtSetValues(). It's the same one: The widget must be written to allow you to set the resources. Well then, how will you know if you can or can't set resources? Hopefully, the widget writer gave you an accurate facts sheet, or better still, the source code (Athena is free, OSF/Motif costs a little money). In Chapter 6, you will see how a widget handles the XtSetValues( )/XtGetValues( ) requests.

5.4.9.2. Translations and Actions This use of callbacks is fairly nice stuff, but it would be nice to know how the Intrinsics "wizard" pulls off these tricks. You know XtCallCallbacks() is used, but who calls it? You can see for sure that it isn't the client. Or is it?

The answer is "No." The widget does the calling. How is this done? To demonstrate, you will add a keyboard interface to the "xawlist" client. That is, you would like to move around the list using the Up and Down arrow keys, then make the selection using the Return key. This client is shown in Figure 5-8. Its code is as follows:

```
/*    FILE:          xawlistTM.c
 */
#include "XbkUtil.h"
#define XbkShellName       "xawlistTM"
#define XbkApplClass       "XawlistTM"
#include <X11/Form.h>
```

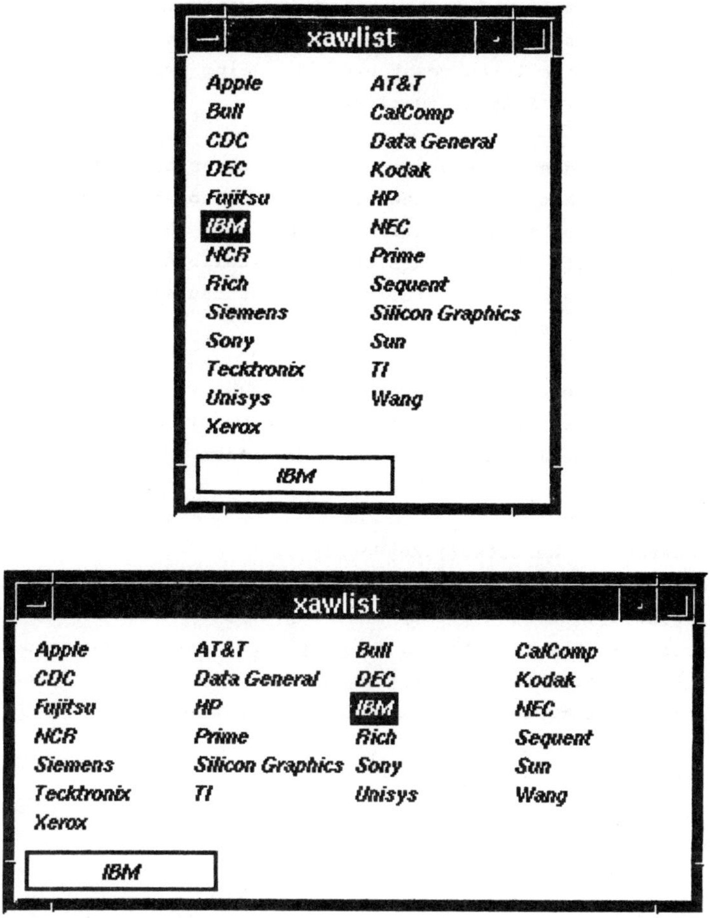

Figure 5-8a and b XawlistTM.

```
#include <X11/List.h>
#include <X11/Label.h>
/*
 * This is the forward declaration of our callback
 */
static void selection_callback();
/* In xawlist.c we introduced the concept of the callback procedure
 * and hinted at some magic going on behind the scenes.  In this
 * client we introduce the translation mechanism for getting things
 * done.
 *
 * Translations are ways of performing actions based on some
```

```
 * events. We simply define the action to watch for and the
 * action(s) to take when the event occurs.  This is much easier
 * than writing the large messy event-handling switch statement
 * that you see in Xlib-based clients.
 *
 * In the listWidgetClass you would see a translation table that
 * kicks off an ActionProc (the type of function that is invoked by
 * the translation manager) called Notify when the mouse button is
 * pressed. Notify then invokes the XtCallCallbacks on the widget.
 * That is the magic behind the scenes that causes the callbacks
 * registered to be invoked.
 *
 * As in the case of the callback procedures, we must first
 * forward-declare the functions.  Notice we are sticking with the
 * safe way of declaring this kind of function by using
 * XtActionProc.
 */
XtActionProc     NextItem(),KeyNotify();
/* The next thing we will have to do is set up an action table.
 * Essentially, we need to map a string representation of a
 * function to the real thing. So we provide the string used in
 * the translation table, dropping the parameter part and the
 * function the translation manager will invoke.
 */
XtActionsRec    listAxns[] = {
{"NextItem",NextItem},
{"KeyNotify",KeyNotify},
{NULL, NULL},
};
/* The next step is to define a translation table.  It is a static
 * string with a defined format.  The first part is the event you
 * want to watch. You then place a semicolon between the event and
 * the list of action procedures that will be called (in our case
 * we call NextItem passing a parameter) then separate each entry
 * with a \n. The '\' after the \n is used to instruct the
 * compiler that we are continuing the line.
 */
static String   list_actions =
      "#override \
      <Key>Up: NextItem(Up) \n\
      <Key>Down: NextItem(Down)\n\
      <Key>Return: KeyNotify()";
/* Finally, we need to define a variable that will contain the
 * parsed translations.
 */
XtTranslations     listTrans;
```

```
static String str[] = {
      "Apple","AT&T","Bull","CalComp","CDC",
      "Data General","DEC","Kodak","Fujitsu",
      "HP","IBM","NEC","NCR","Prime","Rich",
      "Sequent","Siemens","Silicon Graphics",
      "Sony","Sun","Tecktronix","TI","Unisys",
      "Wang","Xerox"};

Widget lbl;    /* Need to make it global so the callback can
                * use it.
                */
main(argc,argv)
int argc; char *argv[];
{
      Widget    top,container,lst;
      int    i;
      Arg     args[3];
      top = XtInitialize(XbkShellName,XbkApplClass,
             NULL,0,&argc,argv);
/*
 *     Install our new actions and compile the list.
 */
      XtAddActions(listAxns,XtNumber(listAxns));
      listTrans = XtParseTranslationTable(list_actions);

      container = XtCreateManagedWidget("container",
                  formWidgetClass,top,NULL,(Cardinal)0);
      XtSetArg(args[0],XtNlist,str);
      XtSetArg(args[1],XtNnumberStrings, XtNumber(str));
      lst = XtCreateManagedWidget("list",listWidgetClass,
                  container,args,(Cardinal)2);
      XtAddCallback(lst,XtNcallback,selection_callback, NULL);
/*
 * Now install the new translations overriding any that may be
 * defined.
 */
      XtOverrideTranslations(lst,listTrans);
      XtSetArg(args[0],XtNfromVert,lst);
      XtSetArg(args[1],XtNlabel,"No selection yet !!");
      lbl = XtCreateManagedWidget("lbl",
                  labelWidgetClass,container,args,(Cardinal)2);
      XtRealizeWidget(top);
      XtMainLoop();
}
```

```
/*
 * These are the Action Procs.  These are Intrinsic-specific
 * functions and as such have predefined mechanisms for writing
 * them.
 */
XtActionProc KeyNotify(w,event,param,num_params)
        Widget w;
        XEvent *event;
        String *param;
        Cardinal num_params;
{
     XtListReturnStruct *now = XtListShowCurrent(w);
     XtCallCallbacks(w,XtNcallback, now);
}
typedef enum {Up = 'U',Down ='D'} Axn;
XtActionProc NextItem(w,event,param,num_params)
        Widget w;
        XEvent *event;
        String *param;
        Cardinal num_params;
{
     Axn action;
     Arg arg[2];
     XtListReturnStruct *now;
     int nstr,idx;
     action = (Axn)param[0][0];
/* By using the C enum type it is easy to determine the action to
 * be taken.  You will notice that the parameters passed are
 * strings.  In our case we pass either Up or Down.
 */
        if (islower((char)action))
                action = (Axn)toupper((char)action);
/* Now we can check on the action and set highlight the next list
 * item.
 */
     now = XtListShowCurrent(w);
     idx = now->index;
     XtSetArg(arg[0],XtNnumberStrings,&nstr);
     XtGetValues(w,arg,1);
        switch(action) {
                case Up:
               XtListHighlight(w,(idx == 0) ? --nstr : --idx);
                        break;
                case Down:
               XtListHighlight(w,(idx == --nstr) ? 0 : ++idx);
               break;
```

```
        }
}
static void selection_callback(w,client_data,call_data)
        Widget w;
        caddr_t *client_data;
        XtListReturnStruct *call_data;
{
        Arg args[1];
        XtSetArg(args[0],XtNlabel,(XtArgVal)call_data->string);
        XtSetValues(lbl,args,(Cardinal)1);
}
```

The important points in this client are the translation table definitions, the installation of new actions, the parsing of the translation table, the installation of the new translations, and the action procedures.

Every widget has provisions for one translation table. The translation table may be provided either in the source (as in "xawlistTM") or through the resource database (discussed in Chapter 9). The Xt Intrinsics manual describes the syntax of the translation table in detail, but you need to remember a few things:

1. :<Key>a refers to the lowercase a.
2. <Key>a refers to either lowercase or uppercase a.
3. If you want to define a key, simply use the definition of the keysym in keysymdef.h and remove the "XK_." XK_a becomes a and XK_tilde becomes tilde.
4. A tilda (~) means "not this." So if you saw ~Alt<Key>f: Action it reads "do the Action when any key is pressed with the 'f' key *except* Alt."
5. More specific entries must come first in the list.
6. You may use shorthand for repeated events. For example, <Btn1Down>,<Btn1Down>,<Btn1Down>: MultiClick() could be replaced by <Btn1Down>(3): MultiClick().
7. The caret (^) means Ctrl, the dollar sign ($) means Meta, and the backslash (\) is used to indicate a quote.

Table 5-5
Key and Button Abbreviations

Abbreviation	What It Means
Ctrl	KeyPress and Ctrl modifier
Meta	KeyPress and Meta modifier
Shift	KeyPress and Shift modifier
Alt	KeyPress and Alt modifier
Btn[1,2,3,4,5]Down	ButtonPress with detail specified
Btn[1,2,3,4,5]Up	ButtonRelease with detail specified
Btn[1,2,3,4,5]Motion	MotionNotify with button modifier
BtnMotion	MotionNotify with any button

Table 5-6
Event Types for Translation Tables

Use in Table	Event Corresponding to Entry
Key	KeyPress
KeyDown	KeyPress
KeyUp	KeyRelease
BtnDown	ButtonPress
BtnUp	ButtonRelease
Motion	MotionNotify
PtrMoved	MotionNotify
MouseMoved	MotionNotify
Enter	EnterNotify
EnterWindow	EnterNotify
Leave	LeaveNotify
LeaveWindow	LeaveNotify
FocusIn	FocusIn
FocusOut	FocusOut
Keymap	KeymapNotify
Expose	Expose
GrExpose	GraphicsExpose
NoExp	NoExpose
Visible	VisibilityNotify
Create	CreateNotify
Destroy	DestroyNotify
Unmap	UnmapNotify
Map	MapNotify
MapReq	MapRequest
Reparent	ReparentNotify
Configure	ConfigureNotify
ConfigureReq	ConfigureRequest
Grav	GravityNotify
ResReq	ResizeRequest
Circ	CirculateNotify
CircReq	CirculateRequest
Prop	PropertyNotify
SelClr	SelectionClear
SelReq	SelectionRequest
Select	SelectionNotify
Clrmap	ColormapNotify
Message	ClientMessage
Mapping	MappingNotify

Place the less-than and greater-than signs around the event that you are watching for. So, if you were interested in the ColormapNotify event, you would have the following table entry:

```
<Clrmap>:          DoSomethingAboutColormap()
```

5.4.10. Alternative Procedures

Now that you are an expert at setting and dealing with events, you need to explore three additional units of work that can be done using the Intrinsics: the timeout procedure, the alternative input procedure, and the background work procedure.

5.4.10.1. Timeout Procedures There are times in applications when you would like to have a reminder to do something. For instance, suppose you wanted to reread a database every five minutes. This could be a separate process running that would sleep for that time, then wake up and perform the job. In Xt this job could be performed by XtTimeoutProc.

To demonstrate this, let's create a client that uses this function. The client is called "alarm" and will use several of the mechanisms you have already used in previous clients. One neat feature is added to this client: the ability to display a clock. This is very easy to do since the Athena Widget Set has a clockWidgetClass (if you've seen xclock, you've seen this widget in action). This client simply lets the user set an alarm to ring at a specific time.

To add a timeout procedure use

```
id = XtAddTimeOut(delay,proc,data)
```

where delay is the number of milliseconds to wait before timing out, proc refers to the Intrinsics-specific timeout procedure, and data is information to give to the procedure. To remove this procedure, use

```
XtRemoveTimeOut(id)
```

where id refers to an id returned from a previous XtAddTimeOut() call. This client is shown in Figure 5-9. The code is given here:

```
/* FILE:    alarm.c
 */
/* Our utility header file */
#include "XbkUtil.h"
/* Widget headers to be used in this client */
#include <X11/Form.h>
#include <X11/Box.h>
#include <X11/Clock.h>
```

```
#include <X11/Command.h>
#include <X11/Label.h>

#define XbkShellName      "alarm"
#define XbkApplClass      "Alarm"

/* We set up a structure that will have this applications default.
*/
struct _myAppRes {
        Boolean     viewClock;
} myAppRes;

XrmOptionDescRec myCmdOpts[] = {
{ "-viewClock", "*viewClock", XrmoptionNoArg, "TRUE" },
};

#define OFFSET(field)  XtOffset(struct _myAppRes*, field)
static XtResource myAppResOpts[] = {
   {"viewClock", "ViewClock", XtRBoolean, sizeof(Boolean),
       OFFSET(viewClock),XtRString, "False"},
};
#undef OFFSET
/* Here are a bunch of callbacks */
XtCallbackProc     set_hour(),set_minute(),set_ampm(),set_alarm();
```

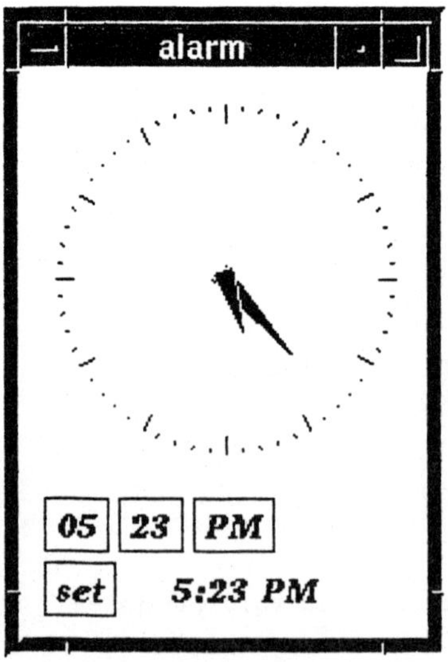

Figure 5-9 Alarm.

```
/* This is a forward declare for the time out proc */
XtTimerCallbackProc     TellThem();

#define ALARMRANG "Alarm Rang !!"
#define DISABLE    "Alarm is Off"
#define AM     0
#define PM     1
/* Set up the globals for use in the callback routines.
 */

struct tm tm, *localtime();
long      tv;
char      scratch[10];
/* We need to keep around some 'state' data. */
struct   {
    Boolean   alarmSet;
    int       hour;
    int       min;
    int       amOrpm;
    XtIntervalId    id;
} alarmData;

Widget setLbl;

main(argc,argv)
     int argc;
     char **argv;
{
     Widget top,container,clk,
          button_container,hr,min,am_pm,set;
     char     scratch[10];
     Arg arg[MAXARGS];
     int n;

     top = XtInitialize(XbkShellName,XbkApplClass,
                 myCmdOpts,XtNumber(myCmdOpts),
                 &argc, argv);
/* We've used this before  */
      XtGetApplicationResources(top, &myAppRes, myAppResOpts,
                  XtNumber(myAppResOpts),NULL, 0);
/* Now if the user wants the clock, then create a container to
 * hold the clock and the button box.  Otherwise, just create the
 * button box.
 */
```

```
    if (myAppRes.viewClock) {
        container =
            XtCreateManagedWidget("container",boxWidgetClass,
                        top,NULL,0);
 /* Can you believe this is all we had to do to get an analog
clock?  */
        clk = XtCreateManagedWidget("clk",clockWidgetClass,
                    container,NULL,0);
        button_container =
            XtCreateManagedWidget("button_container",
                formWidgetClass,container,NULL,0);
    } else {
        button_container =
            XtCreateManagedWidget("button_container",
                formWidgetClass,top,NULL,0);
    }
    (void) time(&tv);
    tm = *localtime(&tv);
/*
 * Set the alarm data
 */
    alarmData.alarmSet = False;
    alarmData.hour   = (tm.tm_hour > 12) ? tm.tm_hour - 12 :
                       tm.tm_hour;
    alarmData.min    = tm.tm_min;
    alarmData.amOrpm = (tm.tm_hour > 12) ? PM : AM;

    memset(scratch,'\0',sizeof(scratch));
    if (alarmData.hour <= 9)
        sprintf(scratch,"0%ld",alarmData.hour);
    else
        sprintf(scratch,"%2d",alarmData.hour);
    n = 0;
    XtSetArg(arg[n],XtNleft,XtChainLeft); n++;
    XtSetArg(arg[n],XtNlabel,scratch); n++;
    hr = XtCreateManagedWidget("hour",commandWidgetClass,
                    button_container,arg,n);
    XtAddCallback(hr,XtNcallback,set_hour,NULL);

    memset(scratch,'\0',sizeof(scratch));
    if (alarmData.min <= 9)
        sprintf(scratch,"0%ld",alarmData.min);
    else
        sprintf(scratch,"%2d",alarmData.min);
```

```
    n = 0;
    XtSetArg(arg[n],XtNfromHoriz,hr); n++;
    XtSetArg(arg[n],XtNlabel,scratch); n++;
    min=XtCreateManagedWidget("minute",commandWidgetClass,
                button_container,arg,n);
    XtAddCallback(min,XtNcallback,set_minute,NULL);
    memset(scratch,'\0',sizeof(scratch));
    sprintf(scratch,(alarmData.amOrpm == PM) ? "PM" : "AM");
    n = 0;
    XtSetArg(arg[n],XtNfromHoriz,min); n++;
    XtSetArg(arg[n],XtNlabel,scratch); n++;
    am_pm = XtCreateManagedWidget("am_pm",commandWidgetClass,
                button_container,arg,n);
    XtAddCallback(am_pm,XtNcallback,set_ampm,NULL);
    n = 0;
    XtSetArg(arg[n],XtNfromVert,hr); n++;
    set = XtCreateManagedWidget("set",commandWidgetClass,
                button_container,arg,n);
    XtAddCallback(set,XtNcallback,set_alarm,NULL);
    n = 0;
    XtSetArg(arg[n],XtNfromHoriz,set); n++;
    XtSetArg(arg[n],XtNfromVert,am_pm); n++;
    XtSetArg(arg[n],XtNlabel,DISABLE);n++;
    setLbl = XtCreateManagedWidget("setLabel",labelWidgetClass,
                button_container,arg,n);
    XtRealizeWidget(top);
    XtMainLoop();
}
/* These are the callbacks that increment the number and toggle
* AM/PM.
*/
XtCallbackProc set_hour(w,call_data,client_data)
    Widget w; caddr_t call_data,client_data;
{
    Arg arg[1];
    alarmData.hour = (alarmData.hour == 12) ? 1 : alarmData.hour
+ 1;
    memset(scratch,'\0',sizeof(scratch));
    if (alarmData.hour  9)
        sprintf(scratch,"0%1d",alarmData.hour);
    else
        sprintf(scratch,"%2d",alarmData.hour);
    XtSetArg(arg[0],XtNlabel,scratch);
    XtSetValues(w,arg,(Cardinal)1);
```

```
}
XtCallbackProc set_minute(w,call_data,client_data)
     Widget w; caddr_t call_data,client_data;
{
     Arg arg[1];
     alarmData.min = (alarmData.min == 59) ? 0 : alarmData.min + 1;
     memset(scratch,'\0',sizeof(scratch));
     if (alarmData.min <= 9)
          sprintf(scratch,"0%ld",alarmData.min);
     else
          sprintf(scratch,"%2d",alarmData.min);
     XtSetArg(arg[0],XtNlabel,scratch);
     XtSetValues(w,arg,(Cardinal)1);
}
XtCallbackProc set_ampm(w,call_data,client_data)
     Widget w; caddr_t call_data,client_data;
{
     Arg arg[1];
     switch(alarmData.amOrpm) {
     case PM:
          memset(scratch,'\0',sizeof(scratch));
          sprintf(scratch,"AM");
          XtSetArg(arg[0],XtNlabel,scratch);
          XtSetValues(w,arg,(Cardinal)1);
          alarmData.amOrpm = AM;
          break;
     default:
          memset(scratch,'\0',sizeof(scratch));
          sprintf(scratch,"PM");
          XtSetArg(arg[0],XtNlabel,scratch);
          XtSetValues(w,arg,(Cardinal)1);
          alarmData.amOrpm = PM;
          break;
     }
}
/*
 * This is where we use the timeout.  If the alarm was previously
 * set we remove the timeout, if not we add it.
 */
XtCallbackProc set_alarm(w,call_data,client_data)
     Widget w; caddr_t call_data,client_data;
{
     Arg arg[1];
     unsigned long delay, hr_delay;
```

```
        long min_delay;
        if (alarmData.alarmSet) {
             XtRemoveTimeOut(alarmData.id);
             alarmData.alarmSet = False;
             memset(scratch,'\0',sizeof(scratch));
             sprintf(scratch,"%s",DISABLE);
             XtSetArg(arg[0],XtNlabel,scratch);
             XtSetValues(setLbl,arg,(Cardinal)1);
        } else {
             (void) time(&tv);
             tm = *localtime(&tv);
             switch(alarmData.amOrpm){
             case PM:
/* This says, if the current time is greater than the alarm request
 * time then set the delay.
 */
                  if ((tm.tm_hour > 12) &&
                      ((tm.tm_hour == alarmData.hour+12) &&
                       (tm.tm_min  <  alarmData.min)) ||
                       (tm.tm_hour <  alarmData.hour+12)){
                      hr_delay = (unsigned long)
                        (tm.tm_hour-(alarmData.hour+12))*60;
                      min_delay =
                        (tm.tm_min - alarmData.min);
                      delay = hr_delay +
                           (min_delay < 0 ? min_delay*-1 :
                                min_delay);
                      alarmData.alarmSet = True;
/* Here it is!  We install the timeout to ring at some delay
 * found by that nasty logic above.  Since the timeout proc
 * requires milliseconds we need to do the multiplication
 * to instruct the Intrinsics.
 */
                       alarmData.id =
                            XtAddTimeOut(delay*60*1000,
                                 TellThem,NULL);
                       memset(scratch,'\0',sizeof(scratch));
                       if (alarmData.min <= 9)
                         sprintf(scratch,"%2d:0%1d PM",
                         alarmData.hour,alarmData.min);
                       else
                         sprintf(scratch,"%2d:%2d PM",
                             alarmData.hour,alarmData.min);
                             XtSetArg(arg[0],XtNlabel,scratch);
```

```
                              XtSetValues(setLbl,arg,(Cardinal)1);
        } else {
                      BEEP(w);
                      BEEP(w);
                      return;
              }
              break;
        case AM:
              if ((tm.tm_hour < 12) &&
                  ((tm.tm_hour == alarmData.hour+12) &&
                   (tm.tm_min  <  alarmData.min)) ||
                   (tm.tm_hour <  alarmData.hour+12)){
                  hr_delay = (unsigned long)
                   (tm.tm_hour-(alarmData.hour+12))*60;
                  min_delay = (tm.tm_min - alarmData.min);
                  delay = hr_delay +
                        (min_delay < 0 ? min_delay*-1 :
                             min_delay);
                  alarmData.alarmSet = True;
                  alarmData.id =
                       XtAddTimeOut(delay*60*1000,
                            TellThem,NULL);
                  memset(scratch,'\0',sizeof(scratch));
                  sprintf(scratch,"%2d:%2d AM",
                       alarmData.hour,alarmData.min);
                  XtSetArg(arg[0],XtNlabel,scratch);
                  XtSetValues(setLbl,arg,(Cardinal)1);
              } else {
                  BEEP(w);
                  BEEP(w);
                  return;
              }
              break;
        }/*endofswitch*/
      }/*endofif*/
}
/*
 * And here is the actual code!  Notice, it is very
 * trivial.  In our case, we issue a beep and change the label
 * to ALARMRANG.
 */

XtTimerCallbackProc TellThem(call_data,id)
     caddr_t call_data; XtIntervalId    id;
```

```
{
    Arg arg[1];
    alarmData.alarmSet = False;
    memset(scratch,'\0',sizeof(scratch));
    sprintf(scratch,"%s",ALARMRANG);
    XtSetArg(arg[0],XtNlabel,scratch);
    XtSetValues(setLbl,arg,(Cardinal)1);
    BEEP(setLbl);
}
```

The three most important aspects of this client are the easy addition of a "fancy" display by simply creating an instance of its widget (clockWidgetClass), the installation of the timeout, and the removal of the timeout.

You used XtAddTimeOut(delay,proc,data) to install the timeout and return its id. Notice that delay is in milliseconds, proc is XtTimeoutCallbackProc, and data is for passing any information to the proc. To remove a timeout, use XtRemoveTimeOut(id), where id is returned from a previous XtAddTimeOut() call. Figure 5-10 shows the results at three different stages.

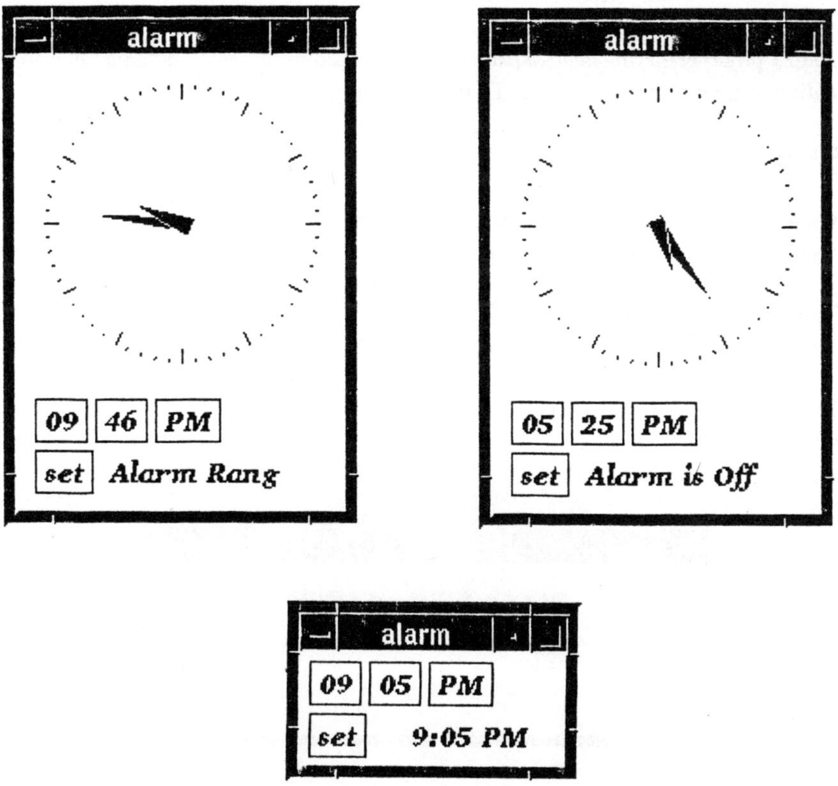

Figure 5-10a, b, and c Alarm clocks.

5.4.10.2. Background Work Procedures There are times when you need to have some additional work performed while you wait for events. After all, you could wait around for quite some time before the next event arrives. If you needed to do some work and still handle events, you could run into some serious problems because you didn't give either enough time.

This problem of giving work to both event processing and application processing is partly addressed by the Intrinsics background work procedure. Essentially, you install a work procedure similarly to the way you did it for the timeout procedure.

To demonstrate, let's create a client called "calcit." This client displays a list of securities (stocks). When you click on the issue, you will kick off a background work procedure that reads a file, calculates the average high, low, and closing price, and then displays the results. While the work is being performed, you set the list to be insensitive, effectively disabling it by using the XtSetSensitive() function.

The work procedure in this client is *re-entrant* or state-driven. It is important to write your work procedures this way since you do not want to do too much work before you check the event queue.

To add a work procedure, use the following:

```
id = XtAddWorkProc(proc,data);
```

where "proc" is the Intrinsics-specific work procedure name, and "data" is information to give to the work proc. To remove a procedure, use this:

```
XtRemoveWorkProc(id);
```

where "id" refers to the id returned from a previous XtAddWorkProc() call. The client is shown in Figure 5-11. The code is as follows:

```
/* FILE:  calcit.c
 */

/* Our utility header file */
#include "XbkUtil.h"
```

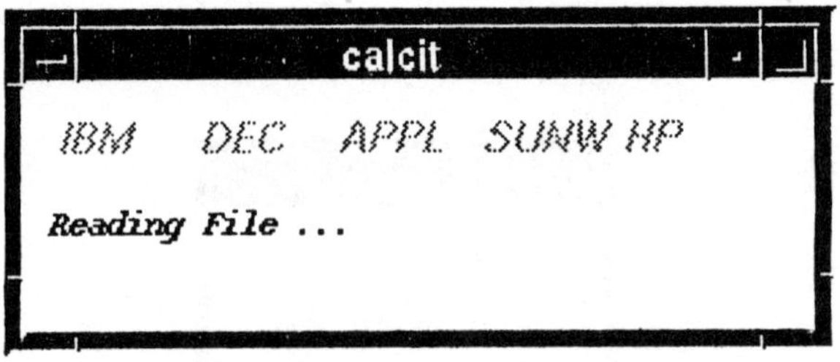

Figure 5-11 Calcit.

```
/* Widget headers to be used in this client */
#include <X11/Form.h>
#include <X11/List.h>
#include <X11/Label.h

#define XbkShellName     "Calcit"
#define XbkApplClass     "Calcit"

/** These are the states used for managing the WorkProcs
 */
#define NOSTATE     0
#define READFILE    1
#define CALCIT      2
#define RESULT      3

/* Some messages we want to display */
#define NOTHING "                    "
#define READ   "Reading File ..."
#define CALC   "Calculating ... "
#define DONE   "Done !!          "
#define ERROR  "No Data File !! "

static char *list[] = {"IBM","DEC","APPL","SUNW","HP"};
/* A structure for reading in the data file (recall Chapter 2) */
typedef struct _TRADEREC{
     float     high;
     float     low;
     float     close;
} TRADEREC;

/* We initialize this "table" that corresponds to the list
 * defined above.  In this way we may refer to the information
 * through the list index that is returned when we make
 * the selection.
 */
struct {
     int            state;    /* state data */
     char           *file;    /* file to read */
     XtWorkProcId   wp_id;    /* the workproc's id */
     float          high;
     float          low;
     float          close;
     int       num_recs;
} choice_data[] = {
```

```
        {NOSTATE,"ibm.dat",0,0.00,0.00,0.00,0},
        {NOSTATE,"dec.dat",0,0.00,0.00,0.00,0},
        {NOSTATE,"apple.dat",0,0.00,0.00,0.00,0},
        {NOSTATE,"sun.dat",0,0.00,0.00,0.00,0},
        {NOSTATE,"hp.dat",0,0.00,0.00,0.00,0}
};

XtCallbackProc      selection_callback();
Boolean             calcit();
Widget              lst,lbl,result;
char                rslt[40];

/* These are some handy macros to perform some clean-up work
 */
#define CLEAN(it)    memset(it,' ',sizeof(it))
#define INIT(it)     memset(it,'\0',sizeof(it))
#define CLRRSLT(it) {Arg arg[1]; CLEAN(it);\
                XtSetArg(arg[0],XtNlabel,it); \
                XtSetValues(result,arg,(Cardinal)1);}
main(argc,argv)
        int argc;
        char **argv;
{
        Widget top,container;

        Arg        args[MAXARGS];
        int n;
        top = XtInitialize(XbkShellName,XbkApplClass,
                NULL,0, &argc, argv);
        container = XtCreateManagedWidget("container",
                formWidgetClass,top,NULL,0);
        n = 0;
        XtSetArg(args[n],XtNlist,list); n++;
        XtSetArg(args[n],XtNnumberStrings, XtNumber(list)); n++;
        lst = XtCreateManagedWidget("list",
                listWidgetClass,container,args,(Cardinal)n);
        XtAddCallback(lst,XtNcallback,selection_callback, NULL);

        n = 0;
        XtSetArg(args[n],XtNfromVert,lst); n++;
        XtSetArg(args[n],XtNlabel,NOTHING); n++;
        lbl = XtCreateManagedWidget("status",
                labelWidgetClass,container,args,(Cardinal)n);
        INIT(rslt);
```

```
    CLEAN(rslt);
    n = 0;
    XtSetArg(args[n],XtNfromVert,lbl); n++;
    XtSetArg(args[n],XtNlabel,rslt); n++;
    result = XtCreateManagedWidget("result",
              labelWidgetClass,container,args,(Cardinal)n);
    XtRealizeWidget(top);
    XtMainLoop();
}

XtCallbackProc selection_callback(w,client_data,call_data)
    Widget w;
    caddr_t *client_data;
    XtListReturnStruct *call_data;
{
    Arg args[1];
    CLRRSLT(rslt);
    if (choice_data[call_data->index].wp_id == NULL) {
         choice_data[call_data->index].state = READFILE;
         choice_data[call_data->index].wp_id =
              XtAddWorkProc(calcit,call_data->index);
         XtSetArg(args[0],XtNlabel,READ);
         XtSetValues(lbl,args,(Cardinal)1);
         XtSetArg(args[0],XtNsensitive,False);
         XtSetValues(w,args,(Cardinal)1);
    } else {
         BEEP(w); BEEP(w);
    }
}
Boolean calcit(idx)
    int idx;
{
    Arg        args[1];
    FILE       *fp;
    TRADEREC   rec;
    char       rslt[40];

    switch(choice_data[idx].state) {
/* The first state is to read and store the information from
 * the data file for the list entry selected.
 */
    case READFILE:
         CLRRSLT(rslt);
         choice_data[idx].num_recs = 0;
```

```
        choice_data[idx].high = choice_data[idx].low =
         choice_data[idx].close = (float)0.00;
        sleep(5); /* this is simply to slow it down */
        if ((fp = fopen(choice_data[idx].file,"r")) == NULL) {
             choice_data[idx].state = NOSTATE;
             choice_data[idx].wp_id = NULL;
             XtSetArg(args[0],XtNlabel,ERROR);
             XtSetValues(lbl,args,(Cardinal)1);
             XtSetArg(args[0],XtNsensitive,True);
             XtSetValues(lst,args,(Cardinal)1);
             XtListHighlight(lst,idx);
             return TRUE;
        } else {
             while((fscanf(fp,"%f %f %f",
                  &rec.high,&rec.low,&rec.close)) != EOF){
                  choice_data[idx].num_recs++;
                  choice_data[idx].high =
                   choice_data[idx].high + rec.high;
                  choice_data[idx].low =
                   choice_data[idx].low + rec.low;
                  choice_data[idx].close =
                   choice_data[idx].close + rec.close;
             }
             fclose(fp);
             choice_data[idx].state = CALCIT;
             XtSetArg(args[0],XtNlabel,CALC);
             XtSetValues(lbl,args,(Cardinal)1);
/* By returning FALSE we tell the Intrinsics to call us again.
 * If we return TRUE, the Intrinsics removes us.
 */
             return FALSE;
        }
        break;
/* The next state is to perform the averages...
 */
    case CALCIT:
        sleep(5); /* Just to slow us down */
        choice_data[idx].high =
              choice_data[idx].high/choice_data[idx].num_recs;
        choice_data[idx].low =
              choice_data[idx].low/choice_data[idx].num_recs;
        choice_data[idx].close =
           choice_data[idx].close/choice_data[idx].num_recs;
        choice_data[idx].state = RESULT;
```

```
          return FALSE;
          break;
     case RESULT:
/* The last state is to display the results.
 */
          XtSetArg(args[0],XtNlabel,DONE);
          XtSetValues(lbl,args,(Cardinal)1);
          choice_data[idx].state = NOSTATE;
          choice_data[idx].wp_id = NULL;
          CLEAN(rslt);
          sprintf(rslt,"%s High %.3f Low %.3f Close %.3f",
               list[idx],choice_data[idx].high,
               choice_data[idx].low,choice_data[idx].close);
          XtSetArg(args[0],XtNlabel,rslt);
          XtSetValues(result,args,(Cardinal)1);
/* We instruct the widget to become sensitive again !!  We could
 * have used XtSetSensitive(lst,True) instead.
 */

          XtSetArg(args[0],XtNsensitive,True);
          XtSetValues(lst,args,(Cardinal)1);
          XtListHighlight(lst,idx);


/* Now we are done so inform the Intrinsics of it so we won't be
 * called again.
 */
          return TRUE;
          break;
   }
}
```

This client is fairly simple, yet it introduces an area that you, as an application writer, will no doubt want to exploit. The important points are: Do not stay in the work proc for long periods of time; if you want to re-enter the work proc, return false; and if you need to remove the work procedure, use XtRemoveWorkProc(id) where id is the id returned from a previous XtAddWorkProc(). Figure 5-12 shows the client at two stages of work.

5.4.10.3. Alternative Input Procedures The last of the three additional units of work is using alternative input devices. This corresponds to using files or pipes to be informed of information. You may watch the pipe/file for four different things:

1. XtInputNoneMask, an OS-dependent condition.
2. XtInputReadMask when there is info to read.

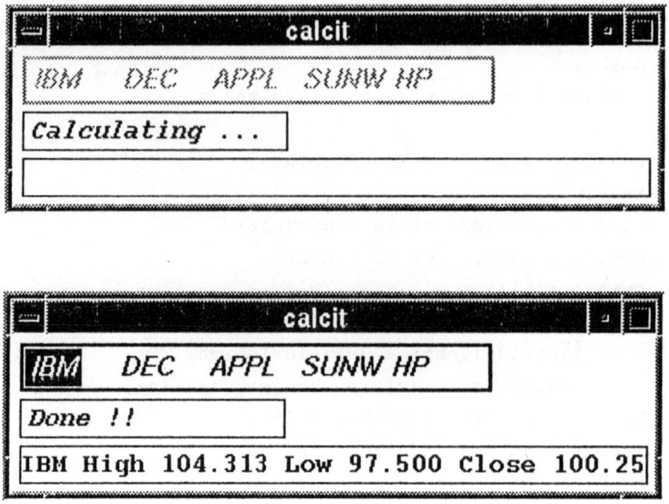

Figure 5-12a and b Calcit.

3. XtInputWriteMask when it is available to write.
4. XtInputExceptMask when an OS exception occurs.

To get set up to watch, you use the following:

```
id = XtAddInput(src,condition,proc,data);
```

where "srs" is a UNIX file descriptor, "condition" is one of the four just listed, "proc" is the Intrinsics-specific name, and "data" is the data to provide the proc. To remove this procedure, use the following:

```
XtRemoveInput(id);
```

where "id" refers to an id obtained from a previous XtAddInput() call.

To demonstrate this, you will create a client called "watch." This client will simply "keep an eye out" for data in a file. The Athena AsciiText widget is employed in this client to display the information. The AsciiText Widget is a very useful widget that provides quite a bit of text support. The client is shown in Figure 5-13. The code is shown here:

```
/* FILE:    watch.c
 */
#include "XbkUtil.h"

/* Widget Headers to be used in this client */
```

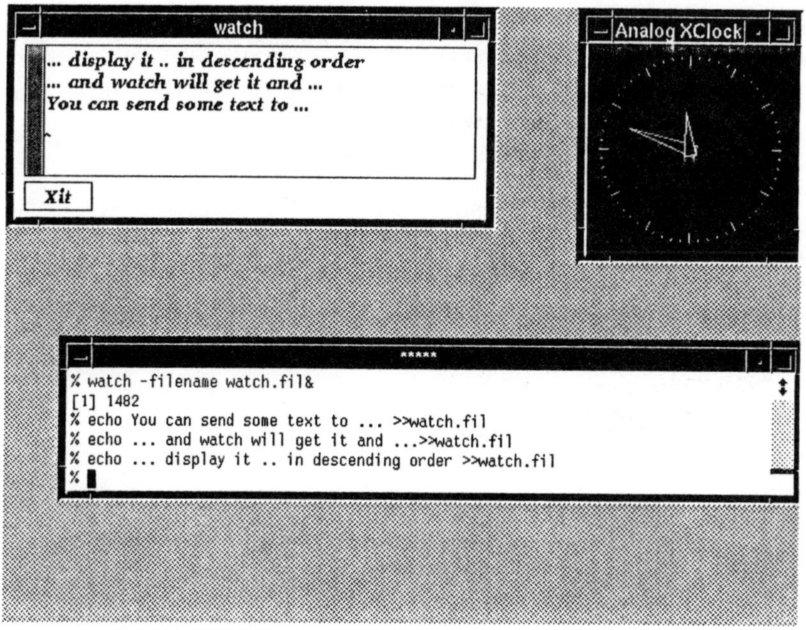

Figure 5-13 Watch.

```
#include <X11/Form.h>
#include <X11/AsciiText.h>
#include <X11/Command.h>

#define XbkShellName    "watch"
#define XbkApplClass    "Watch"

#define BUFFER_SIZE 2000
#define NO_FILE          "File given was not found !!!"

Widget    fileOutput;          /* This widget will display the file
                                * output
                                */
int    watch_file();      /* forward declaration */
XtCallbackProc Xit();

struct _myAppRes {
        String filename;
} myAppRes;
XrmOptionDescRec myCmdOpts[] = {
{ "-filename", "*fileName", XrmoptionSepArg, NULL },
};
```

```
#define OFFSET(field)  XtOffset(struct _myAppRes*, field)
static XtResource myAppResOpts[] = {
   {"fileName", "FileName", XtRString, sizeof(String),
         OFFSET(filename), XtRString, "watch.txt"},
};
#undef OFFSET

main(argc, argv)
int argc; char **argv;
{
     Widget top, container, exit;
     FILE *fd;
     Arg  args[MAXARGS];
     int  n;

        top = XtInitialize(XbkShellName,XbkApplClass,
                              myCmdOpts,XtNumber(myCmdOpts),&argc,
argv);
        XtGetApplicationResources(top, &myAppRes, myAppResOpts,
                              XtNumber(myAppResOpts),NULL, 0);

/* Set up a manager for the display and exit button */

    container = XtCreateManagedWidget("container",formWidgetClass,
          top,NULL,0);
/* Set up a place for the file to be read to. We are using
 * the asciiStringWidgetClass and informing the widget that we
 * want a scrollbar and would like the user to be able to edit it.
 * Warning:  There is some logic in the source (the part used
 * to get data) that says not to deal with updates to the string
 * if we are not editable.  Since we will be adding data to the
 * display, we need to allow for changes and hence the editable
nature.
 */
     n = 0;
     XtSetArg(args[n],XtNlength, 4000); n++;
     XtSetArg(args[n],XtNeditType,XttextEdit);n++;
     XtSetArg(args[n],XtNtextOptions,scrollVertical|editable); n++;
     fileOutput =

XtCreateManagedWidget("fileOutput",asciiStringWidgetClass,
               container,args,n);

/* Let's have an exit button */
     n = 0;
```

```
    XtSetArg(args[n],XtNfromVert,fileOutput); n++;
    exit = XtCreateManagedWidget("Xit",commandWidgetClass,
            container,args,n);

    XtAddCallback(exit, XtNcallback, Xit, top);
    if ((fd = fopen(myAppRes.filename, "r")) == NULL) {
        XtxuTextInsertString(NO_FILE)'
    }
/*
 * Now set up a proc to watch the file
 */
    XtAddInput(fileno(fd), XtInputReadMask, watch_file, NULL);

    XtRealizeWidget(top);

    XtMainLoop();
}
XtCallbackProc  Xit(w,call_data,client_data)
    Widget w;
    caddr_t    call_data,client_data;
{
    XtUnmapWidget(w);
    XtCloseDisplay(XtDisplay(w));
    exit(0);
}
/* This is our alternative input procedure.  You will notice that
 * it is quite simple.
 */
int watch_file(client_data, fid, id)
caddr_t client_data;
int *fid;
XtInputId *id;
{
    char buf[BUFSIZ];
    int nbytes;
/* Notice that the file id is gotten as an argument. */

    if ((nbytes = read(*fid, buf, BUFSIZ)) == -1)
        perror("read_watched_file");

/* If we read the data simply "slap" it to the screen using our
 * text utilities.
 */
    if (nbytes) XtxuTextInsertString(buf);
}
```

This is a very simple program, and watching a file isn't really that hard. You might have seen this technique used for taking data from "pipes" and providing front ends to some of the UNIX utilities. That is all well and good, but application writers need practical uses of alternative input mechanisms. The "watch" client could be used with the client in Chapter 8 (the "trade" client) to record transactions, etc.

If you are wondering what XtxuTextInsertString() does, read on to the next chapter. I discuss those tools when I talk about widget crafting.

5.4.11. Miscellaneous Stuff This has been quite a chapter. We've touched on just about everything you will run into when you start to code your own Xt clients. Before you get into building widgets and developing more complete clients, you should look at two interesting items. The first demonstrates how to install an icon so that the window manager can give your client some meaning. The second creates a scrolling list.

Chapter 4 discussed things called bitmaps and pixmaps. It was mentioned that bitmaps could be used for installing icons on top-level windows. To make it easy, let's create a macro for XbkUtil.h that will do this for you:

```
#define INSTALLICON(w,bits,width,height) {                    \
          Arg marg;                                           \
          XtSetArg(marg,XtNiconPixmap,                        \
            XCreateBitmapFromData(XtDisplay(w),               \
                       XtScreen(w)-root,                      \
                       bits,width,height));                   \
          XtSetValues(w,&marg,1);                             \
}
```

Notice that you pass down the widget (w), the bits, width, and height of the bitmap to use. You then use an Xlib primitive that creates the bitmap from that information and sets it as a resource. Lastly, you invoke the set_values method of the widget to install the icon.

To install an icon, you create a bitmap either by hand or using the X client bitmap. Include the file that is written in your client, and pass the appropriate elements to the macro. A sample of the file generated and used is given below, with the result shown in Figure 5-14:

```
#define iconic_width 16
#define iconic_height 16
static char iconic_bits[] = {
  0xff, 0xff, 0x03, 0xc0, 0xfd, 0xbf, 0x05, 0xa0, 0x05,
  0xa0, 0x05, 0xa0, 0x05, 0xa0, 0x05, 0xa0, 0x05, 0xa0,
  0x05, 0xa0, 0x05, 0xa0, 0x05, 0xa0, 0x05, 0xa0, 0xfd,
  0xbf, 0x03, 0xc0, 0xff, 0xff};
```

Figure 5-14 Icon.

The last thing to discuss is how to make a list into a scrolled list. In the OSF/Motif set, you will find a nice convenience function called XmCreateScrolledList() to do that. However, in the Athena Widget Set, no such "niceness" exists. That's okay, since it isn't such a bad idea to understand how these things are created anyway. To make a list a scrolled list, you simply make it a child of a viewportWidgetClass.

What's a viewport? Well, a viewport is a container widget that allows its children to scroll around. By setting up the resource correctly, you can make the list into a scrolled list. Figure 5-15 shows an example of a scrolled list.

The following client "xawlistScr" demonstrates how to produce this list:

```
/*  FILE:            xawlistScr.c
 */


#include "XbkUtil.h"
```

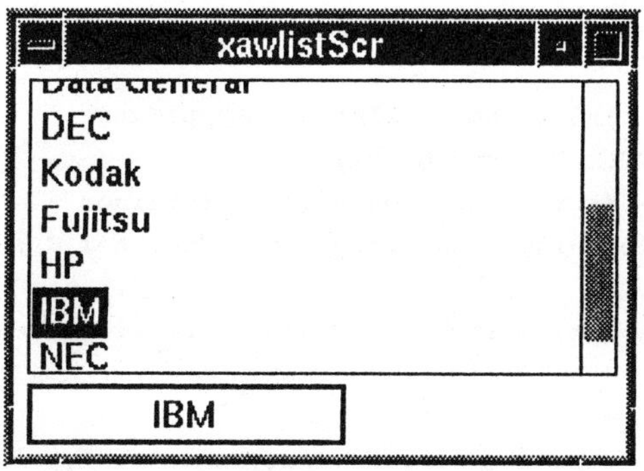

Figure 5-15 Scrolled list.

```
#define XbkShellName     "xawlistScr"
#define XbkApplClass     "XawlistScr"

#include <X11/Form.h>
#include <X11/List.h>
#include <X11/Label.h>
#include <X11/Viewport.h> /* Athena Scrolling Window */

/*
 * This is the forward declaration of our callback
 */
static void selection_callback();

static String str[] = {
     "Apple","AT&T","Bull","CalComp","CDC",
     "Data General","DEC","Kodak","Fujitsu",
     "HP","IBM","NEC","NCR","Prime","Rich",
     "Sequent","Siemens","Silicon Graphics",
     "Sony","Sun","Tecktronix","TI","Unisys",
     "Wang","Xerox"};

Widget lbl;     /* Need to make it global so the callback can
                 * use it. */

main(argc,argv)
int argc; char *argv[];
{
     Widget      top,container,scrollIt,lst;
     int  i;
     Arg  args[3];
     int  wth,iwth;          /* holders for widths */

     top = XtInitialize(XbkShellName,XbkApplClass,
               NULL,0,&argc,argv);
     container = XtCreateManagedWidget("container",
               formWidgetClass,top,NULL,(Cardinal)0);
/*
 * Create a viewport, which is a widget that will scroll its
 * children.
 */
     scrollIt  = XtCreateManagedWidget("scrollIt",
               viewportWidgetClass,container,NULL,(Cardinal)0);
/*
```

```
 * Create the list as a child of the viewport.
 */
     XtSetArg(args[0],XtNlist,str);
     XtSetArg(args[1],XtNnumberStrings, XtNumber(str));
     XtSetArg(args[2],XtNverticalList, True);
     lst = XtCreateWidget("list",listWidgetClass,
             scrollIt,args,(Cardinal)3);

     XtAddCallback(lst,XtNcallback,selection_callback, NULL);
/*
 * Set the width of the list widget to be the width of the
 * longest item plus the internalWidth in the list. This will
 * give us a nice vertical list to start off with.
 */
     XtSetArg(args[0],XtNlongest,&wth);
     XtSetArg(args[1],XtNinternalWidth,&iwth);
     XtGetValues(lst,args,(Cardinal)2);
     XtSetArg(args[0],XtNwidth,wth+iwth);
     XtSetValues(lst,args,(Cardinal)1);
/*
 * Since we created the list as Unmanaged the geometry
 * negotiation between it and the parent has yet to occur.  This
 * gave us the chance to get a better width to set the widget
 * with.
 */
     XtManageChild(lst);
     XtSetArg(args[0],XtNfromVert,scrollIt);
     XtSetArg(args[1],XtNlabel,"No selection yet !!");
     lbl = XtCreateManagedWidget("lbl",
                labelWidgetClass,container,args,(Cardinal)2);
     XtRealizeWidget(top);
     XtMainLoop();
}
static void selection_callback(w,client_data,call_data)
     Widget w;
     caddr_t *client_data;
     XtListReturnStruct *call_data;
{
     Arg args[1];
     XtSetArg(args[0],XtNlabel,(XtArgVal)call_data-string);
     XtSetValues(lbl,args,(Cardinal)1);
}
```

The application defaults are as follows:

```
! XawlistScr
*font:     *-helvetica-*-100-*
*scrollIt.allowVert:      True
*scrollIt.useRight: True
*scrollIt.height:    120
*lbl.borderWidth: 2
*lbl.borderColor: white
```

These basically instruct the Viewport to use the scrollbar and place it on the right side. So as you can see, creating scrolled anythings are fairly simple. OSF/Motif provides a similar mechanism called xmScrolledWindow.

6

Building Widgets: Primitive Widgets

The first five chapters of this book have laid the foundation for the remainder. You have been introduced to most of those mechanisms that application writers need to know about. This was done by creating clients that demonstrated resource setting, resource gathering, translation management, actions, callbacks, timeouts, event handlers, background work procedures, and alternative input mechanisms. In each case, you were lucky enough to have a widget that could do the job. What would you have done if none of the widgets suited your needs? The answer is to craft your own.

In this chapter you will construct a "field editor" by using the inheritance mechanism of the Intrinsics. You will learn the structure of all primitive widgets, the requirements for this widget, and how to construct such a widget.

6.1. Structure of a Primitive Widget

As we discussed in Chapter 3, all widgets are subclasses of the Core widget. Recall from that chapter that a widget has two components, the class part and the instance part. The class part contains those things that all widgets in the class share, while the instance part has information specific to the occurrence of a widget. Recall also that there is a single instance of the class part per application, while there will be *n* number of instance records for each widget of the class created.

The class part structure of the Core widget is as follows:

```
typedef struct _CoreClassPart {
    WidgetClass         superclass;              (data)
    String              class_name;              (data)
    Cardinal            widget_size;             (data)
    XtProc              class_initialize;        (method)
    XtWidgetClassProc   class_part_initialize;   (method)
    XtEnum              class_inited;            (data)
```

```
    XtInitProc          initialize;             (method)
    XtArgsProc          initialize_hook;        (method)
    XtRealizeProc       realize;                (method)
    XtActionList        actions;                (data/method)
    Cardinal            num_actions;            (data)
    XtResourceList      resources;              (data)
    Cardinal            num_resources;          (data)
    XrmClass            xrm_class;              (data)
    Boolean             compress_motion;        (data)
    XtEnum              compress_exposure;      (data)
    Boolean             compress_enterleave;    (data)
    Boolean             visible_interest;       (data)
    XtWidgetProc        destroy;                (method)
    XtWidgetProc        resize;                 (method)
    XtExposeProc        expose;                 (method)
    XtSetValuesFunc     set_values;             (method)
    XtArgsFunc          set_values_hook;        (method)
    XtAlmostProc        set_values_almost;      (method)
    XtArgsProc          get_values_hook;        (method)
    XtAcceptFocusProc   accept_focus;           (method)
    XtVersionType       version;                (data)
    XtPointer           callback_private;       (data/method)
    String              tm_table;               (data/method)
    XtGeometryHandler   query_geometry;         (method)
    XtStringProc        display_accelerator;    (method)
    XtPointer           extension;              (data/method)
} CoreClassPart;
```

As you can see, the CoreClassPart structure contains both data and methods. The methods are actually pointers to C functions that are invoked by the Intrinsics. Let's take a moment to understand each of the members.

Table 6-1
CoreClassPart Members and Descriptions

Member	Description
superclass	A pointer to the class record of the class that the widget belongs to. In the case of Core, you cannot go any higher; therefore, this is null.
class_name	The string representation for the class. This is used by the resource manager for matching resource specifications.
widget_size	This informs the world how many bytes this widget's instance record is.

Member	Description
class_initialize	This is a method that is invoked at widget creation time. It has the responsibility of adding anything that could not be done at compile time. Most often it installs any type converters the widget requires.
class_part_initialize	After the class_initialize method is through, this method is invoked. It is used by widgets that have added fields for their class.
class_inited	This is a flag that informs the Intrinsics of whether the class has been intialized or not.
initialize	This method is called for the creation of a widget instance. Its job is to fill in the instance part.
initialize_hook	Another method that may be used at initialize time.
realize	A method used to bring the widget to life.
actions	This is both data and methods. It is actually a list of actions that this widget adds.
num_actions	The number of actions.
resources	Provides instructions to the resource manager in how to fill the widget structure.
num_resources	The number of resources.
xrm_class	An internal representation of the class used by the resource manager.
compress_motion	A flag to instruct the Intrinsics to compress motion events into a single motion event.
compress_exposure	A flag to instruct the Intrinsics to compress exposure events into a single exposure event.
compress_enterleave	A flag to instruct the Intrinsics to compress crossing events (pairs of enter/leave events).
visible_interest	A flag to instruct the Intrinsics to inform the widget when it has become visible.
destroy	A method invoked when the widget is being destroyed (removed). It has the responsibility of giving back any dynamically allocated memory, graphics contexts, or file handles the widget is using. You can consider this a widget clean-up routine.
resize	A method to adjust the widget's configuration due to a resize request.
expose	A method that handles the display needs of the widget.
set_values	A method that allows for setting of widget resources. Invoked by XtSetValues().
set_values_hook	A method to add additional value-setting processing.
set_values_almost	A method used to adjust values during geometry negotiations with a parent.
get_values_hook	A method to return widget resources. It is invoked by XtGetValues( ).

Member	Description
accept_focus	A method for accepting the input focus.
version	Data informing the Intrinsics of what version the widget was built using.
callback_private	The callback list for the widget. It contains a list of procedures to invoke.
tm_table	The translation table for this widget.
query_geometry	A method for assisting parent widgets in geometry negotiations.
display_accelerator	A method to display the representation of the currently installed accelerators.
extension	Used to add to the widget without changing the other elements.

You will find that many of the methods in the ClassPart are inherited by the widgets. In the case of the CoreWidget, it must provide some of the functionality:

```
typedef struct _WidgetClassRec {
    CoreClassPart core_class;
} WidgetClassRec, CoreClassRec;
```

The ClassPart of each widget is "tacked on" to the end of the CoreClassPart. So, if you had your own widget called "OurWidgetClass," you would create the widget's class record by doing the following:

```
typedef struct _OurWidgetClassRec {
    CoreClassPart core_class;
    OurClassPart  our_class;
} OurWidgetClassRec;
```

The second part of a widget is the instance part (record). The CoreWidget's is defined as follows:

```
typedef struct _CorePart {
    Widget              self;
    WidgetClass         widget_class;
    Widget              parent;
    XrmName             xrm_name;
    Boolean             being_destroyed;
    XtCallbackList      destroy_callbacks;
    XtPointer           constraints;
    Position            x, y;
    Dimension           width, height;
    Dimension           border_width;
    Boolean             managed;
    Boolean             sensitive;
```

```
    Boolean             ancestor_sensitive;
    XtEventTable        event_table;
    XtTMRec             tm;
    XtTranslations      accelerators;
    Pixel               border_pixel;
    Pixmap              border_pixmap;
    WidgetList          popup_list;
    Cardinal            num_popups;
    String              name;
    Screen              *screen;
    Colormap            colormap;
    Window              window;
    Cardinal            depth;
    Pixel               background_pixel;
    Pixmap              background_pixmap;
    Boolean             visible;
    Boolean             mapped_when_managed;
} CorePart;
```

This structure provides the instance-specific data. When you look at the members in the structure, you can see it makes a lot of sense. For instance, you would not want to share the window id with all widgets of the class. It makes sense to have an expose method shareable, since all widgets of the class are defined exactly the same, but when it comes to resources, no chance. Let's examine each of the members of the CorePart structure in the following table.

Table 6-2
CorePart Members and Descriptions

Member	Description
self	A pointer to this instance record.
widget_class	A pointer to this widget's class record. This gives the connection to the expose, realize, and other shareable methods.
parent	A pointer to the parent's widget id.
xrm_name	The internal resource manager's version of the widget's instance name.
being_destroyed	A flag informing the Intrinsics that you are in the destruction process.
destroy_callbacks	Provisions for the application writer to add additional clean-up activities.
constraints	A pointer to constraint records placed in the widget by a container widget.
x,y	Pixel offsets for the position of the window that the widget owns.

Member	Description
width,height	Dimensions for the window.
border_width	The width, in pixels, of the window's border.
managed	A flag to inform the Intrinsics if this widget is managed or not.
sensitive	A flag to inform the Intrinsics if this widget is to be informed of events. Expose and some other events are processed.
ancestor_sensitive	A flag telling the Intrinsics if the widget's parent is sensitive or not. If the parent is insensitive, the child is insensitive.
event_table	The event mask and handlers for this widget.
tm	The compiled translations.
accelerators	Accelerators installed on this widget.
border_pixel	The color of the border.
border_pixmap	The kind of representation for the border.
popup_list	Pop-up children associated with this widget.
num_popups	Number of pop-ups placed on this widget.
name	A string representation of the instance name for this widget. It is used by the resource manager to obtain resource settings for this widget.
screen	A pointer to the screen this widget is on.
colormap	The colormap that is being used by the widget.
window	The window id of the window associated with this widget.
depth	The depth of the screen being used.
background_pixel	The background color.
background_pixmap	The background pixmap.
visible	A flag used to tell if the widget is visible or not.
mapped_when_managed	A flag to instruct the Intrinsics if the widget should be mapped when it is managed.

A widget's record is created as follows:

```
typedef struct _WidgetRec {
    CorePart    core;
} WidgetRec,  CoreRec;
```

Just as you did for the ClassPart, the CorePart (instance) is "tacked on" to the end of the CorePart. So, if you had your own widget called "OurWidget," you would create the widget's instance record by doing the following:

```
typedef struct _OurWidgetRec {
    CorePart core;
    OurPart  our;
} OurWidgetRec;
```

6.2. Inheritance in Xt

The Xt Intrinsics provide for a powerful notion termed *inheritance*. This is a way of creating a new class of widget that has similar features to another class. In fact, all of the data and methods of the superclass are available to the subclass, as illustrated in Figure 6-1.

The mechanics for inheritance involve five steps, as follows:

1. Define a new ClassPart. If there aren't any class fields to add, you simply create an empty one. This is needed by the Intrinsics.

```
typedef struct {
     int  empty;
} ExampleClassPart;
```

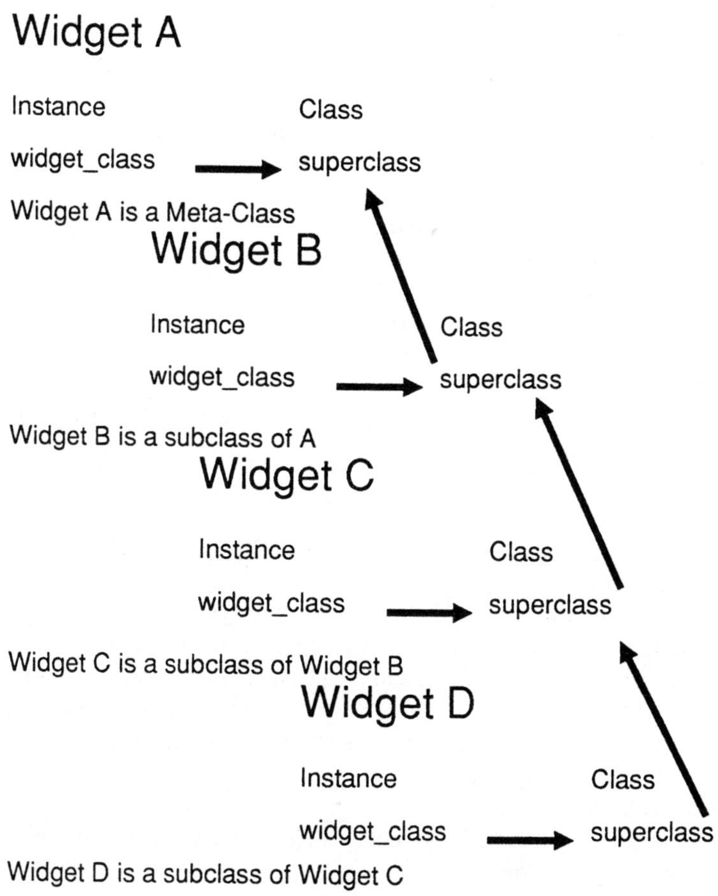

Figure 6-1 How widgets connect.

2. Tack it on to the back of the ClassPart of the superclass:

```
typedef struct {
     CoreClassPart          core_class;
     SimpleClassPart        simple_class;
     ExampleClassPart       example_class;
} MyWidgetClassRec;
```

3. Define the class pointer:

```
ExampleWidgetClass exampleWidgetClass;
```

4. Define a new instance part:

```
typedef struct {
     int  new_data;
     int  more_new_data;
} ExamplePart;
```

5. Tack it on to the back of the instance part of the superclass:

```
typedef struct {
     CorePart        core;
     SimplePart      simple;
     ExamplePart     example;
} ExampleRec, *ExampleWidget;
```

Later in this chapter, you will build a new widget that demonstrates the inheritance mechanism.

6.3. Requirements for the FieldEdWidget

If you look in the Athena or OSF/Motif widget sets, you find many useful widgets. Yet they are lacking in one key area: field editing. *Field editing* refers to the ability to define a field of a certain type, and then have all the editing actions performed for that field. For instance, if you had a field that was to contain alphabetic characters only, it would be useful to instruct the widget to look for just those characters. Additionally, we would like to have a field action routine so that you could provide enhanced edit checking.

Since this "dream" widget does not exist, you have to craft it yourself. To start, let's define the requirements:

1. It must be fully extensible. That is, if the client writer does not like the internal editing routines for the various field types, a client-provided procedure may be installed.
2. It must provide a field action procedure.
3. It must allow focus in, focus out, and enter window event procedures to be installed by the client writer.
4. It must allow intra-field movement. That is, it must have control sequences for moving the cursor within the field.
5. It must provide a clear field mechanism.
6. It must allow the client writer to obtain the widget resources through "standard" Xt mechanisms (XtGetValues()) as opposed to "convenience" routines.

Since there is a widget that handles most of the editing activities such as figuring out text width, height, offsets in the window, colors for the text, fonts, clearing out text in a source, and so on, you should employ the power of inheritance to construct your widget.

6.4. Constructing the Widget

All widgets are constructed using at least three files:

1. Public header file.
2. Private header file.
3. Implementation file.

The public header file is intended for client writers, the private header is intended for this widget writer, and those widget writers who will subclass this widget (see Figure 6-2). The implementation file has all the standard methods and widget-specific procedures needed to support the widget.

6.4.1. The Public Header File

The first file to be created when you build your own widget is the private header file. This is where both the new ClassPart and the widget's instance part will be defined:

```
/* FILE:  FieldEdP.h
 * PURPOSE:     Private header file for the FieldEd Widget.
 */

#ifndef _FieldEdP_h
#define _FieldEdP_h
```

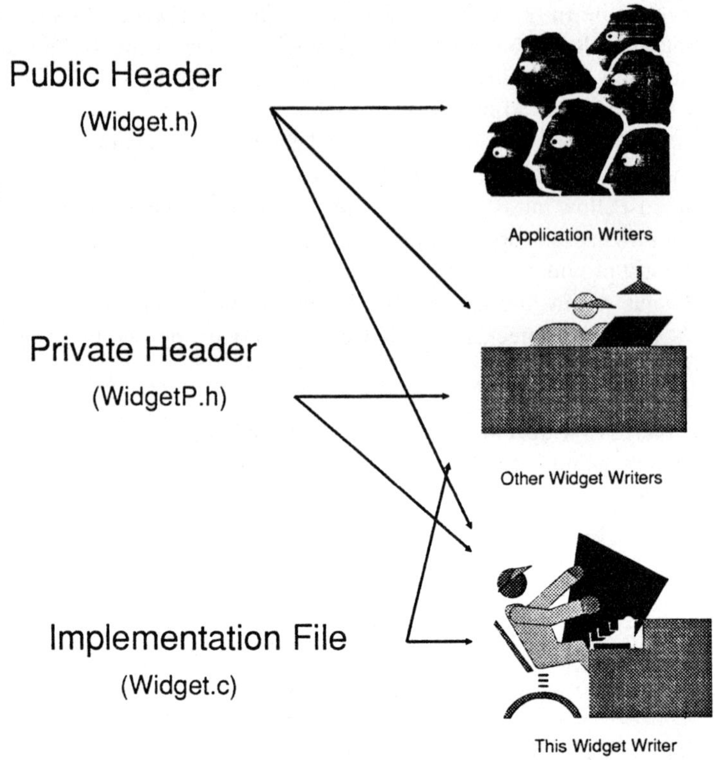

Figure 6-2 Who uses what part of a widget's code?

```
/* We will always include our public header file so we can get the
 * definitions for the resources, etc.  Additionally, we will need
 * our superclass's private header for definitions of the structure
 * that makes it up.
 */

#include "FieldEd.h"
/*
 * If you haven't seen this before, this is a C compile directive.
 * When compiling I pass a symbolic to determine which part of
 * the code to consider.  You do it using -DX11R3 on the compile
 * line.
 */

#ifdef X11R3
#include <X11/TextP.h>
#else
```

```
#include <X11/Xaw/TextP.h>
#endif
/* If we were adding additional fields to the class, this is the
 * time to do it.  In our case, we are not; therefore, we simply
 * enter a dummy field ("nothing"). This keeps the compiler happy
 * and allows the daisy chaining to continue correctly.
 */

/* Step One ... Define the new class part ..........
 */

typedef struct {int nothing;} FieldEdClassPart;
/* We define the class part as the "chain" of core, simple (has the
 * window type operations), text (our superclass), and finally
 * field_editor_class (us).
 */

/* Step Two ... Tack it to the back of the superclass's ClassPart
 */

typedef struct _FieldEdClassRec {
    CoreClassPart               core_class;
    SimpleClassPart             simple_class;
    TextClassPart               text_class;
    FieldEdClassPart            field_editor_class;
} FieldEdClassRec;
/* Notice the use of conventions here!  As you can see, the members
 * of the structure use lowercase and compound words use the
 * underline as the separator.
 */

/* Step Three ... Define the Class Pointer ........
 */

extern FieldEdClassRec fieldEdClassRec;
/* Now we define the instance-specific fields for this widget.
 * Notice we have five FwProcs available.  We provide FocusIn,
 * FocusOut, EnterWindow, editor, and FieldAxn.
 *  FocusIn     is for setting the field active via highlighting,
 *              inversing, etc.
 *  FocusOut    would reset the field.
 *  EnterWindow is similar to FocusIn except it supports pointer
 *              traversal and could set the focus to itself.
 *
```

```
 * The editor proc has the job of handling four cases of editing:
 *    case DeleteFwdChar:
 *         Based on the kind of editor you are and where you
 *         are in the string, delete the character where the cursor
 *         is.
 *    case DeletePrvChar:
 *         Based on the kind of editor you are and where you
 *         are in the string, delete the character just behind the
 *         cursor.
 *    case DeleteField:
 *         Clear the field.
 *    case InsertChar:
 *         The "real" editor.  Decide if entry is valid and insert
 *         it into the string using the correct format.
 *
 * And lastly, there is a FieldAxn proc.  This proc is invoked when
 * the Return Key is pressed.  This allows for edit checking, next
 * field traversal, etc.
 *
 * The procs are invoked using a Notifier.  A Notifier is an action
 * proc that will invoke (notify) functions (callbacks or internal
 * procs).  This widget requires only one, and depends on the
 * parameters passed to it for finding out which proc to call.
 */

/* Step Four ..... Define the instance specific record
 */
typedef struct {
    FwProc          focusIn_proc;        /* Focus in event proc   */
    FwProc          focusOut_proc;       /* Focus out event proc  */
    FwProc          enterWindow_proc;    /* EnterWindow event proc*/
    FwProc          editor_proc;         /* Editor for the widget */
    FwProc          field_axn_proc;      /* After return key has
                                            been pressed */
    char            *str;                /* string value          */
    int             editor_type;         /* Type of editor        */
    Pixel           active_color;        /* Pixel for highlight   */
    Pixel           inactive_color;      /* Original BorderColor */
    caddr_t         editor_extension;    /* For use by editor procs
*/
} FieldEdPart;

/* Create the widget structure by daisy chaining the needed
 * components. Core (because you must), Simple (because Text did),
```

```
 * Text (because we want to use a lot of its source), and finally
 * Field ('cause that's us).
 */

/* Step Five ... Tack the new instance part to the back of the
 * superclass's.
 */

typedef struct _FieldEdRec {
    CorePart        core;
    SimplePart      simple;
    TextPart        text;
    FieldEdPart     field_editor;
} FieldEdRec;

#endif  _FieldEdP_h
```

6.4.2. The Private Header File

Now that you have the private header file defined, your next step is to create the public header. This is the header that will be used by client writers who want to employ this widget. The resources names, resource class names, and any new representation types are defined in this file:

```
/* FILE:  FieldEd.h
 * PURPOSE:    Public Header file for the FieldEd Widget.
 */

/* This first part of the public header is a little trick used so
 * that if this header is included many times only one copy will
 * show up in your source.
 */

#ifndef _FieldEd_h
#define _FieldEd_h
/* We need to include the superclass's public header so that we can
 * inherit all of its public stuff.
 */

#ifdef X11R3
#include <X11/Text.h>
#else
#include <X11/Xaw/Text.h>
#endif  /* We are a subclass of Text */
```

```
/* These are the editing options that the editor procedure
 * recognizes. Since, client writers may add their own editor
 * procedures we need to let them have access to these internal
 * representations.
 */

#define DeleteFwdChar          (int)-1
#define DeletePrvChar          (int)-2
#define DeleteField            (int)-3
#define InsertChar             (int)1
/* These are constants for the editor types.  We have provided for
 * application-added editors and internal ones.  If this widget
 * grew to include a basic set of internal editors, we would add
 * to the list.
 */

#define FE_APPL             -1   /* Tells us the client provided it */
#define FE_ALPHA             0   /* Use the alpha editor            */
#define FE_ALPHANUMERIC      1   /* Use the alphanumeric editor     */
#define FE_INT               2   /* Use the int editor              */
#define FE_FLOAT             3   /* Use the float editor            */
/* Widgets can provide additional C function invocation via the
 * Intrinsics "callback" mechanism or supply their own notion.
 * We have chosen to create our own function call mechanism.
 * So to be consistent with implementations we provide our own
 * procedure type.
 */

typedef void (*FwProc)();     /* Our own procedure type */

/* These #defines are the resource, class, and representation
 * strings that the resource manager will need.  They help
 * eliminate spelling mistakes and give the programmer a hand in
 * not caring about what this stuff really means.
 */

/*
 * XtN ... is for the instance resource
 */
#define XtNstring              "string"
#define XtNeditorProc          "editorProc"
#define XtNeditorType          "editorType"
```

```
#define XtNintVal               "intVal"
#define XtNfloatVal             "floatVal"
#define XtNstringVal            "stringVal"
#define XtNfocusInProc          "focusInProc"
#define XtNfocusOutProc         "focusOutProc"
#define XtNenterWindowProc      "enterWindowProc"
#define XtNfieldAxnProc         "fieldAxnProc"
#define XtNactiveColor          "activeColor"
#define XtNinActiveColor        "inActiveColor"
/*
 * XtC ... is for the class resource.
 */
#define XtCString               "String"
#define XtCEditorProc           "EditorProc"
#define XtCEditorType           "EditorType"
#define XtCFocusInProc          "FocusInProc"
#define XtCFocusOutProc         "FocusOutProc"
#define XtCEnterWindowProc      "EnterWindowProc"
#define XtCFieldAxnProc         "FieldAxnProc"
#define XtCIntVal               "IntVal"
#define XtCFloatVal             "FloatVal"
#define XtCStringVal            "StringVal"
#define XtCActiveColor          "ActiveColor"
#define XtCInActiveColor        "InActiveColor"
/*
 * XtR ... is a representation type.  This is used for converting
 *         resources.  The resource manager will match the
 *         to and from types with the correct resource converter.
 *         In FieldEd.c you will find an example of a resource
 *         converter.
 */
#define XtRFwProc          "FwProc"
/*
 * Now we create the definitions that will be used for the instance
 * and class records.
 */
typedef struct _FieldClassRec *FieldEdWidgetClass;
typedef struct _FieldEdRec    *FieldEdWidget;

extern WidgetClass fieldEdWidgetClass;

#endif  _FieldEd_h  /* Do not, repeat do not add after this point
*/
```

6.4.3. The Implementation File

Now that you have the data set down, you can begin your implementation. The first thing to point out is that you are a subclass of the TextWidget. As such, the X11R3 version (the one used for developing this widget) fails to provide access to all of the handy features internal to the widget. To overcome this, you can create a set of utilities to help out.

6.4.3.1. Utilities As is often the case with software provided by other individuals or companies, there are times when the software developer left out some functions that would be useful. This is the case with the Athena Text widget (R3) which has prompted the need for some software to supplement that code. The following is the source code for a few utilities used to assist in implementing the Athena Text widget:

```
/* FILE:        TextUtils.h
 * PURPOSE:     Header for TextUtils.c source.
 *
 */

#ifndef _TextUtil_h
#define _TextUtil_h
/* We need the private headers so we can get access to the
 * structure members.  Since public headers are intended to
 * mask the programmer from those details, we have no other
 * recourse.
 */
#include <X11/IntrinsicP.h>
#include <X11/TextP.h>
#include <X11/AsciiText.h>

/* This is a little trick that makes code maintenance much easier.
 * In the code that actually defines the functions we add:
 *
 * #define DEFSOURCE
 *
 * prior to including this header file.  By doing that, the
 * symbol EXT is defined to "dead space."  In the source that
 * uses this header for support, they wouldn't use the #define,
 * thus making EXT equal to extern.
 */
#ifdef DEFSOURCE
#define EXT
#else
```

```
#define EXT extern
#endif

/* Export the functions from TextUtil.c
 */
EXT XtTextPosition XtxuTextGetLastPos();
EXT void XtxuInstallInsertCursor();
EXT void XtxuBlankCursor();
EXT char *XtxuTextGetString();
EXT char *XtxuTextGetPartOfString();
EXtTextPosition XtxuTextScan();
EXT int XtxuTextGetMaxHeight();
EXT void XtxuTextClearAll();
EXT void XtxuTextClearPos();
EXT int   XtxuTextInsertString();
#endif
```

And now for the implementation file. Essentially, you want to provide a higher level interface to the text widget, so that when you port the "FieldEd" widget you need only concern yourself with these utilities rather than the entire source of the widget. Here is the file:

```
/* FILE:        TextUtils.c
 * PURPOSE:     Various utilities for the Athena Text Widget(R3&R4).
 *
 */

#define DEFSOURCE yes
#include "TextUtils.h"

extern _XtTextGetText();


#ifdef X11R3
#define REPLACE(w,spos,epos,tb)     XtTextReplace(w,spos,epos,tb)
#define TextBlock                   XtTextBlock
#define TextPosition                XtTextPosition
#else
#define REPLACE(w,spos,epos,tb)     XawTextReplace(w,spos,epos,tb)
#define TextBlock                   XawTextBlock
#define TextPosition                 XawTextPosition
#endif
/* Handy tool to insert text.  This allows us to forget about
 * making sure we have the correct setup for doing this.
```

```
 */

int XtxuTextInsertString(w,str)
     Widget w;
     char *str;
{
     TextBlock tb;
     tb.firstPos = 0;
     tb.length   = strlen(str);
     tb.ptr      = str;
     REPLACE(w,0,0,&tb);
}

char *XtxuTextGetString(w)
     Widget w;
{
/*
 * Get the string from the widget.  We should probably use the
 * convenience routine provided by Xaw.
 */
     TextPosition lastPos = XtxuTextGetLastPos(w);
     return (char *) _XtTextGetText(w,(Position)0,lastPos);
}

char *XtxuTextGetPartOfString(w,spos,epos)
     Widget w;
     TextPosition spos,epos;
{
/*
 * Just get a part of the string.
 */
    return (char *) _XtTextGetText(w,spos,epos);
}
TextPosition  XtxuTextScan(w,pos,sType,dir,count,include)
  Widget w;
  TextPosition pos;
  XtTextScanType sType;
  XtTextScanDirection dir;
  int             count;
  Boolean         include;
{
/*
 * It would have been nice for Xaw to export an interface to all
 * of the parts of the widget.  However, that wasn't the case.
```

```
 * Therefore, we have to do it ourselves.
 */
     XtTextSource source = ((TextWidget)w)->text.source;
     return (source->Scan)(((TextWidget)w)->text.source,pos,sType,
               dir, count, include);
}
int XtxuTextGetMaxHeight(w,hgt)
     Widget w; int hgt;
{
     XtTextSink sink = ((TextWidget)w)->text.sink;
     return (int)(sink-MaxHeight)(w, hgt);
}
TextPosition XtxuTextGetLastPos(w)
     Widget w;
{
   XtTextSource source = ((TextWidget)w)->text.source;
   return (source-Scan)(source, 0, XtstAll, XtsdRight, 1, TRUE );
}

void XtxuTextClearPos(w,spos,epos)
     Widget w;
     Position spos,epos;
{
/*
 * Clear the area specified by the position.
 */
     TextBlock tb;
     tb.length = tb.firstPos = 0;
     REPLACE(w,spos,epos,&tb);
}
void XtxuTextClearAll(w)
     Widget w;
{
     TextBlock tb;
     TextPosition lastPos = XtxuTextScan(w, (XtTextPosition)0,
                                 XtstAll,XtsdRight, 1, TRUE);
     tb.length = tb.firstPos = 0;
     REPLACE(w,0,lastPos,&tb);
}
```

6.4.3.2. Including Header Files for the Widget With these handy tools, you are ready to craft the widget. The first thing to do in constructing any widget is to include the header files that you will need for its implementation. The following are used for this widget:

```
#include <X11/IntrinsicP.h>
#include <X11/StringDefs.h>
#include <X11/keysym.h>

/* We will need our private header.  Note we will also get our
 * public since the private gets the public.  Additionally, we
 * will get our superclass's information.
 */

#include "FieldEdP.h"
#include "TextUtils.h"     /* here are utilities */
```

6.4.3.3. Setting Up Helpful Macros The next thing to do is set up any useful macros that you might need:

```
#define BEEP(w)    XBell(XtDisplay(w),50)
/* We set up some helpful macros for our editing functions.  These
 * are based on the LATIN1 definition.  Note: We make some
 * assumptions that the keysyms will have the "correct" ASCII
 * values.  This is not completely accurate since things can be
 * changed, but the design choice is to live with it.
 */
#define IsUpperAlphaKey(keysym) \
     (((unsigned)(keysym) >= XK_A) && ((unsigned)(keysym) <= XK_Z))

#define IsLowerAlphaKey(keysym) \
     (((unsigned)(keysym) >= XK_a) && ((unsigned)(keysym) <= XK_z))

#define IsNumericKey(keysym) \
((((unsigned)(keysym) >= XK_0) && ((unsigned)(keysym) <= XK_9))||
\
 (((unsigned)(keysym) >= XK_KP_0) && ((unsigned)(keysym) <=
XK_KP_9)))

#define IsDecimalKey(keysym) \
     (((unsigned)(keysym) == XK_period) || \
      ((unsigned)(keysym) == XK_KP_Decimal))

#define IsAlphaKey(keysym) \
     (IsUpperAlphaKey(keysym) || IsLowerAlphaKey(keysym))
```

6.4.3.4. Forward Declarations Next, you would need all of the forward declarations for any function that will be used in the widget. Forward declarations are part of the ANSI standard and are generally good programming practice. The forward declarations are given here:

```
/* Define any forward reference we care about.
 */

extern char FieldEdTrans[]; /* fwd reference */
#ifdef X11R3
extern void ForceBuildLineTable();
#endif

/*
 * This is our added converter.  Converters are registered and
 * installed by widgets that need them.  If the Intrinsics have
 * the kind of conversion you need, then it makes little sense to
 * create your own. This converter is very simple and is more for
 * demonstration of how to do it.
 */
void FwCvtFunctionToFwProc();

/*
 * These procedures are our built-in editors and event routines.
 * Often widgets provide a "base" functionality for applications
 * or other widgets who subclass off of them.
 */
FwProc     AlphaEd(),AlphaNumEd(),IntEd(),FloatEd(),DefFIProc(),
           DefFOProc(),DefEWProc();
/* The nice thing about forward declarations is that they indicate
 * the programmer's intentions.  In widgets this makes life easy.
 * If we see that only two of the several class methods are
 * forward declared, we can see right away that the writer is
 * using (inheriting) many things from the superclass.
 */
static void  FieldEdClassInitialize(),
             FieldEdInitialize(),
             FieldEdCreateSourceSink(),
             FieldEdGetValuesHook(),
             FieldEdDestroy();
static Boolean FieldEdSetValues();

XtActionProc   MoveInsert(),NotifyEditor(),RedrawDisplay(),
               NotifyProcs();
```

6.4.3.5. Setting Up the Widget Resources The next part of the implementation file is the resource table. Setting resources for widgets is done exactly the same way as it was done in Chapter 5 for applications. (If any of this is unclear, refer to the previous chapter.) Here is the implementation file:

```
/*
 * These variables will be used in the resource table.  They
 * are defaults.
 */
static int defType = FE_ALPHA;
FwProc defEdProc = AlphaEd;
FwProc defFIProc = DefFIProc;
FwProc defFOProc = DefFOProc;
FwProc defEWProc = DefEWProc;

/*
 * One of the most powerful things in the toolkit is the notion of
 * resource management.  Widgets set up their "defaults" in the
 * instance file so that there are some known values.
 * Additionally, when the resource manager needs to find the
 * correct converter to use when getting the information from the
 * resource databases, it will use this table.
 *
 * The resource record (XtResource) has six components:
 *    1. The resource name (XtN)
 *    2. The resource class name (XtC)
 *    3. The representation we would like to get to
 *    4. The place where the value should go
 *    5. The representation we are coming from
 *    6. A default value if neither XtN or XtC are found
 *          in the databases.
 *
 * XtN is a string representation (following X conventions) of
 * the resource.  This is defined in the public header file or
 * shares one in StringDefs.h.
 *
 * XtC is the class name and follows the X conventions.
 *
 * XtR in the third field is part of the resource manager's look-up
 * mechanism.  Coupled with the fifth field, the resource manager
 * can search an internal table of converters to get the address
 * of the correct one.  It will then provide the appropriate
 * arguments with the result landing in the fourth field.
 */

#define INSET(fld) XtOffset(FieldEdWidget, fld)
static XtResource fieldEdRes[] = {
```

```
{XtNstring, XtCString, XtRString, sizeof(String),
  INSET(field_editor.str), XtRString, NULL},
{XtNeditorType,XtCEditorType,XtRInt,sizeof(int),
  INSET(field_editor.editor_type), XtRInt,(caddr_t)&defType},
{XtNfocusInProc,XtCFocusInProc,XtRFunction,sizeof(caddr_t),
  INSET(field_editor.focusIn_proc),
  XtRFunction,(caddr_t)&defFIProc},
{XtNfocusOutProc,XtCFocusOutProc,XtRFunction,sizeof(caddr_t),
  INSET(field_editor.focusOut_proc),
  XtRFunction,(caddr_t)&defFOProc},
{XtNenterWindowProc,XtCEnterWindowProc,XtRFunction,sizeof(caddr_t),
  INSET(field_editor.enterWindow_proc),
  XtRFunction,(caddr_t)&defEWProc},
{XtNfieldAxnProc,XtCFieldAxnProc,XtRFwProc,sizeof(caddr_t),
  INSET(field_editor.field_axn_proc), XtRFunction,(caddr_t)NULL},
{XtNeditorProc,XtCEditorProc,XtRFwProc,sizeof(caddr_t),
  INSET(field_editor.editor_proc),
XtRFunction,(caddr_t)&defEdProc},
{XtNactiveColor,XtCActiveColor,XtRPixel,sizeof(Pixel),
  INSET(field_editor.active_color), XtRString,
XtDefaultForeground},
};
#undef INSET
```

6.4.3.6. Setting Up Action Tables for a Widget Recalling the discussion in the previous chapter on action tables, you can apply the same technique for creating an action table for the widget. Unlike the actions for the application, widget actions live with the widget. That is, these actions are necessary for the widget implementation, while the ones for the application are necessary for the application. The action table follows:

```
/*
 * One of the fields in the class record is for the actions that
 * the widget needs to get its work done.  The actions coupled with
 * the translation table give the widget its behavior for
 * specific events (i.e., how do we want to look when EnterWindow
 * events are received).
 */
XtActionsRec  FieldEdAxnTbl[] = {
  {"MoveInsert",          MoveInsert},
  {"RedrawDisplay",       RedrawDisplay},
  {"NotifyProcs",         NotifyProcs},
  {"NotifyEditor",        NotifyEditor},
};
```

6.4.3.7. Using Look-up Tables in Widgets When reading the Intrinsics code (the actual XtI), you will find the use of look-up tables. This concept is very useful, and one that is employed in this widget. The table helps your NotifyEditor action procedure in informing the editor_proc of the correct action. You'll see this in more detail when you get to that part of the code. The table is defined here:

```
typedef struct _LookupRec {
     char *cmd;
     int  val;
} LookupRec;
static LookupRec editorCmds[] = {
     {"DC", DeleteFwdChar},
     {"DP", DeletePrvChar},
     {"DF", DeleteField},
     {"IN", InsertChar},
     {NULL,NULL},
};
```

6.4.3.8. Filling in the Class Record The class record is the next item to be completed. Recall from the discussion earlier that it contains the shareable elements of the widget. This includes the exposure handling method and initialization method. The class record is also the place to connect with any superclasses. In this case, it was decided to be a subclass of the Athena Text widget because this widget provided a fair amount of the code needed for the basic editing of text data. What it lacked was the notion of fields and the things needed for field editing. With that, this is a perfect example of using the inheritance mechanisms of the Intrinsics, as shown here:

```
/* We always need to fill out the ClassRecord in our implementation
 * file.  You will notice that we do not have the same mechanics
 * for the instance part, because the creation
 * process fills in the data at run time.
 */
FieldEdClassRec fieldEdClassRec = {
{ /* core fields   */
  /* superclass          */      (WidgetClass) &textClassRec,
  /* class_name          */      "FieldEd",
  /* widget_size         */      sizeof(FieldEdRec),
  /* class_initialize    */      FieldEdClassInitialize,
  /* class_part_init     */      NULL,
  /* class_inited        */      FALSE,
  /* initialize          */      FieldEdInitialize,
  /* initialize_hook     */      FieldEdCreateSourceSink,
  /* realize             */      XtInheritRealize,
  /* actions             */      FieldEdAxnTbl,
```

```
  /* num_actions          */      XtNumber(FieldEdAxnTbl),
  /* resources            */      fieldEdRes,
  /* num_ resource        */      XtNumber(fieldEdRes),
  /* xrm_class            */      NULLQUARK,
  /* compress_motion      */      TRUE,
  /* compress_exposure    */      FALSE,
  /* compress_enterleave  */      TRUE,
  /* visible_interest     */      FALSE,
  /* destroy              */      FieldEdDestroy,
  /* resize               */      XtInheritResize,
  /* expose               */      XtInheritExpose,
  /* set_values           */      FieldEdSetValues,
  /* set_values_hook      */      NULL,
  /* set_values_almost    */      XtInheritSetValuesAlmost,
  /* get_values_hook      */      FieldEdGetValuesHook,
  /* accept_focus         */      XtInheritAcceptFocus,
  /* version              */      XtVersion,
  /* callback_private     */      NULL,
  /* tm_table             */      FieldEdTrans,
  /* query_geometry        */     XtInheritQueryGeometry
},
{ /* text fields */
  /* empty              */     0
},
{ /* fieldEd fields */
  /* empty              */     0
}
};
WidgetClass fieldEdWidgetClass = (WidgetClass)&fieldEdClassRec;
```

6.4.3.9. Creating a Type Converter The Intrinsics provides many type converters that are used by the resource manager when it needs to convert a value provided for a widget resource to the type that the resource is expecting to be in. For many cases the internal Intrinsic converters will be sufficient, but it wouldn't be prudent not to show at least an example of one.

This converter takes what is provided in the "from" argument and assigns it to the "to" argument. Nothing special needs to happen since you are providing the pointer to a function and the resource is expecting a pointer:

```
void FwCvtFunctionToFwProc(args,num_args,fromVal,toVal)
     XrmValue *args; Cardinal *num_args;
     XrmValue *fromVal,*toVal;
{
     toVal->size = fromVal->size;
     toVal->addr = fromVal->addr;
}
```

6.4.3.10. The Class_initialize Method This method is responsible for setting up anything that the class will require. This includes initializing any data that is required and installing any converters that the class needs. In this example, the widget needs a converter installed:

```
static void FieldEdClassInitialize()
{
    XtAddConverter(XtRFunction, XtRFwProc,
                FwCvtFunctionToFwProc,NULL,  0 );
}
```

6.4.3.11. The Initialize Method The initialize method is responsible for setting up any data that the widget instance needs. All initialize methods should make sure that the width and height of the widget are nonzero values. The reason for doing this is that the Intrinsics just doesn't like widgets that have no width or height. This function is invoked by the XtCreateWidget( ) or XtCreateManagedWidget( ) functions. The code is as follows:

```
static void FieldEdInitialize(request, new)
    Widget request, new;
{
/* We use the casting mechanism in C to get the correct
 * information. Widget is an opaque pointer, thus we can have it
 * assume several roles (Chapter 2 covered this).
 */
     FieldEdWidget fwr = (FieldEdWidget)request;
     FieldEdWidget fwn = (FieldEdWidget)new;
     FwProc useProc;
     XrmValue to;

/* The initialize method of the superclass will not have known the
 * source or sink we are using.  Therefore we need to establish the
 * default height.
 */
    if (fwr->core.height == DEFAULT_TEXT_HEIGHT)
      fwn->core.height = DEFAULT_TEXT_HEIGHT;

/* We will set the inactive color to the desired border color.
 * This can then be used to inform the user of an unfocused field.
 * This resource is not setable. If the user changes the border
 * color after creation, the inactive_color will not be changed.
 */

    fwn->field_editor.inactive_color = fwr->core.border_pixel;
```

```
/* Now we check for the kind of editor the client writer wants.
 */
   switch(fwr->field_editor.editor_type) {
     case FE_ALPHA:
          useProc = AlphaEd;
          break;
     case FE_ALPHANUMERIC:
          useProc = AlphaNumEd;
          break;
     case FE_INT:
          useProc = IntEd;
          break;
     case FE_FLOAT:
          useProc = FloatEd;
          break;
     case FE_APPL:
/* If they want to install their own, they'd better!  Otherwise,
 * we kill the client.
 */
          if (fwr->field_editor.editor_proc == NULL)
               XtError("FATAL!! You must supply your own \
                    editor proc !!");
               exit(-1);
          useProc = NULL;
          break;
     default:
          fwr->field_editor.editor_type = FE_ALPHA;
          useProc = AlphaEd;
          XtWarning("FieldEd Init..Unknown editor_type defaulting \
                    to FE_ALPHA !!!");
          break;

    }
    /* Set up the field editor type */
    fwn->field_editor.editor_type = fwr->field_editor.editor_type;
    fwn->field_editor.editor_proc = useProc;
}
```

6.4.3.11.1. The Initialize_hook Method As an additional start-up method, the initialize_hook can be used to finish any part of the job that the initialize method did not. In this example, the R3 Text widget does not create a sink or source when it is created, so any widget or application must do so itself. To avoid this, use the initialize_hook method to create a sink and source. The *sink* is the part of the text object that provides display capabilities, while the *source* is used for the data part of the widget. The code is as follows:

```
static void FieldEdCreateSourceSink(widget, args, num_args)
    Widget widget;
    ArgList args;
    Cardinal *num_args;
{
#ifdef X11R3
   FieldEdWidget w = (FieldEdWidget)widget;

    w->text.source = XtStringSourceCreate( widget, args, *num_args
);
    w->text.sink = XtAsciiSinkCreate( widget, args, *num_args );
    w->text.lastPos = XtxuTextGetLastPos(widget);
    ForceBuildLineTable( (TextWidget)w );
#endif

/* Now we can readjust the height since the sink will let us know
 * the information regarding the height.
 */
    if (w->core.height == DEFAULT_TEXT_HEIGHT)
        w->core.height = (2*yMargin) + 2
                  + XtxuTextGetMaxHeight(widget,1);
}
```

6.4.3.12. The Set_values Method As you saw in the previous chapter, widgets provide a mechanism for altering their resources. The set_values method has that responsibility. Whenever the XtSetValues() function is invoked, the Intrinsics will call the set_values method. Most widgets do not tell the client writer that the resources requested to be set are not setable. As a client writer, this can be annoying. The widget shown here will inform the client writers by warning them:

```
static Boolean FieldEdSetValues(current, request, new)
    Widget current, request, new;
{
     FieldEdWidget fwc = (FieldEdWidget)current;
     FieldEdWidget fwr = (FieldEdWidget)request;
     FieldEdWidget fwn = (FieldEdWidget)new;
/* We will not allow changes to the procs that have been set up.
 */
     if ((fwc->field_editor.focusIn_proc !=
          fwr->field_editor.focusIn_proc)       ||
         (fwc->field_editor.focusOut_proc !=
          fwr->field_editor.focusOut_proc)       ||
         (fwc->field_editor.enterWindow_proc !=
```

```
        fwr->field_editor.enterWindow_proc)       ||
       (fwc->field_editor.editor_proc !=
        fwr->field_editor.editor_proc)       ||
       (fwc->field_editor.str !=
        fwr->field_editor.str)       ||
       (fwc->field_editor.editor_type !=
        fwr->field_editor.editor_type)){
        XtWarning("Cannot alter FieldEdPart Values");
    }
/*
 * The only setable FieldEdParts is the "active" color.
 */
     if (fwc->field_editor.active_color !=
         fwr->field_editor.active_color)
         fwn->field_editor.active_color =
         fwr-field_editor.active_color;
    return True;
}
```

6.4.3.13. The Get_values Method The counterpart to set_values is get_values. This method should give back those widget resources that the widget writer cares to give back to the client writer. Client writers cannot assume that just because they follow the rules for an XtGetValues() request, the values requested will be returned. The reason is that the widget might not provide a get_values method, or the get_values method provided might not return the request.

Looking at the following function, you can see that there are resources that this widget will not return. They are the addresses of the "proc" pointers. The point here for client writers is: Don't assume anything with respect to widgets. Make sure that the widget writer has carefully documented the code, or better still, gives you a copy of the source. The function is as follows:

```
static void FieldEdGetValuesHook(wdg, args, num_args)
     Widget wdg;
     ArgList args;
     Cardinal *num_args;
{
     FieldEdWidget fw = (FieldEdWidget)wdg;
     int i = 0;
     int ival;float fval;
/* We look through the list of arguments to find the requests.
 * Based on the request we will return the value.  Notice that
 * the field is a string representation, therefore we need to
 * convert to the one the client desires.
 */
```

```
    while(i< *num_args) {
         if (strcmp(args[i].name, XtNintVal) == 0) {
         fw->field_editor.str = XtxuTextGetString(wdg);
         if (strlen(fw->field_editor.str)) {
              sscanf(fw->field_editor.str,"%d",&ival);
              *((int *)args[i].value) = ival;
         } else {
              *((int *)args[i].value) = (int)0;
         }
    } else if (strcmp(args[i].name, XtNfloatVal) == 0) {
         fw->field_editor.str = XtxuTextGetString(wdg);
         if (strlen(fw->field_editor.str)) {
              sscanf(fw->field_editor.str,"%f",&fval);
              *((float *)args[i].value) = fval;
         } else {
              *((float *)args[i].value) = (int)0;
         }
    } else if (strcmp(args[i].name, XtNstringVal) == 0) {
         fw->field_editor.str = XtxuTextGetString(wdg);
         if (strlen(fw->field_editor.str)) {
              *((char **)args[i].value) =
                fw->field_editor.str;
         } else {
              *((char **)args[i].value) = "";
         }
    } else if (strcmp(args[i].name, XtNheight) == 0) {
         args[i].value = fw->core.height;
    } else if (strcmp(args[i].name, XtNwidth) == 0) {
         args[i].value = fw->core.width;
    } else if (strcmp(args[i].name, XtNactiveColor) == 0) {
         args[i].value = fw->field_editor.active_color;
    } else if (strcmp(args[i].name, XtNinActiveColor) == 0)
{
         args[i].value = fw->field_editor.inactive_color;
    } else if (strcmp(args[i].name, XtNeditorType) == 0) {
         args[i].value = fw->field_editor.editor_type;
    }
    i++;
    }
}
```

6.4.3.14. The Destroy Method The purpose of the destroy method is to give back any system-related resources that it has taken. This includes freeing dynamically allocated memory or file handles. In this example, you need to free up the sink and the source since each has "malloced" some space:

```
/* When a widget is told to kill itself, its destroy method is
 * invoked.  This method has the responsibility of cleaning up
 * any dynamic things it took.  In our case, we will free the
 * sink and the source.
 */
static void FieldEdDestroy(w)
    Widget w;
{
    XtStringSourceDestroy( ((FieldEdWidget)w)->text.source );
    XtAsciiSinkDestroy( ((FieldEdWidget)w)->text.sink );
}
```

6.4.4. Support Functions for the Widget: The Flavor of the Widget

The basic implementation of the widget consists of defining all those elements in the widget. That involves including any header files needed, defining helpful macros, defining action and translation tables, filling out the class record, and creating all the methods to support the widget. The last part is to add the "flavor" of the widget by writing the action procedures, callbacks, internal routines, or whatever is needed to pull off the widget magic. This section contains all of the source code for the functional part of the widget.

6.4.4.1. Portability Concerns To make the widget as adaptable as possible to change and minimize the effect on the code created, #define is employed to handle "generic" things. This should make the migration from X11R3 to X11R4 and to OSF/Motif fairly painless:

```
#ifdef X11R3
#define SETINSERTIONPOINT(w,loc)    XtTextSetInsertionPoint(w,loc)
#define GETINSERTIONPOINT(w)  XtTextGetInsertionPoint(w)
#define GETLASTPOS(w)         XtxuTextGetLastPos(w)
#define DISPLAY(w)        XtTextDisplay(w)
#define REPLACE(w,spos,epos,tb)  XtTextReplace(w,spos,epos,tb)
#else
#define SETINSERTIONPOINT(w,loc)    XawTextSetInsertionPoint(w,loc)
#define GETINSERTIONPOINT(w)  XawTextGetInsertionPoint(w)
#define GETLASTPOS(w)         XawTextGetLastPos(w)
#define DISPLAY(w)        XawTextDisplay(w)
#define REPLACE(w,spos,epos,tb) XawTextReplace(w,spos,epos,tb)
#endif
```

6.4.4.2. Managing the Insertion Position The Text widget has the notion of an insert position. The action procedure in this section is a higher-level version of the Text widget's. It moves the insertion position for four cases, FW (forward one character), BK (backward one character), BG (beginning of the field), and ED (end of the field). The code is as follows:

```
/* MoveInsert is responsible for managing the insert position.
 * It takes as a parameter the kind of movement that is desired,
 * then figures out how to do it.
 */
XtActionProc MoveInsert(w, event, params,num_params)
  Widget w;
  XEvent *event;
  String *params;
  Cardinal num_params;
{
    int lastPos = GETLASTPOS(w);
    int insertPos = GETINSERTIONPOINT(w);
    /* Forward Movement */
    if (strcmp("FW",params[0]) == 0) {
         if (insertPos == lastPos)
              BEEP(w);
         else
              SETINSERTIONPOINT(w,++insertPos);
    /* Backward Movement */
    } else if (strcmp("BK",params[0]) == 0) {
         if (insertPos == 0)
              BEEP(w);
         else
              SETINSERTIONPOINT(w,--insertPos);
    /* Go to the beginning of the string */
    } else if (strcmp("BG",params[0]) == 0) {
              SETINSERTIONPOINT(w,0);
    /* Go to the end of the string */
    } else if (strcmp("ED",params[0]) == 0) {
              SETINSERTIONPOINT(w,lastPos);
    } else {
         XtWarning("MoveInsert of FieldEdWidget .. bad param !");
              BEEP(w);
    }
}
```

6.4.4.3. Redisplay Mechanism If the field needs to be redisplayed, this action procedure will perform the necessary task:

```
/* Provide a mechanism for cleaning up the screen. */

XtActionProc RedrawDisplay(w, event, params,num_params)
 Widget w;
 XEvent *event;
```

```
 String *params;
 Cardinal num_params;
{
     DISPLAY(w);
}
```

6.4.4.4. Using Notifiers to Manage Procedures This widget borrows a concept from the Athena Command widget called the notifier. A *notifier* is a function (action proc) that manages the calling of subordinate functions. In the case of the "FieldEditor" widget there are two notifiers, one for handling editing functionality, and the other for event handling.

The NotifyEditor() procedure uses a look-up table to match the parameter passed as an argument by the translation manager. This parameter corresponds to the kind of editing that is to be performed. Editing takes the form of deletion or insertion.

The NotifyProcs() procedure simply uses the parameter passed to call one of the installed functions for the widget. Recall that there are four event procedures that are installed by the client: enter window, focus in, focus out, and field action (activated by a Return keypress). Here is the code for the notifiers:

```
/* This notifier is constructed to pass to the editor the correct
 * command.  Recall the definition in FieldEd.h.
 */
XtActionProc NotifyEditor(w, event, params,num_params)
 Widget w;
 XEvent *event;
 String *params;
 Cardinal num_params;
{
      FieldEdWidget fw = (FieldEdWidget)w;
      int i,cnt = XtNumber(editorCmds);

      if (num_params != 0) {
            for (i = 0; i  cnt; i++) {
                  if (strcmp(editorCmds[i].cmd,params[0]) == 0) {
                        (*fw->field_editor.editor_proc)(fw,
                              event,editorCmds[i].val);
                        return;
                  }
            }
      }
      XtWarning("Bad param to NotifyEditor in FieldEdWidget !!");
}
/* This notifier manages which FwProc to invoke. */
XtActionProc NotifyProcs(w, event, params,num_params)
```

```
 Widget w;
 XEvent *event;
 String *params;
 Cardinal num_params;
{
     FieldEdWidget fw = (FieldEdWidget)w;
     if (strcmp(params[0],"FI") == 0) {
          if (fw->field_editor.focusIn_proc != NULL)
               (*fw->field_editor.focusIn_proc)(w);
     } else if (strcmp(params[0],"FO") == 0) {
          if (fw->field_editor.focusOut_proc != NULL)
               (*fw->field_editor.focusOut_proc)(w);
     } else if (strcmp(params[0],"EW") == 0) {
          if (fw->field_editor.enterWindow_proc != NULL)
               (*fw->field_editor.enterWindow_proc)(w);
     } else if (strcmp(params[0],"FA") == 0) {
          if (fw->field_editor.field_axn_proc != NULL)
               (*fw->field_editor.field_axn_proc)(w);
     } else {
          XtWarning("Bad param to NotifyProcs \
          in FieldEdWidget !!");
     }
}
```

6.4.4.5. Default Procedures All widgets should supply some default level that will exist if the application writer does not add anything new. The following functions provide the base functionality for all of the procedures that are installable:

```
/* These are some default procedures for FocusIn (FI), FocusOut
 * (FO), and EnterWindow (EW).
 */
FwProc  DefFIProc(w)
     Widget w;
{
     Arg arg[1];

XtSetArg(arg[0],XtNborderColor,WhitePixelOfScreen(XtScreen(w)));
XtSetValues(w,arg,(Cardinal)1);
}
FwProc  DefFOProc(w)
     Widget w;
{
     Arg arg[1];
```

```
XtSetArg(arg[0],XtNborderColor,BlackPixelOfScreen(XtScreen(w)));
XtSetValues(w,arg,(Cardinal)1);
}
FwProc  DefEWProc(w)
     Widget w;
{
/* Get the keyboard focus for the field */
     XSetInputFocus(XtDisplay(w), XtWindow(w),
          RevertToPointerRoot,  CurrentTime);
}
```

6.4.4.6. Internal Editors At this point in the source code, the entire widget has been constructed. You will now construct the internal editors that allow the widget to be a useful tool for screen creation. If you are going to build your own editing procedures to go with this widget, you will need to pay close attention to these four.

The editors are all identical except for the insertion part of the code. In each case, they check the value of the key pressed to determine if it is allowed. Recall the macros defined in the header part of the code; they are used heavily in this part of the code:

```
#define SBUFSIZE    100
XComposeStatus comp_stat = {NULL,0};

FwProc  AlphaEd(w,event,EditorAxn)
     Widget w;
     XEvent *event;
     int EditorAxn;
{
     XtTextPosition insertPos,nxtPos;
     XtTextBlock    tb;

     switch(EditorAxn) {
          case DeleteFwdChar:
               insertPos = GETINSERTIONPOINT(w);
               nxtPos = XtxuTextScan(w,insertPos, XtstPositions,
                         XtsdRight, 1, TRUE);
               if (insertPos == nxtPos) {
                    BEEP(w);
               } else {
                    tb.length = tb.firstPos = 0;
                    REPLACE(w,insertPos,nxtPos,&tb);
               }
               break;
          case DeletePrvChar:
```

```
                insertPos = GETINSERTIONPOINT(w);
                nxtPos = XtxuTextScan(w,insertPos,XtstPositions,
                                XtsdLeft, 1, TRUE);
                if (insertPos == 0) {
                     BEEP(w);
                } else {
                     tb.length = tb.firstPos = 0;
                     REPLACE(w,nxtPos,insertPos,&tb);
                }
                break;
           case DeleteField:
                tb.length = tb.firstPos = 0;
                nxtPos = XtxuTextScan(w, (XtTextPosition)0,
                                XtstAll,XtsdRight, 1, TRUE);
                REPLACE(w,(XtTextPosition)0,nxtPos,&tb);
                break;
           case InsertChar: {
                char sbuf[SBUFSIZE];
                int keysym;
/*
 * Look up the "value" of the key pressed and check if it is
 * allowed. If it is, then insert it.  Otherwise, do nothing.
 */
                tb.length = XLookupString(event,sbuf,SBUFSIZE,
                              &keysym,&comp_stat);
                if (tb.length == 0) break;
                if (IsAlphaKey(keysym)){
                      tb.ptr = &sbuf[0];
                      tb.firstPos = 0;
                      insertPos = GETINSERTIONPOINT(w);
                      REPLACE(w,insertPos,insertPos,&tb);
                }
                break;
           }
     }
}
FwProc  AlphaNumEd(w,event,EditorAxn)
     Widget w;
     XEvent *event;
     int EditorAxn;
{
     XtTextPosition insertPos,nxtPos;
     XtTextBlock    tb;
```

```
switch(EditorAxn) {
     case DeleteFwdChar:
          insertPos = GETINSERTIONPOINT(w);
          nxtPos = XtxuTextScan(w,insertPos,XtstPositions,
                         XtsdRight, 1, TRUE);
          if (insertPos == nxtPos) {
               BEEP(w);
          } else {
               tb.length = tb.firstPos = 0;
               REPLACE(w,insertPos,nxtPos,&tb);
          }
          break;
     case DeletePrvChar:
          insertPos = GETINSERTIONPOINT(w);
          nxtPos = XtxuTextScan(w,insertPos, XtstPositions,
                         XtsdLeft, 1, TRUE);
          if (insertPos == 0) {
               BEEP(w);
          } else {
               tb.length = tb.firstPos = 0;
               REPLACE(w,nxtPos,insertPos,&tb);
          }
          break;
     case DeleteField:
          tb.length = tb.firstPos = 0;
          nxtPos = XtxuTextScan(w, (XtTextPosition)0,
                         XtstAll,XtsdRight, 1, TRUE);
          REPLACE(w,(XtTextPosition)0,nxtPos,&tb);
          break;
     case InsertChar:
     {
          char sbuf[SBUFSIZE];
          int keysym;
          tb.length = XLookupString(event,sbuf,SBUFSIZE,
                    &keysym,&comp_stat);
          if (tb.length == 0) break;
          if (IsAlphaKey(keysym) || IsNumericKey(keysym)){
               tb.ptr = &sbuf[0];
               tb.firstPos = 0;
          insertPos = GETINSERTIONPOINT(w);
          REPLACE(w,insertPos,insertPos, &tb);
          }
     }
          break;
```

```
    }
}
FwProc  IntEd(w,event,EditorAxn)
     Widget w;
     XEvent *event;
     int EditorAxn;
{
     XtTextPosition insertPos,nxtPos;
     XtTextBlock    tb;

     switch(EditorAxn) {
          case DeleteFwdChar:
               insertPos = GETINSERTIONPOINT(w);
               nxtPos = XtxuTextScan(w,insertPos,XtstPositions,
                              XtsdRight, 1, TRUE);
               if (insertPos == nxtPos) {
                    BEEP(w);
               } else {
                    tb.length = tb.firstPos = 0;
                    REPLACE(w,insertPos,nxtPos,&tb);
               }
               break;
          case DeletePrvChar:
               insertPos = GETINSERTIONPOINT(w);
               nxtPos = XtxuTextScan(w,insertPos, XtstPositions,
                              XtsdLeft, 1, TRUE);
               if (insertPos == 0) {
                    BEEP(w);
               } else {
                    tb.length = tb.firstPos = 0;
                    REPLACE(w,nxtPos,insertPos,&tb);
               }
               break;
          case DeleteField:
               tb.length = tb.firstPos = 0;
               nxtPos = XtxuTextScan(w, (XtTextPosition)0,
                              XtstAll,XtsdRight, 1, TRUE);
               REPLACE(w,(XtTextPosition)0,nxtPos,&tb);
               break;
          case InsertChar:
          {
               char sbuf[SBUFSIZE];
               int keysym;
               tb.length = XLookupString(event,sbuf,SBUFSIZE,
```

```
                    &keysym,&comp_stat);
            if (tb.length == 0) break;
            if (IsNumericKey(keysym)){
                tb.ptr = &sbuf[0];
                tb.firstPos = 0;
                insertPos = GETINSERTIONPOINT(w);
                REPLACE(w,insertPos,insertPos,&tb);
            }
        }
            break;
    }
}
FwProc  FloatEd(w,event,EditorAxn)
    Widget w;
    XEvent *event;
    int EditorAxn;
{
    XtTextPosition insertPos,nxtPos;
    XtTextBlock    tb;
    FieldEdWidget fw = (FieldEdWidget)w;
    switch(EditorAxn) {
        case DeleteFwdChar:
            insertPos = GETINSERTIONPOINT(w);
            nxtPos = XtxuTextScan(w,insertPos,XtstPositions,
                        XtsdRight, 1, TRUE);
            if (insertPos ==  nxtPos) {
                BEEP(w);
            } else {
                tb.length = tb.firstPos = 0;
                REPLACE(w,insertPos,nxtPos,&tb);
            }
            break;
        case DeletePrvChar:
            insertPos = GETINSERTIONPOINT(w);
            nxtPos = XtxuTextScan(w,insertPos,XtstPositions,
                        XtsdLeft, 1, TRUE);
            if (insertPos == 0) {
                BEEP(w);
            } else {
                tb.length = tb.firstPos = 0;
                REPLACE(w,nxtPos,insertPos,&tb);
            }
            break;
        case DeleteField:
```

```
                tb.length = tb.firstPos = 0;
                nxtPos = XtxuTextScan(w,(XtTextPosition)0,
                               XtstAll,XtsdRight, 1, TRUE);
                REPLACE(w,(XtTextPosition)0,nxtPos,&tb);
                break;
            case InsertChar:
            {
                char sbuf[SBUFSIZE];
                int keysym;
                char *sb;
                nxtPos = XtxuTextScan(w,(XtTextPosition)0,
                               XtstEOL,XtsdRight, 1, TRUE);
                sb = XtxuTextGetString(w,0,nxtPos);
                tb.length = XLookupString(event,sbuf,SBUFSIZE,
                         &keysym,&comp_stat);
                if (tb.length == 0) break;
                if (IsNumericKey(keysym) ||
                   (IsDecimalKey(keysym) &&
                    (strstr(sb,".")==NULL))){
                     tb.ptr = &sbuf[0];
                     tb.firstPos = 0;
                     insertPos = GETINSERTIONPOINT(w);
                     REPLACE(w,insertPos,insertPos,&tb);
                }
                XtFree(sb);
            }
                break;
        }
}
```

6.4.4.7. Default Translations The following are the default translations set up for the widget:

```
/* FILE:        FieldEdTr.c
 * PURPOSE:     Hold the default translations for the field editor
 *              widget class.
 * FW - Forward Char
 * BK - Backward Char
 * DC - Delete Char, DP - Delete Prv Char, DF - Delete Field
 * IN - Insert Char, FI - Focus In, FO - FocusOut, EW - Enter
 * Window
 */
char FieldEdTrans[] =
"\
```

```
Ctrl<Key>F:         MoveInsert(FW) \n\
Ctrl<Key>B:         MoveInsert(BK) \n\
Ctrl<Key>D:         NotifyEditor(DC) \n\
Ctrl<Key>A:         MoveInsert(BG) \n\
Ctrl<Key>E:         MoveInsert(ED) \n\
Ctrl<Key>H:         NotifyEditor(DP) \n\
Ctrl<Key>K:         NotifyEditor(DF) \n\
Ctrl<Key>L:         RedrawDisplay() \n\
<Key>Right:         MoveInsert(FW) \n\
<Key>Left:          MoveInsert(BK) \n\
<Key>Delete:        NotifyEditor(DP) \n\
<Key>Backspace:     NotifyEditor(DP) \n\
<Key>Return:        NotifyProcs(FA) \n\
<Key>:              NotifyEditor(IN) \n\
<FocusIn>:          NotifyProcs(FI) \n\
<FocusOut>:         NotifyProcs(FO) \n\
<EnterWindow>:      NotifyProcs(EW)";
```

6.5. Summing Up

This has been a heavyweight chapter. The widget created here is rather useful (as you will see in Chapter 8), and demonstrates the power and ease of creating widgets. You simply define the class, define the instance things, then provide the procedures to handle the standard mechanics (realize, expose), and add the action procedures that give your widget character.

If you can find a superclass that has many of the traits that you need, use it! In this case, TextWidget was perfect. Imagine how complicated things would have gotten if it didn't exist.

You should take some time and read TextWidget's source code. It will give you valuable insight into how widgets work. As of X11R4, it has been given a facelift, so you may want to check out that version.

7

Building Widgets: Container Widgets

In the previous chapter you constructed a primitive widget that was useful for field editing. You did this by using the Intrinsic inheritance mechanism as subclassed off of the Athena Text widget. As you can tell, primitive widgets are the "worker" widgets, and as such are the most important ones to understand how to construct. This chapter discusses the two additional kinds of widgets: composite and constraint.

7.1. Composite Widget

The *composite* widget is a layout-manager type of abstraction. Essentially, it provides client writers with some useful layout mechanisms so that the details of laying out widgets are somewhat removed. In the Athena Widget Set, the BoxWidgetClass is an example of this kind of widget. The client writer simply defines a few resources to instruct the BoxWidget about how spacing should be handled for the children widgets, and then proceeds to add/delete children. In the Motif Widget Set, the MenuShellWidget is an example of this kind of widget.

One thing you may find interesting about composite widgets is that there aren't that many written. Hard to believe, isn't it? Well, to put your mind at ease, take a look in Appendix A of this book in the part that shows the "classing" of both Athena and Motif widgets. How many did you find that were *just* composite widgets? You will find several constraint widgets (which just happen to be subclasses of composite widgets), but few composites.

7.2. Structure of a Composite Widget

The composite widget is one of the protocol widgets found in the Intrinsics. It is much like the primitive widget in that it too has an instance and class part. The instance part is as follows:

```
typedef struct _CompositePart {
  WidgetList  children;      /* array of ALL widget children     */
  Cardinal    num_children; /* total number of widget children */
  Cardinal    num_slots;     /* number of slots in children array */
  XtOrderProc insert_position; /* compute position of new child */
} CompositePart,*CompositePtr;
```

The instance record is defined as follows:

```
typedef struct _CompositeRec {
    CorePart      core;
    CompositePart composite;
} CompositeRec;
```

Notice that this is very straightforward. The “children” member refers to the list of widgets that are being managed. The “num_children” member is the number of children in the list. The “num_slots” member indicates the maximum size of the list. The “insert_position” member is a pointer to a function that informs the widget of the index into the list where the next child will go.

The class part is equally simple, and is given here:

```
typedef struct _CompositeClassPart {
 XtGeometryHandler geometry_manager; /* geometry manager */
 XtWidgetProc      change_managed;   /* change managed state of
                                        child */
 XtWidgetProc      insert_child;     /* physically add child to
                                        parent */
 XtWidgetProc      delete_child;     /* physically remove child */
 XtPointer         extension;        /* pointer to extension
                                        record */
} CompositeClassPart,*CompositePartPtr;
```

The X11R4 definition for the extension record is defined as:

```
typedef struct {
 XtPointer next_extension; /* 1st 4 mandated for all extension
                              records */
 XrmQuark record_type;      /* NULLQUARK; on CompositeClassPart */
 long version;              /* must be XtCompositeExtensionVersion*/
 Cardinal record_size;      /* sizeof(CompositeClassExtensionRec) */
 Boolean accepts_objects;
} CompositeClassExtensionRec, *CompositeClassExtension;
```

and the class record defined as:

```
typedef struct _CompositeClassRec {
     CoreClassPart      core_class;
     CompositeClassPart composite_class;
} CompositeClassRec;
```

The first member of the class structure is a pointer to "geometry_manager." This is a method that performs the negotiation between the widget's children and itself. If you recall from the previous chapter, the CoreClassPart contained a member for a method called query_geometry. This is the method that is invoked by a composite widget's geometry_manager when attempting a layout. The important point here is to have an understanding of how these widgets work, not how to build your own.

The next members are "change_managed," "insert_child," and "delete_child." These methods worry about the state of the children under management. The change_managed method is responsible for redoing the layout whenever the composite widget detects a change in its children. The insert_child and delete_child methods simply provide the capability to add/delete children from the list.

In the actual implementation file of a composite widget you would find the standard "class" record to fill out. Typically, the only methods that are required to be created are Initialize( ), Resize( ), and QueryGeometry( ).

The Initialize() method would probably make sure that the widget has nonzero width and height. (That sounds real tough!) In the Resize( ) method, you would probably find a call to a function that performs the layout. This layout function would be coupled with a "sister" function that tries the layout prior to applying it. Lastly, the QueryGeometry() method would be crafted. All widgets should provide one of these (though most don't) so that children are easier to manage, since the parent will "discuss" things via the QueryGeometry() method of the child. This routine has the chore of checking on the intentions of the parent, which entails determining what the parent is trying to change, and seeing if it can be allowed to happen.

Now then, since Initialize(), Resize(), and QueryGeometry() are done, what next? As you can see, the composite widget has additional class parts. In the previous chapter, your widget did not have anything new to add to the class. For composites, however, this is not the case. They add the four previously mentioned members. The only one of concern is the GeometryManager() method; the others are usually inherited. As stated before, this method calls the child's QueryGeometry() method to conduct a negotiation. There is an exchange of dialog between the parent and child that informs each of the other's wishes. Eventually, a result will be obtained with the parent having the right to enforce any changes on the child.

Granted, this discussion on composite widgets is brief, but this book is a practical guide, and in the real world almost all programmers work with what is available. Therefore, this discussion is intended purely for "understanding's" sake, not to provide comprehensive knowledge.

7.3. Structure of a Constraint Widget

The last of the protocol widgets is the constraint widget. It is a subclass of composite, and is also used for layout. It provides an added degree of layout mechanics through the use of constraints applied to each of the widgets it manages.

If you recall, the CorePart (instance) has a member that is a pointer to a constraint record. You might have wondered what that was all about. Where would the widget get these constraints? The answer is from a constraint widget that is managing the child.

The instance and class structures are as follows:

```
typedef struct _ConstraintPart {
    XtPointer   mumble;
} ConstraintPart;

typedef struct _ConstraintRec {
    CorePart        core;
    CompositePart   composite;
    ConstraintPart  constraint;
} ConstraintRec, *ConstraintWidget;
```

The class part is given as:

```
typedef struct _ConstraintClassPart {
  XtResourceList resources;    /* constraint resource list */
  Cardinal    num_resources;  /*  number of constraints in list */
  Cardinal    constraint_size;  /* size of constraint record */
  XtInitProc initialize;       /* constraint initialization */
  XtWidgetProc destroy;        /* constraint destroy proc */
  XtSetValuesFunc set_values; /* constraint set_values proc */
  XtPointer        extension; /* pointer to extension record */
} ConstraintClassPart;
```

The extension definition is given as:

```
typedef struct {
 XtPointer next_extension;   /*1st 4 mandated for all extension */
 XrmQuark record_type;       /* NULLQUARK; on ConstraintClassPart */
 long version; /* must be XtConstraintExtensionVersion */
 Cardinal record_size;    /* sizeof(ConstraintClassExtensionRec) */
 XtArgsProc get_values_hook;
} ConstraintClassExtensionRec, *ConstraintClassExtension;
```

The class record is given as:

```
typedef struct _ConstraintClassRec {
    CoreClassPart       core_class;
    CompositeClassPart  composite_class;
    ConstraintClassPart constraint_class;
} ConstraintClassRec;
```

The class members should be familiar to you: "resources" and "num_resources" are used by the resource manager (see Chapter 5 and Chapter 6), and "constraint_size" tells the Intrinsics how many bytes long the constraint record is. The remainder are methods: initialize, destroy, and set_values. These behave just like those in Chapter 6, namely, "initialize" sets up the constraint values, "destroy" cleans up, and "set_values" assigns values to constraint resources.

You should notice the extension record. This creature is a common piece of equipment now, with X11R4 defining the protocol for how to lay it out. The reason for extensions (and standards for their use), is that they eliminate core Intrinsics changes.

It is easy to see that the structures of the protocol widgets are quite lengthy. Now that you are familiar with the Intrinsics, you can also see that there are fairly well-defined mechanisms for interaction with Xt. If that is true, then imagine what a change would do to the Intrinsic code, if the members of the structures were toyed with.

Remember that the constraint widget is a subclass of the composite, making it a manager type. Therefore, the things that occur when using a composite widget will hold true for a constraint widget. Additionally, the constraint widget adds more layout information which it must consider during its layout management.

7.4. Summing Up

Container widgets are confusing, hard to write, and something most application writers will not have to do. Fortunately, most of the widget sets provide a good base of layout managers (containers) that application writers may employ. The key points to remember are as follows:

1. Composite and constraint widgets manage children.
2. Geometry management can be lengthy.
3. If you will be creating several children of a manager at one time, it is wise to create them as unmanaged and then manage all of them at one time.

If you have the desire to explore this topic further, the Athena BoxWidget and FormWidget are useful examples in the "how" of writing container widgets.

8

Sample Application: A Character-Oriented Client

In Chapter 5 you wrote several clients, each an application in its own right. However, none had all of the features that most applications tend to have. In this chapter, you will construct a complete application, with field entry, pop-up help, pop-up menu, pop-up option list, and field traversal without the mouse.

8.1. Designing an Xt Application

Since X clients are event-driven, the way you think about application design must change. For instance, in the "old" style of programming, it was fairly easy to write an editing screen. Each field would be entered in sequence, with the program "watching" the keystrokes so that the user added the right information. In some cases, a field action routine would "fire" after a Return keypress, with some editing feedback given. In other cases, the entire form would be filled in, and then a "form action" routine would validate each field. These techniques were tried and true and fairly straightforward. Those were the days of keyboards.

When graphical user interfaces (GUIs) came along, so did the use of a mouse. The mouse (not to be confused with a hairy little animal) took the old model of programming and put a kink in it. Those days of simply watching a keyboard are gone. No longer can you assume that the entire form will be filled in, nor can you assume a sequence of field traversal. Of course, programs can be written to force the user to comply with the applications-defined policy, but that goes against the grain of "productivity." So, how do you keep the users happy? With a great deal of pain, sometimes.

Designing an Xt client encompasses three things: application flow, layout policy, and construction tools. The first step in your design is to understand the application flows and decide what components are needed (such as a menu, or a command button). Next, you must determine the interface policy that the application warrants. Is it like Presentation Manager? Does the user department have a policy? The next decision is on the widget set. Athena? Motif? XWIN? Or a hybrid of several? Once you know the policy, widget set, and application flows, you can construct the application.

8.2. Standardizing the Interface

The idea behind standardizing the user interface is not new. Many companies have devoted many hours researching this subject and have their own versions. On top of X we have OSF/Motif (Presentation Manager-like), AT&T/XWIN (Open Look), and Sun/XView (another Open Look), with perhaps more to follow. Interface policies have become such a concern that corporations are suing other corporations over "look and feel!"

In Figure 8-1 you can see one type of interface. The top-left corner contains the application title. Next to it, there is an exit button, followed by a min/max button. Below the application title is an options area with the first item being help, followed by system options (i.e., kill, restart, etc.), and finished by any application-specific options. In the window are dotted lines that represent pop-ups. Pop-up menus will always pop up next to the options area, while other pop ups will center in the backdrop.

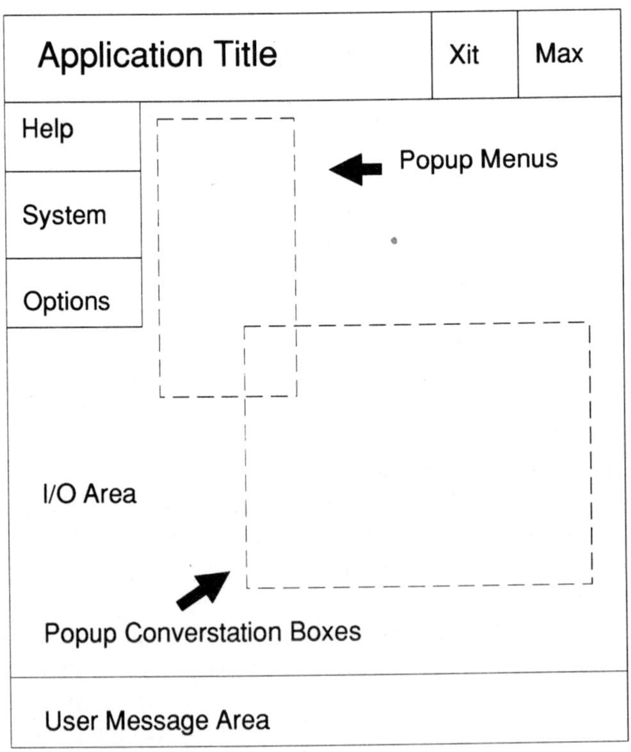

Figure 8-1 One kind of GUI.

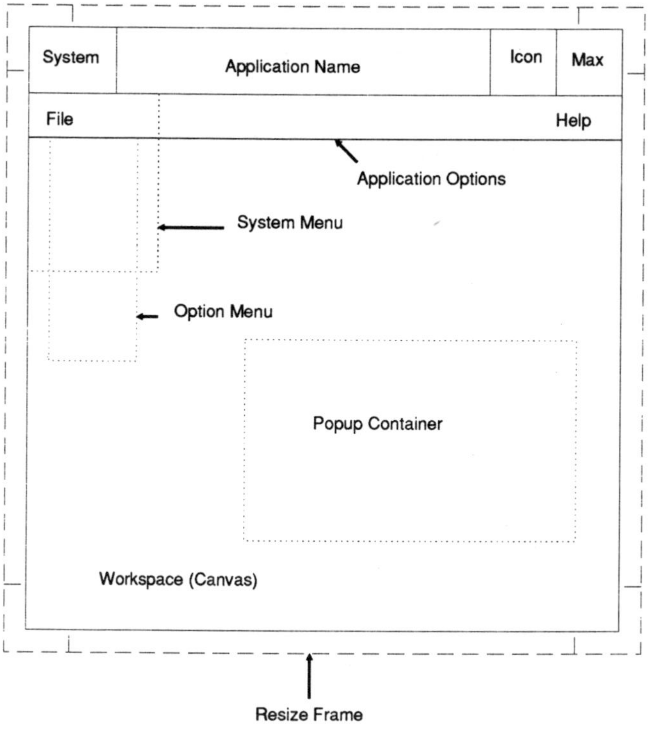

Figure 8-2 Another kind of GUI.

Figure 8-2 demonstrates the OSF/Motif style of interface. As you can see, the resize borders are on the outermost frame of the window (they are placed there by the OSF/Motif window manager, "mwm"). In the upper-left corner is a button for the system menu, followed by the application title, followed by an icon button, and lastly, a min/max button. Below this "system bar" is the application-specific "menu bar." When a menu item from the menu bar is selected, a menu will pull down beneath it (the same is true for the system menu off of the system button). The "workspace" will hold additional pop-up windows or perhaps static display windows.

To show you how to create your own interface policies, independent of any policy body, we will adopt the style in Figure 8-3. It has a "menu/system bar" with the system button in the upper-left corner. Proceeding from that is an exit button so that the user can quickly kill the client. The exit functionality will also be available in system menu. The backdrop will contain containers (entry and display) along with any pop-ups that may occur.

Standardizing the user interface has many advantages. It provides consistent program structure, minimizes user re-education, and streamlines program development.

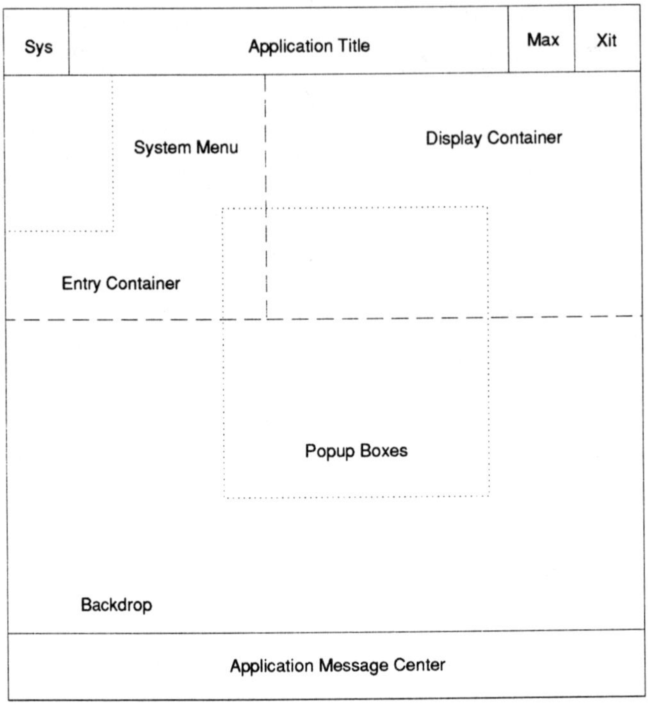

Figure 8-3 Our standard GUI.

Consistent program structure is obtained through the use of common construction tools. Additionally, application writers need not deal with the issues of interface style; they simply adapt whatever is the current policy and use the available tools to abide by it.

With a consistent user interface for applications, the re-education process for users is reduced. Users can spend more time using the application rather than trying to figure out all of the new interface guidelines.

Program development is streamlined due to the reuse of interface "routines" or "objects" that would be created for easing the building of the interface. Additionally, re-creation of interface components is eliminated. An example of this is found in the OSF/Motif Widget Set in the form of the convenience routine CreateMainWindow() (discusses and used in Chapter 11) which creates a standard main window that adheres to the OSF/Motif Style Guide.

8.3. Selecting From the Widget Sets

When developing applications, it is very important to have libraries of routines that provide the functionality you need. Often, software departments will create libraries of routines specific to their needs. These might include standard data calculations, mathematical calculation routines, or database access routines. These libraries go a long way in easing development, and this same notion can be applied to widget set selection.

Each widget set contains the core components to create user interfaces. The Athena Widget Set was the first to arrive. It was developed by the X folks when the Toolkit was created. The intention was to show other people how to construct interface components. The original set contained components such as the scrollbar, command button, label, and text editing. In addition, a few layout assistants were available: box, form, viewport, and vpaned. Soon after this set was created, vendors stepped in to provide their versions of a scrollbar, command button, and the rest. Looking at Athena, Motif, XWIN, or whatever, you can see that each set has a standard collection of useful interface components. Given this, it almost doesn't matter very much which kit you select so long as most of your needs are met.

The important point to make is to select the widget set that works for you. If 3D visuals turn you on, or if "pushpins" and "sliders" are your fancy, go for it. Just remember, when you select a set, you are kind of stuck with it. For the most part, you cannot swap widgets from other sets. There are exceptions (in Chapter 9 we see the Athena Clock widget used with Motif widgets), especially if the widget is a direct class of the Core.

Most widget sets provide a "union" widget. This widget has the special features (such as keyboard traversal) that the widget set uses. If the widget you would like to use is a direct class of Core, that union widget is not in the way, thus the widget is completely usable. If, however, the widget is a subclass of a union widget, the union must be brought over. This may not be possible due to conflicts.

8.3.1. Our Selection

In this client, the Athena Widget Set is used. As has been pointed out earlier, this set is free, and the source code is widely available.

While you develop the code, you should become familiar with the components being used. In this client you will use the following:

1. OverrideShellWidgetClass (for pop-ups).
2. FormWidgetClass (for layout management).
3. BoxWidgetClass (for layout management).
4. ListWidgetClass (for the pop-up option selection list).
5. CommandWidgetClass (for buttons and menu panes).
6. LabelWidgetClass (for the menu titles, message area, and field labels).
7. FieldEdWidgetClass (for field entry).
8. AsciiDiskWidgetClass (for help).

8.3.1.1. OverrideWidgetClass

This widget is a member of the ShellWidgetClass. It is one of the built-in widgets provided by the Intrinsics. Its role is to override window managers. As you have seen in all of your previous clients, the window manager places "adornments" (such as resize bars) around the top-level windows. The OverrideShellWidgetClass is used to get around this. It is used most often for creating pop-ups.

8.3.1.2. FormWidgetClass

This widget is a member of the ConstraintWidgetClass. Essentially, it contains layout policies that are useful for assembling interfaces. In this case, it will be used for controlling the placement of widgets with respect to other widgets, and controlling resizing of the children.

8.3.1.3. BoxWidgetClass

This widget is a member of the CompositeWidgetClass. Its job is to assist in the layout of children. This widget places no constraints on its children. It lays them out by filling in the row first, then continuing down. This is the ideal widget for a button box or a menu.

8.3.1.4. ListWidgetClass

This widget is a member of the SimpleWidgetClass. Its role is to provide a list of items and a callback mechanism for when an item is selected.

8.3.1.5. CommandWidgetClass

This widget is a member of the LabelWidgetClass. Its role is to provide a callback mechanism to the LabelWidgetClass. This is a "button-like" widget. You should not confuse this widget with the command widget from the Motif Set. In Motif, the command widget actually allows for entry and buffering of commands, not button behavior.

8.3.1.6. LabelWidgetClass

This widget is a member of the SimpleWidgetClass. It provides a textual label (justified) or a pixmap in a window. Its main use is to provide a message to the user. It is used in the menu, the message area, and for field labels.

8.3.1.7. FieldEdWidgetClass

This widget is a member of the TextWidgetClass. It provides the necessary mechanisms for field editing. You constructed this widget in Chapter 6.

8.3.1.8. AsciiDiskWidgetClass

This widget is a member of the TextWidgetClass. It can be used to provide editing or display of text files. It is employed here it in its display mode, as a help screen.

8.3.2. Client Requirements

The client requires that the application must have an application bar (which should be optional) containing a system menu button, application title, and exit button. The system menu button will pop down (pull down) a menu that contains an entry for help, exit, and to unpop the menu. When the user clicks a mouse button in the title area, that application should rise to the top. Clicking in the exit button area should kill the client.

There should be five entry fields with labels for editing: Security (alphabetic only), Trader (alphanumeric), Buy/Sell indication (alphabetic field allowing only b, B, s, or S), Quantity (whole number only), and Price (float). The user should be able to move among the fields with or without the mouse. There should be a selection list off of the Security field. Clicking on a selection in the list should fill in the Security field with the selection. Lastly, there should be Commit and Clear buttons. Commit will write the information in the fields to a file. Clear will clean the fields out. Additionally, the user must be able to perform the Commit operation from *any* of the fields.

8.4. Building the Application

As you can see, it's a complete application. To start, you should break the program down into several pieces. You will need to look at building the application resource-gathering mechanism; laying out the menu bar; building a pop-up menu; creating pop-up help, an entry form, an option list, and a button box; and installing accelerators.

In this client most of the widgets have been declared globally. This makes passing to functions easier, but the practice of declaring global variables can make the code hard to read and unmanageable; therefore, use them with care.

The client screen with no menus popped up is shown in Figure 8-4. The main program of the client "trade" is as follows (most of these areas have been explored in one form or another in Chapter 5):

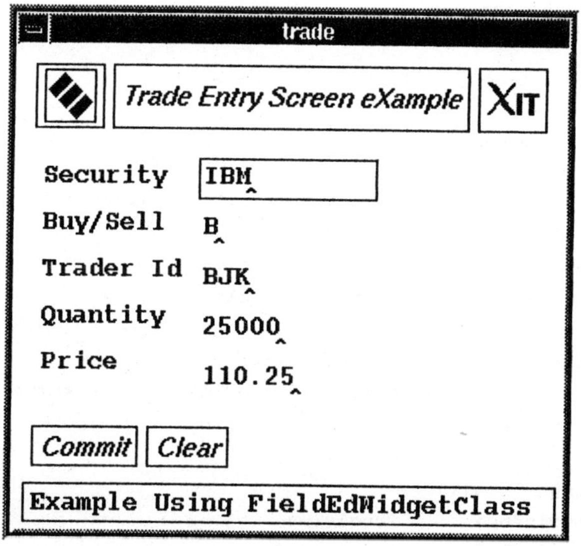

Figure 8-4 Trade with nothing popped.

```
#include "XbkUtil.h"
/* Widget headers to be used in this client */
#include <X11/Shell.h>
#include <X11/Form.h>
#include <X11/Box.h>
#include <X11/Command.h>
#include <X11/List.h>
#include <X11/AsciiText.h> /* This is actually brought in
                             * by FieldEd.h. However, to let
                             * readers understand the code
                             * this is left in. */

/* Add in the header for the fieldEd widget */
#include "FieldEd.h"
#include "TextUtils.h"
/* Some helpful symbols ...
 */
#define TRADESTRSIZE         80
#define SECURITY_SIZE        8
#define TRADER_SIZE          5
/* Our macros for the application shell and class names
 */
#define XbkShellName      "trade"
#define XbkApplClass      "Trade"

/*
 * Forward Declarations.
 */

int PopIt();
XtCallbackProc Chow(),Title(),
               PopMenu(),PopItDown(),PopHelp(),Done(),
               Commit(), Cancel(),selection_callback();

XtActionProc   PopList(),MakePrvFldActive(),
               MakeNxtFldActive(),Toggle();

/* Define the Translations strings...
 *   newAxns (for border setting), stdFldAxns (for keyboard
 *   traversal, and popListAxns (for triggering a pop-up)
 */
static String   newAxns =
     "<EnterWindow>:     Toggle(On) \n\
      <LeaveWindow>:     Toggle(Off)";
```

```
static String  stdFldAxns =
      "Shift<Key>Tab:     MakePrvFldActive() \n\
             <Key>Tab:     MakeNxtFldActive() ";
static String popListAxns = "<Key>F1:   PopList()";

/*
 * Action table for the new actions that we will build.
 */

XtActionsRec     appAxnsTbl[] = {
        {"MakePrvFldActive", MakePrvFldActive},
        {"MakeNxtFldActive", MakeNxtFldActive},
        {"PopList",     PopList},
        {"Toggle",Toggle},
        {NULL, NULL},
};
/*
 * The compiled translation table holders for each of
 * the strings.
 */
XtTranslations  stdFldTrans,popListTrans,newAxnsTrans;

/*
 * Define the widgets to be used in the client.
 */
Widget top;              /* Top-level shell */
Widget backdrop;         /* Application container */
/*
 * Buttons for the menu bar.
 */
Widget menu_bar;         /* Menu bar container */
Widget sys_btn;          /* Button to trigger pop-up */
Widget exit_btn;         /* To kill the client */
Widget title_btn;        /* To raise the window */
/*
 * Widgets to create a pop-up menu.
 */
Widget popup_holder;     /* Pop-up holder */
Widget popup_container;  /* Actual container for menu */
Widget popup_title;      /* Label to contain the name */
/*
 * Help
 */
Widget helpShell;        /* Pop-up shell */
```

```
Widget helpContainer;     /* Container to manage children */
Widget helpText;          /* AsciiDiskWidget */
Widget helpDone;          /* CommandWidget for unpopping */
/*
 * Widgets to create an entry form.
 */
Widget entry_container;   /* Container for fields */
Widget btnBox;            /* Container for commit/cancel */
Widget commit_btn;        /* To accept field entries */
Widget cancel_btn;        /* To clear the screen */
/*
 * List widget stuff...
 */
Widget listShell;         /* Shell for the pop-up */
Widget list;              /* List                 */
/*
 * A "message" label.
 */
Widget label;

main(argc,argv)
     int argc;char **argv;
{
     int i;
     top = XtInitialize(XbkShellName,XbkApplClass,
                    myCmdOpts,XtNumber(myCmdOpts),&argc, argv);
/*
 * Since our application resources may not have come from the
 * command line we need to get them from the database (if we let
 * the user set them in .Xdefaults etc.).
 */
     XtGetApplicationResources(top, &myAppRes, myAppResOpts,
                              XtNumber(myAppResOpts),NULL, 0);
/*
 * Make sure we have a file to write our trades to.  If not,
 * don't start the client.
 */

     if ((fout = fopen(myAppRes.filename,"w+")) == NULL) {
          printf("ERROR: Could not open file !!!");
          XtCloseDisplay(XtDisplay(top));
          exit(-1);
     }
/*
```

```
 * Since we have some new actions to add, we do that now.
 */
     XtAddActions(appAxnsTbl, XtNumber(appAxnsTbl));
/*
 * Now we need to parse the translation table.  This will give us
 * a "compiled table."  The next step would be to set the
 * translations into a widget.  Here we set it to the shell.
 */
     newAxnsTrans = XtParseTranslationTable(newAxns);
     XtOverrideTranslations(top,newAxnsTrans);
/*
 * We are also adding actions for fields.  This is our prv/nxt
 * field handling mechanism.  We do the same as above, but
 * we will set the table to the widgets when they are created.
 * (Refer to later in the code)
 */
     stdFldTrans  = XtParseTranslationTable(stdFldAxns);
     popListTrans = XtParseTranslationTable(popListAxns);
/*
 * Set a manager to manage the various containers to be in the
 * form (i.e., MenuBar, EntryContainer, BtnBox, or Message).
 */
     backdrop = XtCreateManagedWidget("backdrop",
           formWidgetClass,top, NULL,0);
/*
 * If the menu bar is in use then create it along with the pop-ups
 * that correspond to its use (i.e. help and menu).
 */
     if (myAppRes.useMenuBar) {
          create_the_menubar();
          create_the_popup("Simple Menu");
          create_help();
     }
     create_list();                  /* Create the option list */
     create_the_entry_container();   /* Create the entry form  */
     create_the_label();             /* Create the message area */

     XtRealizeWidget(top);           /* "Map" the widgets */
     if (myAppRes.useMenuBar) {
             adjust_menu_bar();      /* Adjust the menu bar size */
     }
     XtMainLoop();                   /* Wait around for events */
}
```

8.4.1. Application Resource Setting

Application resource setting is discussed in Chapter 5. However, as a review, the mechanism involves three steps:

1. Create a structure to hold the application resources.
2. Define the XtResource table.
3. Define the XrmOptionDescRec.

In this application you will need a flag to indicate if the menu bar is wanted, a filename for the trade entry results, and the help filename:

```
struct _myAppRes {
     Boolean    useMenuBar;
     String     filename;
     String     helpFile;
} myAppRes;

#define OFFSET(field)  XtOffset(struct _myAppRes*, field)
static XtResource myAppResOpts[] = {
   {"useMenuBar", "UseMenuBar", XtRBoolean, sizeof(Boolean),
         OFFSET(useMenuBar), XtRString, "False"},
   {"fileName", "FileName", XtRString, sizeof(String),
         OFFSET(filename), XtRString, "trade.dat"},
   {"helpFile", "HelpFile", XtRString, sizeof(String),
         OFFSET(helpFile), XtRString, "trade.hlp"},
};
#undef OFFSET

XrmOptionDescRec myCmdOpts[] = {
{ "-useMenuBar", "*useMenuBar", XrmoptionNoArg, "TRUE" },
{"-filename","*fileName",XrmoptionSepArg,NULL},
{"-helpFile","*fileName",XrmoptionSepArg,NULL},
};
```

8.4.2. Creating the Menu Bar

The menu bar is composed of three command buttons: the system button, the title button, and the exit button. Use the Form widget as the container for the buttons. In this way, you can control the layout and make sure that each button will stay in the correct place relative to the other buttons. The code is as follows:

```
int create_the_menubar()
{
     Arg arg[MAXARGS];
     int cnt = 0;

     XtSetArg(arg[cnt],XtNresizable,FALSE);    cnt++;
     menu_bar = XtCreateManagedWidget("menuBar", formWidgetClass,
               backdrop, arg, cnt);
/* Tell the sys button to attach to the left and top of the form.
 */
     cnt = 0;
     XtSetArg(arg[cnt],XtNx,0);                        cnt++;
     XtSetArg(arg[cnt],XtNy,0);                        cnt++;
     XtSetArg(arg[cnt],XtNleft,XtChainLeft);           cnt++;
     XtSetArg(arg[cnt],XtNtop,XtChainTop);             cnt++;
     XtSetArg(arg[cnt],XtNresizable,FALSE);            cnt++;
     sys_btn = XtCreateManagedWidget("sysBtn",commandWidgetClass,
                    menu_bar, arg, cnt);
/* Add the menu pop-up callback to the button.
 */
     XtAddCallback(sys_btn,XtNcallback,PopMenu, NULL);

/* We will use the sys button height to set the others.
 */
     XtSetArg(arg[0],XtNheight,&height);
     XtGetValues(sys_btn,arg,1);

/* Tell this button to be next to the sys_btn and chain to the top.
 */
     cnt = 0;
     XtSetArg(arg[cnt],XtNfromHoriz,sys_btn);          cnt++;
     XtSetArg(arg[cnt],XtNheight,height);              cnt++;
     XtSetArg(arg[cnt],XtNtop,XtChainTop);             cnt++;
     XtSetArg(arg[cnt],XtNresizable,FALSE);            cnt++;
     title_btn = XtCreateManagedWidget("titleBtn",
          commandWidgetClass, menu_bar, arg, cnt);
/* Add the "raise" callback.
 */
     XtAddCallback(title_btn,XtNcallback,Title, NULL);

/* Tell this button to be next to title_btn and chain to the top.
 */
     cnt = 0;
     XtSetArg(arg[cnt],XtNfromHoriz,title_btn);            cnt++;
```

```
    XtSetArg(arg[cnt],XtNheight,height);                cnt++;
    XtSetArg(arg[cnt],XtNright,XtChainRight);           cnt++;
    XtSetArg(arg[cnt],XtNtop,XtChainTop);               cnt++;
    XtSetArg(arg[cnt],XtNresizable,FALSE);              cnt++;
    exit_btn = XtCreateManagedWidget("Xit", commandWidgetClass,
                    menu_bar, arg, cnt);
/* Add the "exit" callback to it.
 */
    XtAddCallback(exit_btn,XtNcallback,Chow, NULL);

/* This will force the menu bar to have the height we want it to
have.
 */
    XtSetArg(arg[0],XtNheight,height);
    XtSetValues(menu_bar,arg,1);
```

The callbacks we will use are PopMenu() (to bring up the menu), Chow() (to exit), and Title() (to raise the window) and are as follows:

```
XtCallbackProc PopMenu(whoCalledMe,dataFromClient,dataToGiveClient)
    Widget whoCalledMe;
    caddr_t dataFromClient;
    caddr_t dataToGiveClient;
{
    Arg arg[MAXARGS];
    int height = 0;
    int x = y = 0;
    int rx,ry;
    int cnt;

/* To pop up under the place from which we are popped requires
getting
 * the height of the parent. To do this we ask the widget using the
 * GETVALUES method.
 */

    XtSetArg(arg[0],XtNheight,&height);
    XtGetValues(whoCalledMe,arg,1);

/* We want to find out where the pop-up's parent is relative to the
 * root window.  This will give us a pretty good spot to pop up.
 */
    XtTranslateCoords(whoCalledMe, 0, 0, &rx, &ry);

    ry = ry + height;
```

```
/* If the pop-up shell is not realized, then setting values on it
 * does no good.  Therefore, if it is not realized we will realize
 * it so that setting the values on it will work.  Note: after it
 * has been realized it will stay that way.  If we call
 * XtRealizeWidget again it would simply return since it would
 * detect that the widget is already realized.
 */

     if (!XtIsRealized(popup_holder))
          XtRealizeWidget(popup_holder);
/* Tell the pop-up shell where the x,y is.
 */
     cnt = 0;
     XtSetArg(arg[cnt],XtNx,rx);               cnt++;
     XtSetArg(arg[cnt],XtNy,ry);               cnt++;
     XtSetValues(popup_holder,arg,cnt);

/* Pop it up and take an exclusive grab.  The exclusive grab
 * makes sure the user deals with the pop-up prior to doing
 * anything else.
 */
     XtPopup(popup_holder,XtGrabExclusive);
}

XtCallbackProc Title(whoCalledMe,dataFromClient,dataToGiveClient)
     Widget whoCalledMe;
     caddr_t dataFromClient;
     caddr_t dataToGiveClient;
{
/* Simply invoke the Xlib primitive to make the window raise.
 */
     XRaiseWindow(XtDisplay(top),XtWindow(top));
}
XtCallbackProc Chow(whoCalledMe,dataFromClient,dataToGiveClient)
     Widget whoCalledMe;
     caddr_t dataFromClient;
     caddr_t dataToGiveClient;
{
     XtUnmapWidget(top);       /* This yields a "clean" kill look */
     XtDestroyWidget(top);     /* kick off destroy callbacks */
     XtCloseDisplay(XtDisplay(top)); /* Tell the server you're
                                        gone */
     fclose(fout);             /* Close the open file */
     exit(0);                  /* exit without error */
}
```

After the rest of the form is created we will make sure that the menu bar is the size of the form. We do this using the following function:

```
int adjust_menu_bar()
{
     Arg arg[1];

     XtSetArg(arg[0],XtNwidth,&width);
     XtGetValues(top,arg,1);
     XtSetArg(arg[0],XtNwidth,width);
     XtSetValues(menu_bar,arg,1);
}
```

8.4.3. Creating a Pop-up Menu

The first item you need whenever you create any pop-up is a shell. This shell is of the overrideWidgetClass, and will not be subject to the window manager's policy. Pop-ups will only allow one child as a direct descendent, so in most cases, you should add one of the container type widgets and then add children to the container. To get the pop-up shell that will hold the pop-up menu shown in Figure 8-5, do the following:

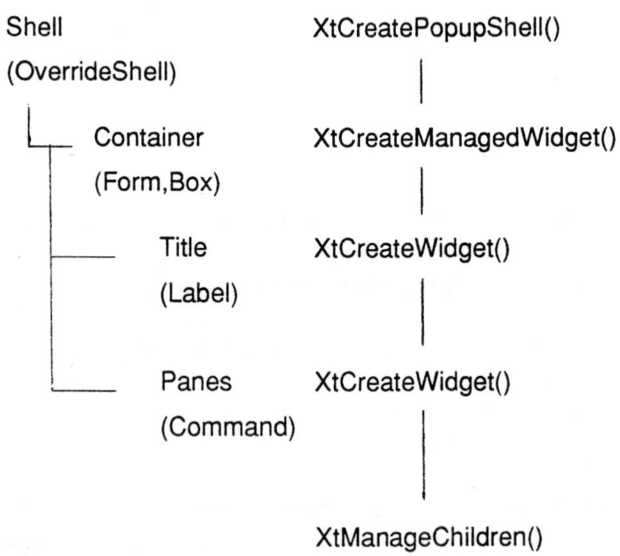

Figure 8-5 Pop-up menu.

```
popup_holder = XtCreatePopupShell("PopupShell",
               overrideShellWidgetClass,top,NULL,0);
```

Notice that you did not use the XtCreateWidget() function. The reason for this is that each widget contains a part that identifies the pop-up children associated with the widget. Using XtCreateWidget() would not fill in that part of the structure. Therefore, the Intrinsics provides XtCreatePopupShell().

The next item is the menu. A menu is composed of a container (to hold the panes), a title, and the panes. Each pane needs a label for some kind of callback that performs an action. The menu in this example uses the Athena boxWidgetClass as the container, labelWidgetClass for the Title, and commandWidgetClass for the panes. As you can see, the menu is fairly structured and the creation of the panes would be repetitive. This implies that you can create a structure to collect the similar information. By doing this, you make the code easier to read and maintain without any significant overhead.

Given that, let's define a structure for each pane:

```
typedef struct _MENUBODY {
     String              label;
     XtCallbackProc      cbProc;
     Widget              pane;
} MENUBODY;
```

A pane would have a label, callback proc, and the widget to hold the command button. With this, you can create an intialized array of these MENUBODY types to represent the menu body. You can then use this array to loop and generate the menu in a nice compact function:

```
MENUBODY pmenu [] = {
     {"Help",       PopHelp,0},
     {"UnPop",      PopItDown,0},
     {"Exit",       Chow,0},
};
```

The routine that creates the menu is:

```
int create_the_popup(tlabel)
     char *tlabel;
{
     Arg arg[MAXARGS];
     int cnt;
     int i;

/* Create the shell */
```

```
    popup_holder = XtCreatePopupShell("PopupShell",
                    overrideShellWidgetClass,top,NULL,0);
/* Now the container */
    popup_container = XtCreateManagedWidget("PopupMenu",
              boxWidgetClass,popup_holder,  NULL, 0);
/* Next, the title */
    cnt = 0;
    XtSetArg(arg[cnt],XtNlabel,tlabel);    cnt++;
    popup_title = XtCreateManagedWidget("popMenuLabel",
               labelWidgetClass,popup_container, arg, cnt);

/* Loop through and make the panes */

    for(i=0;i<XtNumber (pmenu);i++) {
        cnt = 0;
        arg[cnt].name = XtNlabel;
        arg[cnt].value = (XtArgVal)pmenu[i].label;
        cnt++;
        pmenu[i].pane = XtCreateManagedWidget("pane",
                            commandWidgetClass,
                            popup_container,
                            arg,cnt);

/* If a callback was provided add it */

        if (pmenu[i].cbProc != NULL)
            XtAddCallback(pmenu[i].pane,XtNcallback,
                pmenu[i].cbProc, NULL);
    }
}
```

You will no doubt notice the three callbacks used in the initialized array, PopHelp( ),PopItDown( ), and Chow( ). The new callbacks are as follows:

```
XtCallbackProc PopHelp(w,dataFromClient,dataToGiveClient)
    Widget w;
    caddr_t dataFromClient;
    caddr_t dataToGiveClient;
{
    PopIt(w,helpShell); /* This is a handy routine for anchoring
                         * the pop-up shell next to the widget
                         * requesting the pop-up.
                         */
}
```

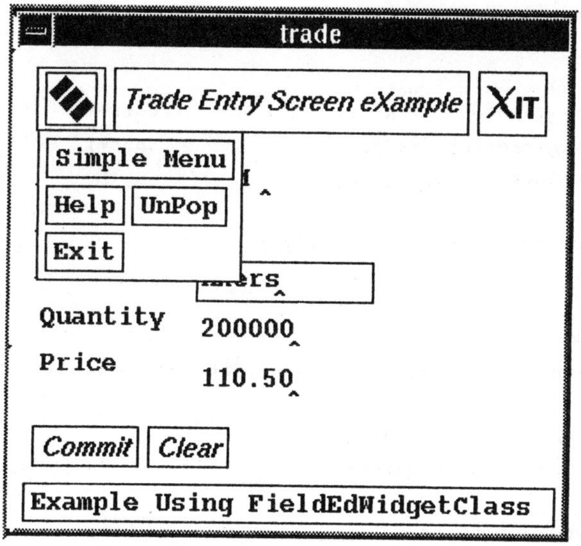

Figure 8-6 Trade with pop-up menu.

The next function is a utility that will be used by another function to place the pop-up in the correct place. It is very much like the previous PopMenu() function. The only change is that instead of being placed below the widget, this goes to the left (Figure 8-6 shows the finished pop-up menu):

```
int PopIt(w,shell)
     Widget w;
     Widget shell;
{
     Arg arg[MAXARGS];
     int width = 0;
     int x = 0;
     int y = 0;
     int rx,ry;
     int cnt;

     XtSetArg(arg[0],XtNwidth,&width);
     XtGetValues(w,arg,1);

     XtTranslateCoords(w, 0, 0, &rx, &ry);

     rx = rx + width;

     if (!XtIsRealized(shell))
```

```
            XtRealizeWidget(shell);

        cnt = 0;
        XtSetArg(arg[cnt],XtNx,rx);              cnt++;
        XtSetArg(arg[cnt],XtNy,ry);              cnt++;
        XtSetValues(shell,arg,cnt);

        XtPopup(shell,XtGrabExclusive);
}

XtCallbackProc
PopItDown(whoCalledMe,dataFromClient,dataToGiveClient)
        Widget whoCalledMe;
        caddr_t dataFromClient;
        caddr_t dataToGiveClient;
{
        XtPopdown(popup_holder);
}
```

8.4.4. Creating Pop-up Help

There are many ways to present help to users. In this application, you will employ a fairly easy one using the asciiDiskWidget. This widget reads the name of a file given as an argument at creation time and provides scrolling when the text is too large to fit the display area. The only thing to add other than the container is a button to "unpop" the help screen. The help screen shown in Figure 8-7 is generated from the following:

```
int create_help()
{
        Arg args[MAXARGS];
        int n;

        helpShell = XtCreatePopupShell("helpShell",
                        overrideShellWidgetClass,top,NULL,0);
        helpContainer = XtCreateManagedWidget("helpContainer",
                        formWidgetClass,helpShell,NULL,0);
/* Give the widget the file name and tell it to use a vertical
 * scrollbar.
 */
        n = 0;
        XtSetArg(args[n],XtNfile,myAppRes.helpFile); n++;
        XtSetArg(args[n],XtNtextOptions,scrollVertical); n++;
        XtSetArg(args[n],XtNheight,320);n++;
        XtSetArg(args[n],XtNwidth,500);n++;
```

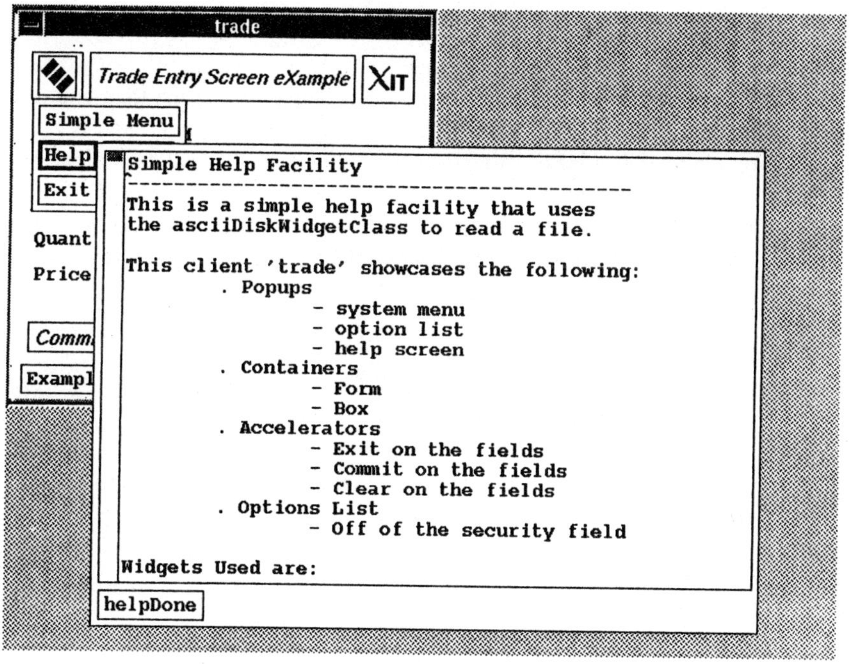

Figure 8-7 Trade with help.

```
     helpText = XtCreateManagedWidget("helpText",
                   asciiDiskWidgetClass,helpContainer,
                   args,(Cardinal)n);
/* Place this widget below the text area.
 */
     n = 0;
     XtSetArg(args[n],XtNfromVert,helpText);n++;
     helpDone = XtCreateManagedWidget("helpDone",
                 commandWidgetClass,helpContainer,args,n);
/* Add the "Done" or unpop callback. */
     XtAddCallback(helpDone,XtNcallback,Done,helpShell);
}
```

The callback for the "done" button simply calls the Intrinsics routine for "unpopping" a pop-up. The code is as follows:

```
XtCallbackProc Done(whoCalledMe,dataFromClient,dataToGiveClient)
     Widget whoCalledMe;
     caddr_t dataFromClient, dataToGiveClient;
{
     XtPopdown(dataFromClient);
/* dataFromClient will be the Widget id of the shell */
}
```

8.4.5. Creating a Pop-up Option List

One of the requirements for this client was to create a pop-up list that would be attached to one of the fields. This is a fairly common requirement, and is rather easy to implement. It is done by using the listWidgetClass and a callback procedure for when the selection is made.

The first thing to do is create the list entries. This can be done by either reading a file or using an initalized array. In this example, use the intialized array:

```
/*
 * List ... define static list of items for the pop-up!
 */
static char *security[] = {"IBM ","DEC ","APPL","SUNW","HP  "};
```

Now you can create the actual list. Notice that it is a pop-up. Therefore, it will need a pop-up shell:

```
int create_list()
{
      Arg args[MAXARGS];
      int n;

      listShell = XtCreatePopupShell("ListShell",
                        overrideShellWidgetClass,top,NULL,0);
      n = 0;
      XtSetArg(args[n],XtNlist,security); n++;
      XtSetArg(args[n],XtNnumberStrings, XtNumber(security)); n++;
      list = XtCreateManagedWidget("list",
               listWidgetClass,listShell,args,(Cardinal)n);
      XtAddCallback(list,XtNcallback,selection_callback, NULL);
}
```

The ListWidget was constructed so that the client writer could attach a callback to find out the value selected. The value is passed in the call_data argument of the callback and is part of a structure. In Chapter 5 you explored the "magic" of filling in such a structure so you need not concern yourself with the mechanics. Here is the remaining code to produce the pop-up list in Figure 8-8:

```
XtCallbackProc  selection_callback(w,client_data,call_data)
        Widget w;
        caddr_t *client_data;
        XtListReturnStruct *call_data;
{
        Arg args[1];
/* Clear the security field then insert the string selected.
*/ XtxuTextClearAll(Fields[0].fe);
```

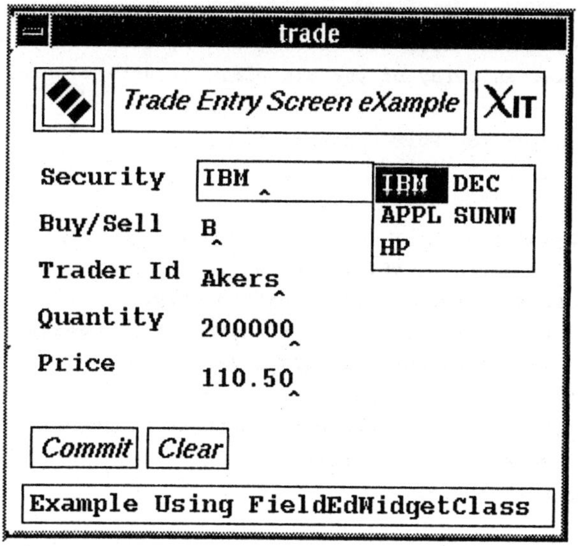

Figure 8-8 Trade with list.

```
    XtxuTextInsertString(Fields[0].fe,call_data->string);
    XtPopdown(listShell);     /* Pop ourselves down */
}
```

8.4.6. Creating an Entry Form

The body of the application is the entry form. This application will employ the widget you crafted in Chapter 6 to act as the editor, and will use the labelWidget-Class to provide a descriptive label for the field.

The easiest way to handle forms is to define a structure (as you did for the menu body) that will be intialized. This provides a nice easy mechanism for creating other forms and lets you change various attributes without going into a function and hacking around the code. The structure for the form is as follows:

```
typedef struct _FIELDINIT {
     String     label;          /* String for the label     */
     int        editor_type;    /* What kind of editor      */
     int        flen;           /* Length to edit           */
     Widget     fe;             /* Widget id of editor      */
     Widget     fl;             /* Widget id of label       */
     FwProc     editor;         /* Ptr to editor proc       */
     FwProc     enter_window;   /* Ptr to enterWindow Proc  */
     FwProc     focus_out;      /* Ptr to focusOut Proc     */
     FwProc     focus_in;       /* Ptr to focusIn  Proc     */
     FwProc     field_axn;      /* Ptr to FieldAxn Proc     */
} FIELDINIT;
```

```
/*
 * We can define the form we are creating by statically
 * initializing an array of the FIELDINIT structure.  This will
 * make defining new forms easy and we will have only one place
 * to go to check for Form definition.
 */

FIELDINIT Fields[] = {
{"Security ",FE_ALPHA,SECURITY_SIZE,0,0,
         NULL,NULL,NULL,NULL,MakeNxtFldActive},
{"Buy/Sell ",FE_ALPHA, 1,0,0,NULL,NULL,NULL,NULL,CheckBuySell},
{"Trader Id",FE_ALPHANUMERIC,TRADER_SIZE,
     0,0,NULL,NULL,NULL,NULL,MakeNxtFldActive},
{"Quantity ",FE_INT,7,0,0,NULL,NULL, NULL,NULL,MakeNxtFldActive},
{"Price    ",FE_FLOAT, 8,0,0,NULL,NULL,
NULL,NULL,MakeNxtFldActive},
};
```

Now you can create the function that generates the form. This function is very specific to this client; it wouldn't be such a bad idea to create a more general one so you can use it with more form definitions. In any event, the function is as follows:

```
int create_the_entry_container()
{
     Arg arg[40],gargs[3], larg[MAXARGS];
     char lblHolder[20];
     int height;
     int cnt = 0,i = 0,marker = 0,lcnt = 0,lmarker = 0;
     int numFlds = XtNumber(Fields);

/* If the menu bar is used, then set the container below it,
 * otherwise we will chain to the top left of the form (backdrop).
*/
     if (myAppRes.useMenuBar) {
          XtSetArg(arg[cnt],XtNfromVert,menu_bar);    cnt++;
     }
     entry_container = XtCreateManagedWidget("entry",
                    formWidgetClass,
                    backdrop, arg,cnt);

/* Set up the FieldEd args that are constant.
 */
     cnt = 0;
     XtSetArg(arg[cnt],XtNeditType,XttextEdit);          cnt++;
```

```
    XtSetArg(arg[cnt],XtNtextOptions,editable);        cnt++;
    XtSetArg(arg[cnt],XtNcursor,NULL);            cnt++;
    marker = cnt;        /* We will use the marker to reset */

/* Set up the label args for all of the labels.
 */
    XtSetArg(larg[lcnt],XtNborderWidth, 0);            lcnt++;
    lmarker = lcnt;    /* We will use the marker to reset */
    for(i=0;i<numFlds;i++){
/* Only the first row needs to be attached to the top, all others
 * should be below the previous row.
 */
        if (i != 0){
           XtSetArg(larg[lcnt],XtNfromVert,Fields[i-1].fl);
           lcnt++;
           XtSetArg(arg[cnt],XtNfromVert,Fields[i-1].fe);cnt++;
        } else {
           XtSetArg(larg[lcnt],XtNtop,XtChainTop); lcnt++;
           XtSetArg(arg[cnt],XtNtop,XtChainTop); cnt++;
        };
        larg[lcnt].name = XtNlabel;
        larg[lcnt].value= (XtArgVal)Fields[i].label;
        lcnt++;
        Fields[i].fl = XtCreateManagedWidget("lbl",
                    labelWidgetClass, entry_container,larg,lcnt);
        lcnt = lmarker;

        XtSetArg(arg[cnt],XtNfromHoriz,Fields[i].fl);cnt++;
/* Install the editor-type procs that will be invoked whenever we
 * are asking to perform character insertion or deletion.
 */
        XtSetArg(arg[cnt],XtNeditorType,Fields[i].editor_type);
        cnt++;
        XtSetArg(arg[cnt],XtNlength,Fields[i].flen);cnt++;
/* Check the remaining procs,  if they are provided then set them
 */
        if (Fields[i].enter_window !=NULL){
             XtSetArg(arg[cnt],XtNenterWindowProc,
                  Fields[i].enter_window); cnt++;
        }
        if (Fields[i].focus_in !=NULL) {
             XtSetArg(arg[cnt],XtNfocusInProc,
                  Fields[i].focus_in); cnt++;
        }
```

```
        if (Fields[i].focus_out !=NULL){
            XtSetArg(arg[cnt],XtNfocusOutProc,
                Fields[i].focus_out); cnt++;
        }
        if (Fields[i].field_axn !=NULL) {
            XtSetArg(arg[cnt],XtNfieldAxnProc,
                Fields[i].field_axn); cnt++;
        }
        Fields[i].fe = XtCreateManagedWidget("flds",
                    fieldEdWidgetClass,
                    entry_container,
                    arg,cnt);

/* We must offset the height of the label for the way the text
 * widget figures out heights.
 */
        XtSetArg(gargs[0],XtNheight,&height);
        XtGetValues(Fields[i].fe,gargs,(Cardinal)1);
        XtSetArg(gargs[0],XtNheight,height);
        XtSetValues(Fields[i].fl,gargs,(Cardinal)1);

/* Install our "prv/nxt" field translations.
 */
        XtOverrideTranslations(Fields[i].fe,stdFldTrans);
        cnt = marker; /* Reset the counter so we don't overwrite
                  * our previous settings */
    }
/* Install the "poplist" translation on the Security field
        (idx =  0)
 */
    XtOverrideTranslations(Fields[0].fe,popListTrans);
/*
 * Create a Button Box to hold the Commit/Clear buttons.
 */
    cnt = 0;
    XtSetArg(arg[cnt],XtNfromVert,entry_container); cnt++;
    btnBox = XtCreateManagedWidget("btnBox",formWidgetClass,
                backdrop, arg,cnt);
/* Create the commit button and add its callback */
    cnt = 0;
    XtSetArg(arg[cnt],XtNtop,XtChainTop);cnt++;
    XtSetArg(arg[cnt],XtNleft,XtChainLeft);cnt++;
    commit_btn = XtCreateManagedWidget("Commit",
                commandWidgetClass,
```

```
                    btnBox, arg,cnt);
     XtAddCallback(commit_btn,XtNcallback,Commit, NULL);
/* Add the cancel (clear) button and its callback */
     cnt = 0;
     XtSetArg(arg[cnt],XtNtop,XtChainTop);cnt++;
     XtSetArg(arg[cnt],XtNright,XtChainRight);cnt++;
     XtSetArg(arg[cnt],XtNfromHoriz,commit_btn);cnt++;
     cancel_btn =
XtCreateManagedWidget("Cancel",commandWidgetClass,
                    btnBox, arg,cnt);
     XtAddCallback(cancel_btn,XtNcallback,Cancel,NULL);
/*
 * We would like to allow the user to use the keyboard (for the
 * most part) rather than the mouse.  The Intrinsics have the
 * notion of an accelerator. Essentially, it is a way of having a
 * widget's actions invoked from a different widget.
 *
 * In this example, we will set the accelerators using the
 * "resource" database.  In this manner, we can adjust the
 * sequence without recompiling.  Also, since the accelerator is a
 * member of the Core it is initialized at "create" time.
 * Therefore, it is perfectly okay to use this method.  If we did
 * not want to use this method we would:
 *   1. Create an accelerator table.
 *        static String accel = "<Key>q:     notify";
 *   2. Compile it by parsing it.
 *        XtAccelerators accelCompiled =
 *             XtParseAcceleratorTable(accel);
 *   3. Then install at PRE create time.
 *        XtSetArg(arg[cnt],XtNaccelerators,accelCompiled); cnt++;
 *
 * A few things to note:
 *    1. Accelerator tables look just like the translations table.
 *    2. Accelerator may use #augment or #override.
 *    3. When #augment is used, the accelerator has a lower
 *       priority than what was there before.
 *    4. The call to XtInstallAccelerators() is:
 *         arg 1 - DESTINATION
 *         arg 2 - SOURCE
 *        Most of us will assume arg 1 is SOURCE and arg 2 is
 *        DESTINATION. Careful!
 *
 */
     for(cnt=0;cnt<XtNumber(Fields);cnt++)
```

```
            XtInstallAccelerators(Fields[cnt].fe,commit_btn);
/*
 * If we are using the menu bar then let the user exit from the
 * fields
 */
     if (myAppRes.useMenuBar)
          for(cnt=0;cnt<XtNumber(Fields);cnt++)
               XtInstallAccelerators(Fields[cnt].fe,exit_btn);
}
```

The support procedures for the form are CheckBuySell( ), PopList( ), Commit( ), and Cancel( ). CheckBuySell( ) is a field action procedure for the Buy/Sell field. It simply makes sure that the field is correctly filled in. If it is, then it invokes the next field action procedure (MakeNxtFldActive( )):

```
FwProc CheckBuySell(w)
     Widget w;
{
     Arg arg[1];
     char *sval,c;

     XtSetArg(arg[0],XtNstringVal,&sval);
     XtGetValues(w,arg,(Cardinal)1);
/* If there is no value then just go to the next field */
     if ((sval == NULL) || strlen(sval))
          MakeNxtFldActive(w,NULL,NULL,NULL);
/* If the field is valid then simply go to the next, otherwise
 * beep at the user.
 */
     if ((strcmp(sval,"B") == 0) ||
          (strcmp(sval,"b") == 0) ||
          (strcmp(sval,"s") == 0) ||
          (strcmp(sval,"S") == 0))
          MakeNxtFldActive(w,NULL,NULL,NULL);
     else
          XBell(XtDisplay(w), 50);
}
```

The Commit() callback writes the trade to a file provided:

```
XtCallbackProc
Commit(whoCalledMe,dataFromClient,dataToGiveClient)
     Widget whoCalledMe;
     caddr_t dataFromClient;
```

```
     caddr_t dataToGiveClient;
{
     int ival; float fval; char *sval;
     Arg arg[1]; int i,numFlds = XtNumber(Fields);
     char out_rec[TRADESTRSIZE];

     memset(out_rec,'\0',sizeof(out_rec));
     sprintf(out_rec+strlen(out_rec), "From File: ");

     for(i=0;i<numFlds;i++) {
          switch(Fields[i].editor_type) {
          case FE_ALPHA:
          case FE_ALPHANUMERIC:
          case FE_APPL:
/* These conditions dictate a "string" return.  Therefore, request
 * one.
 */
               XtSetArg(arg[0],XtNstringVal,&sval);
               XtGetValues(Fields[i].fe,arg,1);
               if (sval != NULL)
                    sprintf(out_rec+strlen(out_rec),
               "%s ",sval);
          break;
     case FE_INT:
          XtSetArg(arg[0],XtNintVal, &ival);
          XtGetValues(Fields[i].fe,arg,(Cardinal)1);
               sprintf(out_rec+strlen(out_rec),
               "%i ",ival);
          break;
     case FE_FLOAT:
          XtSetArg(arg[0],XtNfloatVal, &fval);
          XtGetValues(Fields[i].fe,arg,(Cardinal)1);
               sprintf(out_rec+strlen(out_rec),
               "%.3f ",fval);
          break;
     }
}
/* Write the "constructed" record to a file and flush.  We need
 * to flush so that the data actually gets to the file.  If we
 * don't we will not be sure if the data gets to the file due to
 * the buffering that is being employed.
 */
     fprintf(fout,"%s\n",out_rec);
     fflush(fout);              /* So it gets to the file */
}
```

The Cancel( ) callback simply clears the fields:

```
XtCallbackProc Cancel(whoCalledMe,dataFromClient,dataToGiveClient)
     Widget whoCalledMe;
     caddr_t dataFromClient;
     caddr_t dataToGiveClient;
{

     int i,numFlds = XtNumber(Fields);
     for(i = 0; i < numFlds; i++)
          XtxuTextClearAll(Fields[i].fe);
}
```

Pop List( ) is an action procedure that is used to bring the option list up:

```
XtActionProc PopList(w,event,params,num_params)
        Widget w;
        XEvent *event;
        String *params;
        Cardinal num_params;
{
        PopIt(w,listShell);
}
```

8.4.6.1. Moving Without the Mouse One of the things that many users like in applications is keyboard traversal. This is the movement of the input focus without the mouse. To affect this, widgets must cooperate or the application must be created with some "smarts." The application in this chapter has the intelligence built in, but in Chapter 10 you will see how OSF/Motif handles traversal.

In the code, notice that the entry fields are in an array. By doing this you simply need to determine the current widget to determine which is the next or which was the previous. The functions that determine this are "action procs" which are connected to the fields via the translation manager. They are defined as follows:

```
XtActionProc MakeNxtFldActive(w,event,param,num_params)
        Widget w;
        XEvent *event;
        String *param;
        Cardinal num_params;
{
     Widget ww;
     int i, numFlds = XtNumber(Fields);
```

```
/* The widget that kicked off the action proc defines the current
 * widget.  We look through the array of fields to find it. Once
 * found we simply determine if it is at the end of the list.  If
 * it is, you will set the focus to the "first" widget, otherwise,
 * set it to the next one in the list.
 */
     for(i=0;i<numFlds;i++) {
          if (Fields[i].fe == w){
               if (i == (numFlds - 1))
                    ww = Fields[0].fe;
               else
                    ww = Fields[i+1].fe;
               XSetInputFocus(XtDisplay(ww), XtWindow(ww),
                         RevertToPointerRoot,  CurrentTime);
               break;
          }
     }
}
XtActionProc MakePrvFldActive(w,event,param,num_params)
        Widget w;
        XEvent *event;
        String *param;
        Cardinal num_params;
{
     Widget ww;
     int i,numFlds = XtNumber(Fields);
/* This acts in the same manner except it looks to see if the
 * widget is the top one.  If it is then the bottom widget is the
 * previous, otherwise, it is the one "above."
 */
     for(i=0;i<numFlds;i++) {
          if (Fields[i].fe == w){
               if (i == 0)
                    ww = Fields[numFlds - 1].fe;
               else
                    ww = Fields[i-1].fe;
               XSetInputFocus(XtDisplay(ww), XtWindow(ww),
                         RevertToPointerRoot,  CurrentTime);
               break;
          }
     }
}
```

8.4.7. Miscellaneous

The last two functions are the label-creation function and the Toggle() action procedure. In the case of the label creation, you want it to be just below the button box (Cancel and Commit), so it will simply be set below using one of the constraints provided by the form widget. The Toggle() action procedure simply adjusts the border width. Notice that on window managers that place "special" frames around the client, the toggle effect is not noticed. The functions are defined as follows:

```
int create_the_label()
{
      Arg arg[1];
      XtSetArg(arg[0],XtNfromVert,btnBox);
      label = XtCreateManagedWidget("message", labelWidgetClass,
                         backdrop, arg, (Cardinal)1);
}


typedef enum {On = 'N',Off ='F'} Axn;
XtActionProc Toggle(w,event,param,num_params)
         Widget w;
         XEvent *event;
         String *param;
         Cardinal num_params;
{
      Axn action;
      Arg arg[2];
      Pixel bg,fg;

         action = (Axn)param[0][1];
         if (islower((char)action))
                  action = (Axn)toupper((char)action);
         switch(action) {
                  case On:
                           XtSetArg(arg[0],XtNborderWidth,3);
                           XtSetValues(w,arg,1);
                           break;
                  case Off:
                           XtSetArg(arg[0],XtNborderWidth,1);
                           XtSetValues(w,arg,1);
                           break;
         }
}
```

8.5. Summing Up

This client demonstrated a few features that are often desirable in an application:

1. Field entry (using the widget from Chapter 6).
2. Pop-up help, lists, and menus.
3. Keyboard traversal.
4. Keyboard accelerators.
5. "Form" and "menu" definitions.

By having a widget that handles field entry and is extensible, you have the basis for many applications to follow. As you can see, creating an entry form is fairly simple once the tools are available. Keyboard traversal is "do-able" given the standard Intrinsics functions, and is not too hard to handle. Typedefs and structures make coding much easier by "herding" logical data together and allowing for the creation of arrays of this data. This array creation can make programming extremely easy, especially if generic utilities are created to handle the structures.

9

A Look at OSF/Motif

When X was created, there were no enforced display policies. The creators provided the mechanisms for constructing graphical user interfaces. They really did not care to deal with defining the appearance or behavior of a particular interface component (and probably still don't). Things have changed tremendously since the early days of X. There has been an interface "war" between OSF and Unix International (UI). OSF supports Motif and UI supports Open Look. Both have merits, but many programmers and users like the 3D visuals and Presentation Manager-like behavior of Motif. Given that, and the fact that several vendors bundle it with their presentation software, I have chosen to write about Motif.

9.1. Motif Environment

The Motif environment is composed of three things: a style guide, a window manager, and a widget set. The style guide is what the OSF people believe to be a "good" way to compose Motif clients. It deals with the behavior of clients and the components that make up the client.

Though style guides are important, from a practical point of view most programmers create interfaces that differ from any one style guide. Sure, we adhere to as much of the guide as possible, but if a user doesn't like the placement of a component, should we tell them, "No . . . the style guide says to do it this way"? Probably not. Therefore, a study of the Motif style guide is left to you. The next two items, the window manager and the widget set, are discussed in separate sections of this chapter.

There is actually another part to the Motif environment, called UIL (for User Interface Language). Practically speaking, it will be more important to understand the C interface than UIL. For most application writers the C interface will be much easier to relate to and comprehend. Additionally, user interface building tools will reduce the need for "new" languages, such as UIL, for programmers. Personally, I prefer the C interface to client-writing, therefore UIL is not discussed in this book. If you care to explore this area, I recommend reading the information from OSF.

9.2. Motif Window Manager

The Motif window manager (mwm) often confuses the novice to X into believing that a client with the 3D adornments is a Motif client. This is far from the truth. As you are now aware (from the discussion in Chapter 2), the window manager simply assists the user in managing a desktop and all X clients should be written to work with any window manager. So the next time you see a client being managed by mwm, don't assume it is a Motif client unless you have checked the source code first.

One of the nice features of mwm is the ability to customize its many resources. You can create new menus, change a client's appearance, and move among clients without the mouse. All of these features are fairly easy to do. Changes to a client's appearance would go in the resource database, the others would be in the window manager's resource file (.mwmrc) for frame appearance.

9.2.1. Customizing Using Resources

A window manager is nothing more than a special X client. As such, it will have its own resources and a specific class resource file (Mwm). There are several resources associated with mwm. The following is a table of some of the more useful ones.

Table 9-1
Motif Window Manager Resources

Resource Name	Resource Class	Description
	All Components	
background	Background	Background color
backgroundPixmap	BackgroundPixmap	Pixmap for inactive state
bottomShadowColor	Foreground	Color of lower and right bevels
bottomShadowPixmap	BottomShadowPixmap	Pixmap for lower and right bevels
fontList	FontList	Font used in decorations
foreground	Foreground	Foreground color
saveUnder	SaveUnder	Indicate if saveUnder is active
topShadowColor	Background	Color of upper and left bevels
topShadowPixmap	TopShadowPixmap	Pixmap for upper and left bevels
	For Frame and Icon	
activeBackground	Background	Color for active state
activeBackgroundPixmap	BackgroundPixmap	Pixmap for active state
activeBottomShadowColor	Foreground	Color of lower and right bevels
activeBottomShadowPixmap	BottomShadowPixmap	Pixmap for lower and right bevels
activeForeground	Foreground	Color for active state
activeTopShadowColor	Background	Color of upper and left bevels
activeTopShadowPixmap	TopShadowPixmap	Pixmap for upper and left bevels

Resource Name	Resource Class	Description
	Specific Appearance	
autoKeyFocus	AutoKeyFocus	Turn auto focus on/off
bitmapDirectory	BitmapDirectory	Search path for bitmaps
buttonBindings	ButtonBindings	Bindings from .mwmrc
clientAutoPlace	ClientAutoPlace	Turn auto place on/off
colormapFocusPolicy	ColormapFocusPolicy	explicit, pointer, keyboard
configFile	ConfigFile	Path for .mwmrc
frameBorderWidth	FrameBorderWidth	Width in pixels of client window
iconBoxLayout	IconBoxLayout	firstfit, screenloc
iconPlacement	IconPlacement	top, bottom, left, right
keyBindings	KeyBindings	Bindings from .mwmrc
keyboardFocusPolicy	KeyboardFocusPolicy	explicit, pointer
moveThreshold	MoveThreshold	Number pixels to drag per motion
resizeBorderWidth	ResizeBorderWidth	Total Frame size
useIconBox	UseIconBox	Turn use of box on/off
	Client Specific	
clientDecoration	ClientDecoration	Turn adornments on/off: all, border, maximize, minimize, none, resize, system, title
clientFunctions	ClientFunctions	Turn functions on/off: all, none, resize, move, minimize, maximize, close
iconImage	IconImage	Bitmap file to use as icon
systemMenu	SystemMenu	Menu from .mwmrc to post
useClientIcon	UseClientIcon	Set icon supply policy: true — client wins false — user wins

By editing the mwm class resource file, you can adjust the way your clients appear. For instance, suppose you would like to use the icon box as shown in Figure 9-1. This is accomplished by editing the resource file and adding this line:

Figure 9-1 Icon box.

```
Mwm.useIconBox:     True
```

Now, suppose you want to turn off some of the client decorations. Again, edit the resource file and add something like this:

```
Mwm*XawlistTM.clientDecorations:    +system
```

This would give all clients of the XawlistTM class *only* (Figure 9-2) the system button.

If you would like to add additional key settings that were defined in .mwmrc, you would add them using the "keyBindings" resource as follows:

```
Mwm.keyBindings:     NewKeyBindings
```

where NewKeyBindings was created in the .mwmrc file.

9.2.2. Customizing Using .mwmrc

When mwm starts up, it looks for a file called .mwmrc. It looks for it in the user's $HOME path, the path defined in the configFile resource, or /usr/lib/X11/app-defaults/system.mwmrc. This file contains the menu definitions, key bindings, and button bindings that mwm will use.

9.2.2.1. Menu Format of .mwmrc The format of a menu in .mwmrc is as follows:

```
Menu MenuName
{
      "label"  [mnemonic]  [accelerator]  function
}
```

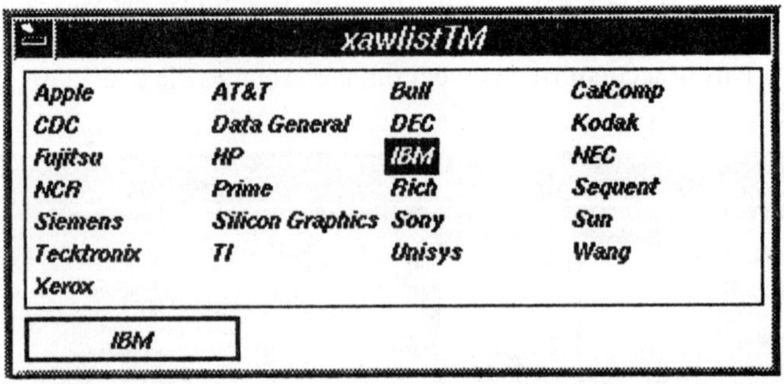

Figure 9-2 XawlistTM.

Mnemonic and accelerator are optional, and function can be one of those in the following table.

Table 9-2
Motif Window Manager Functions

Function	**Description**
f.beep	Beep the user
f.circle_down	Place top icon/window on bottom of the window stack
f.circle_up	Place bottom icon/window on top of the window stack
f.exec	Execute a shell command passed
f.focus_color	Set colormap focus to window/icon
f.focus_key	Set keyboard focus to window/icon
f.kill(IW)	Kill the client
f.lower(IW)	Lower the client to bottom of window stack
f.maximize(IW)	Display client with maximum size
f.menu	Post the menu given by the name
f.minimize(W)	Display client as an icon
f.move(IW)	Cause interactive movement
f.next_cmap	Install next colormap
f.next_key	Set keyboard focus to next icon or window
f.nop	Do nothing
f.normalize(IW)	Restore client to normal state
f.pack_icons	Cause relayout of icons
f.post_wmenu	Post the system menu
f.prev_cmap	Install the previous colormap
f.prev_key	Set keyboard focus to previous icon of window
f.quit_mwm(R)	Kill mwm but not X
f.raise(IW)	Move client to top of stack
f.raise_lower(IW)	If obscured raise client to top of stack, otherwise send to bottom
f.refresh	Redraw all windows
f.refresh_win(W)	Redraw client window
f.resize(W)	Interactively resize the client
f.restart(R)	Restart mwm
f.send_msg(IW)	Send a client message
f.separator	Draw a separator in menu
f.set_behavior	Restart mwm with behavior style default/custom/switch
f.title	Place label as title in menu

Key: IW — Icon and Window; R — Root; W — Window

Each function is constrained to icon, window, or root unless otherwise indicated. Now then, a simple menu could be defined as follows:

```
Menu "ExampleMenu" {
     "Example Menu"                              f.title
     no-label
     "Kill"          _K     Meta<Key>F4     f.kill
     "Refresh"       _R     Meta<Key>F2     f.refresh
     "Directory"     _D     Meta<Key>F10    f.exec "ls -al"
}
```

9.2.2.2. Bindings in .mwmrc You can also create custom button and key bindings in the .mwmrc file. The format for the binding specifications for both button and key are the same with the exception of the name:

```
Button "name" {
     button    buttoncontext    function
}
```

where buttoncontext is [system, border, title, frame, app, minimize, maximize, root, icon, window].

```
Keys "name" {
     key         context      function
}
```

where context is [root, window, icon].

So, to define new bindings, you do the following:

```
Button "NewButtonSet" {
     <Btn1Down>      system           f.post_wmenu
     <Btn2Down>      root             f.exec "xsetroot -solid blue"
}

Keys "NewKeySet" {
     <Key>F9          window|root|icon     f.next_key
     <Key>F10         window|root|icon     f.prev_key
     Meta<Key>F1      icon                 f.normalize
}
```

As window managers go, mwm is rather nice. You can see that customizing it is not very hard, and there is a great deal of flexibility with it. The intent with the coverage in this book is to give you enough to get started. With that, the best way to get acquainted with mwm is to play around with the resource settings and see for yourself what the results are.

9.3. The Motif Widgets

The purpose of this section is to introduce the Motif widgets. It is not intended to be a reference manual, but rather an overview of the different components available. For more specific information, refer to Appendixes A and C of this book or the OSF/Motif *Programmer's Reference Guide*.

The Motif Widget Set (Xm) contains 28 "creatable" widgets, 2 "meta" widgets, 5 gadgets, and 1 "meta" gadget. The following is a table of them.

Table 9-3
Motif Widget Names and ClassPointers

Class Name	Pointer	Type
XmArrowButton	xmArrowButtonWidgetClass	P
XmArrowButtonGadget	xmArrowButtonGadgetClass	P
XmBulletinBoard	xmBulletinBoardWidgetClass	M
XmCascadeButton	xmCascadeButtonWidgetClass	P
XmCascadeButtonGadget	xmCascadeButtonGadgetClass	P
XmCommand	xmCommandWidgetClass	P
XmDialogShell	xmDialogShellWidgetClass	M
XmDrawingArea	xmDrawingAreaWidgetClass	P
XmDrawnButton	xmDrawnButtonWidgetClass	P
XmFileSelectionBox	xmFileSelectionWidgetClass	X
XmForm	xmFormWidget	M
XmFrameWidget	xmFrameWidget	M
XmGadget	xmGadget	P*
XmLabel	xmLabelWidgetClass	P
XmLabelGadget	xmLabelGadgetClass	P
XmList	xmListWidgetClass	P
XmMainWindow	xmMainWindowWidgetClass	X
XmManager	xmManagerWidgetClass	M*
XmMenuShell	xmMenuShellWidgetClass	M
XmMessageBox	xmMessageBoxWidgetClass	X
XmPanedWindow	xmPanedWindowWidgetClass	M
XmPrimitive	xmPrimitiveWidgetClass	P*
XmPushButton	xmPushButtonWidgetClass	P
XmRowColumn	xmRowColumnWidgetClass	M
XmSash	xmSashWidgetClass	PS
XmScale	xmScaleWidgetClass	X
XmScrollBar	xmScrollBarWidgetClass	XPS
XmScrollWindow	xmScrollWindowWidgetClass	X
XmSelectionBox	xmSelectionBoxWidgetClass	X
XmSeparator	xmSeparatorWidgetClass	PS
XmSeparatorGadget	xmSeparatorGadgetClass	P

Class Name	Pointer	Type
XmText	xmTextWidgetClass	P
XmToggleButton	xmToggleButtonWidgetClass	P
XmToggleButtonGadget	xmToggleButtonGadgetClass	P

Key:
P — represents a primitive widget/gadget.
M — represents a manager widget (container).
X — represents a widget composed with other widgets.
PS — represents a primitive widget used to support other widgets.
* — represents a Meta widget.

As you can see there are quite a few. Each widget has its own convenience routine for creating it. The invocation is as follows:

```
XmCreate[Class Name](parent,"instance name",arglist,argcnt)
```

where [Class Name] is replaced by the class name from the table, dropping the "Xm." Therefore, to create xmListWidget you would do the following:

```
list = XmCreateListWidget(parent,"List",arglist,argcnt);
XtManageChild(list);
```

Notice that you need to manage the result since the convenience routines do not create managed widgets. If you prefer to use the Intrinsics mechanism, you would do the following:

```
list = XtCreateManagedWidget("list",xmListWidgetClass,
          parent,arglist,argcnt);
```

The following is a table of the widget creation routines.

Table 9-4
Motif Widget Creation Functions

XmCreateArrowButton( );	XmCreateArrowButtonGadget( );
XmCreateBulletinBoard( );	XmCreateBulletinBoardDialog( );
XmCreateCascadeButton( );	XmCreateCascadeButtonGadget( );
XmCreateCommand( );	XmCreateDialogShell( );
XmCreateDrawingArea( );	XmCreateDrawnButton( );
XmCreateFileSelectionBox( );	XmCreateFileSelectionDialog( );
XmCreateForm( );	XmCreateFormDialog( );
XmCreateFrame( );	XmCreateLabel( );
XmCreateLabelGadget( );	XmCreateList( );

```
XmCreateScrolledList( );            XmCreateMainWindow( );
XmCreateMenuShell( );               XmCreateMessageBox( );
XmCreateMessageDialog( );           XmCreateErrorDialog( );
XmCreateInformationDialog( );       XmCreateQuestionDialog( );
XmCreateWarningDialog( );           XmCreateWorkingDialog( );
XmCreatePanedWindow( );             XmCreatePushButton( );
XmCreatePushButtonGadget( );        XmCreatePushButtonGadget( );
XmCreateRadioBox( );                XmCreateRowColumn( );
XmCreatePopupMenu( );               XmCreatePulldownMenu( );
XmCreateOptionMenu( );              XmCreateMenuBar( );
XmCreateScale( );                   XmCreateScrollBar( );
XmCreateScrolledWindow( );          XmCreateSelectionBox( );
XmCreateSelectionDialog( );         XmCreatePromptDialog( );
XmCreateSeparatorGadget( );         XmCreateSeparator( );
XmCreateText( );                    XmCreateScrolledText( );
XmCreateToggleButton( );            XmCreateToggleButtonGadget( );
```

9.3.1. Motif Widget Resources

The next area of Motif that differs slightly from the Intrinsics mechanism is the setting of resources. In the Intrinsics, you would set, say, the core resources using resource names such as:

```
XtNwidth,XtNheight
```

However, Motif uses the following:

```
XmNwidth,XmNheight.
```

Essentially, the OSF folks took everything from StringDefs.h and changed the "Xt" to "Xm," including the resource classes (XmC) and resource representations (XmR). Additionally, all new resources used by the Motif widgets use "Xm" as a prefix. Refer to Appendix C, "Quick Guide to the OSF/Motif Widget Set," for details on resources and the widget set.

This change was probably intended to eliminate conflicts between other vendor widget sets. Notice, though, that if you wanted to mix widget sets, you would have to handle different resource-naming conventions. There is certainly the potential for nasty administration problems when additional widget sets that "coexist" arrive. In the meantime, note the difference so you will avoid making typing mistakes.

9.3.2. Motif Display Widgets

Display widgets are used for input/output mechanisms that are often needed when developing applications. All display widgets are a subclass of XmPrimitive. This widget is a meta widget, and is never instanciated by itself. It acts as a provider of common functionality for all its subclasses. In this case, XmPrimitive provides foreground, highlighting, traversal, 3D appearance, resolution independence, and help capability.

There are four kinds of buttons available in the widget set: XmArrowButton, XmDrawnButton, XmPushButton, and XmToggleButton. They each provide a callback mechanism for when the user "presses" the button. XmPushButton displays a label and draws a 3D effect when selected. XmArrowButton behaves just like the XmPushButton except it displays an arrow. XmDrawnArea behaves just like XmPushButton except it provides application created graphics. XmToggleButton displays a label and a "toggle" graphic.

XmLabel displays single- or multi-line text strings or pixmaps. It has justification semantics for handling the display of its contents.

XmList displays a list of items and provides two selection policies (single- or multi-selection). When items are selected, the widget invokes callbacks depending on the selection style.

XmScrollBar is used with a "scroller" widget. It provides a visual interaction with the user. Application writers will probably never directly create a scrollbar.

XmSeparator displays a visual separation between widgets. It is most often used in menus, but may be used in other situations.

XmText provides multi-line text editing or display.

9.3.3. Motif Display Gadgets

The following are the gadgets defined in the Motif Set: XmGadget, XmArrowButtonGadget, XmLabelGadget, XmSeparatorGadget, XmToggleButtonGadget. XmGadget is similar to XmPrimitive in that it is a meta class, and provides the same resources. Each of the gadgets behaves just like the widget version.

9.3.4. Motif Container Widgets

The Motif set is rich with layout widgets (containers). All container widgets are subclasses of XmManager. XmManager is a meta class, and provides resources similar to those provided by XmPrimitive. It provides the 3D visuals, traversal mechanisms, and help. It is created from Core, Composite, and Constraint.

XmBulletinBoard provides simple geometry management for its managed children. Unlike other containers, it will not force positions on the children.

XmDrawingArea is an adaptable widget, in that it is an empty widget and can be used to create application-specific displays. It provides callback mechanisms for various events such as expose, resize, keyboard, and button.

XmForm is a strict layout manager that provides several constraints for its children. Unlike XmBulletinBoard, XmForm forces positions on its children.

XmFrame is used to provide 3D appearance for widgets that do not have such capabilities (this is demonstrated in the next section).

XmMainWindow is a complex widget that is actually constructed from several other widgets. It provides a standard layout, including menu bar, command region, and scrollbars. You will use this in Chapter 10.

XmRowColumn supports several layout policies. It may function as a work area, menu bar, pull-down menu, pop-up menu, or an option menu. It is commonly used in the widget set to construct special-case layouts.

XmRadioBox is a special case of the XmRowColumn widget. Its main purpose is to manage a collection of XmToggleButtons.

XmScrolledWindow provides management for its children by allowing them to scroll in both vertical and horizontal directions. It is responsible for displaying scrollbars and moving the children when necessary.

XmScrolledList is a complex widget composed of XmScrolledWindow and XmList. It allows an arbitrary list to be managed in a scrolled region and takes care of setting scrollbars and adjusting the list position.

XmScrolledText is a complex widget composed of XmScrolledWindow and XmText. It provides scrolling capabilities to the XmText widget.

XmVPaned manages its children in a vertically tiled manner. It contains a support widget called XmSash which enables the user to resize the pane.

9.3.5. Motif Dialogs

The OSF folks provided a set of useful interaction constructs referred to as *dialogs*. There are a few creation routines for some of the more common types of dialogs. The following is a table of these functions:

Table 9-5
Motif Dialog Creation Functions

XmCreateBulletinBoardDialog( );	XmCreateDialogShell( );
XmCreateFileSelectionDialog( );	XmCreateFormDialog( );
XmCreateMessageDialog( );	XmCreateErrorDialog( );
XmCreateInformationDialog( );	XmCreateQuestionDialog( );
XmCreateWarningDialog( );	XmCreateWorkingDialog( );
XmCreateSelectionDialog( );	XmCreatePromptDialog( );

Dialogs are created using a few select widgets. XmCommand provides a command input region and a history buffer. XmFileSelectionBox obtains files and provides a list of them along with an entry region, enter, apply, cancel, and help buttons. XmMessageBox provides a symbol and text along with enter, cancel, and help buttons. XmSelectionBox provides a list of alternatives, entry region, enter, apply, cancel, and help buttons. XmDialogShellWidget is a subclass of the Intrinsics transientShellWidgetClass and is used to create all dialog constructs. It provides ICCM* compliance.

With the various widgets discussed in the preceding sections, Motif provides several predefined dialog components that are useful for application development.

BulletinBoardDialog is provided to allow application writers the ability to craft their own dialog.

ErrorDialog is used to warn users of errors made. It provides an error symbol, text message, enter, cancel, and help buttons.

FileSelectionDialog creates an XmFileSelectionBox widget under a dialog shell.

FormDialog is provided to allow application writers the ability to craft their own dialog. Children will be subject to the XmForm widget layout policies.

InformationDialog is used to provide information to the user. It provides an information symbol, message text, enter, cancel, and help buttons.

MessageDialog creates an XmMessageWidget under a dialogShell.

PromptDialog is used to prompt the user for input. It provides a prompt, edit region, enter, cancel, and help buttons.

QuestionDialog is used to get an answer from a user. It provides a question symbol, message text, enter, cancel, and help buttons.

SelectionDialog creates an XmSelectionWidget under a dialogShell.

WarningDialog is used to inform the user of a problem. It provides a warning symbol, message text, enter, cancel, and help buttons.

WorkingDialog is used to inform the user that a task is being performed. It provides a working symbol, message text, enter, cancel, and help buttons.

9.3.6. Motif Menu Widgets

Motif supports the Presentation Manager menu interaction. This includes pull-down, pop-up, and option menus which are constructed using several widgets.

The XmMenuShell widget is a subclass of the Intrinsics overrideShellWidgetClass. It provides ICCM compliance and is used to construct all menus in Motif.

XmCascadeButton is used heavily in the menu system, because it is the only widget that allows a pull-down menu to be attached to it. It can display a label with a cascading symbol, and provides callback mechanisms for when the button is pressed and it is just prior to a menu being mapped.

---

* ICCCM refers to the *Inter-Client Communication Conventions Manual.* This manual defines the mechanisms that are acceptable practice for communication among X clients. The OSF/Motif set provides its own shells so that it ensures compliance with ICCCM.

The XmRowColumn widget is used as the container for the different types of panes (cascade and push-button). Menu creation using the Motif set is discussed in the next chapter.

9.3.7. Motif Traversal Mechanism

In Chapter 6 you saw a type of keyboard traversal. Essentially, the application was intelligent in that it knew the widgets that would get the focus. This is exactly how Motif handles traversing with the keyboard. The only widgets that can accept the focus are the display widgets (and gadgets), because these are the only type with which the user interacts. In the Motif set, the XmManager contains the intelligence for traversing among its children. Just as you had a list of widgets to "look in," so does XmManager. With this list, the manager can move the focus to the previous or next widget in the list.

The only other issue with traversal is how to get from one traversing area to another. A traversing area is a container of traversable widgets. This would be some kind of form such as the one found in the "trade" client. If you had several entry regions in the same client, you would need to get to them so you could fill out those fields. Motif defines these areas as *tab groups*. All you need to do is specify the container widget that is managing the traversable children as a tab group to employ this mechanism. The function call is as follows:

```
XmAddTabGroup(group);
```

Now to get to "group" the user presses the Tab key which sends focus management to the next tab group. XmText widgets must also be added to be traversed to.

9.3.8. Motif Compound String

Motif widgets use a notion of text called a *compound string*. A compound string is a special encoding that allows widgets to handle text with different graphics contexts and of various character sets. Recall the client "XtandGC," which demonstrated how to draw lines of text with several fonts. You could make the same analogy to the Motif Widget Set's handling of text. There is an added level of complexity to the compound string, which is direction. The direction is the way the string will be painted out. The reason for doing this is to allow Motif clients to be written in international languages that require text to be written in different directions.

Appendix C contains a table of the several compound string functions that exist in the widget set. You will need to make "normal" text into a compound string before using it in most of the Motif widgets (the only exception is the XmText widget).

9.3.9. Motif Clipboard

The Motif set has added a higher level of data transfer than the Xlib and Xt mechanisms. It is referred to as a *clipboard*, which is essentially off-screen memory. It is used to allow clients the ability to exchange data back and forth. The Motif clipboard contains several functions for dealing with things such as locking, starting retrieval, stopping retrieval, and copying data to the clipboard. For the most part your applications will probably not require the clipboard, therefore this subject is left to a book specifically on Motif.

9.4. Sample Motif Clients

To demonstrate how easy it is to go from the Athena reference frame to Motif and maintain the Intrinsics creation mechanisms, let's "port" (Sounds sexy!) two clients that have been previously written, namely, "alarm" and "xawlist."

9.4.1. Changing alarm to malarm

The new client is shown in Figure 9-3. The code for the new client is as follows (pay attention to the comments, they tell you what is needed):

```
/* FILE:    malarm.c
 */

#include "XbkUtil.h"
#include <X11/Xos.h>

/* Notice we need to use the Motif headers for their widgets
 */
#include <Xm/Xm.h>
#include <Xm/Form.h>
#include <Xm/PushB.h>
#include <Xm/Label.h>
```

Figure 9-3 Malarm.

```
/*
 * Notice we took out the ClockWidget from this alarm.
 */

#define XbkShellName    "malarm"
#define XbkApplClass    "Malarm"
/*
 * Nothing new here ...
 */
XtCallbackProc      set_hour(),set_minute(),set_ampm(),set_alarm();
XtTimerCallbackProc     TellThem();

#define ALARMRANG "Alarm Rang"
#define DISABLE    "Alarm is Off"
#define AM    0
#define PM    1
#define MILLI      1000
#define SECINHR    3600
#define SECINMIN 60
/* Set up the globals for use in the callback routines.
 */
struct tm tm, *localtime();
long     tv;
char     scratch[10];
struct   {
    Boolean   alarmSet;
    int       hour;
    int       min;
    int       amOrpm;
    XtIntervalId   id;
} alarmData;

Widget setLbl;
/*
 * Something new!  We need to define a compound string variable so
 * when we transform a "normal" string we have a place to put it.
 */
XmString   *cstr;   /* for building Compound String */

main(argc,argv)
    int argc;
    char **argv;
{
    Widget top,button_container,hr,min,am_pm,set;
```

```
    char   scratch[10];
    Arg arg[MAXARGS];
    int n;

    top = XtInitialize(XbkShellName,XbkApplClass,
                NULL,0, &argc, argv);
/*
 * We are using the Motif Form widget as a container.  It provides
 * a nice assortment of layout options that you can make.  My
 * feeling is that this Form widget is a bit nicer then the Athena
 * version.
 *
 * We could easily have used the RowColumn widget since we are
 * dealing with a layout that is grid-like.  The reason for using
 * the Form is to demonstrate how "portable" the client is.
 */
    button_container = XtCreateManagedWidget("button_container",
                xmFormWidgetClass,top,NULL,0);
    (void) time(&tv);
    tm = *localtime(&tv);
/*
 * Set the alarm data
 */
    alarmData.alarmSet = False;
    alarmData.hour    = (tm.tm_hour > 12) ? tm.tm_hour - 12 :
                            tm.tm_hour;
    alarmData.min     = tm.tm_min;
    alarmData.amOrpm = (tm.tm_hour > 12) ? PM : AM;

    memset(scratch,'\0',sizeof(scratch));
    if (alarmData.hour <= 9)
        sprintf(scratch,"0%1d",alarmData.hour);
    else
        sprintf(scratch,"%2d",alarmData.hour);
/*
 * This is perhaps the greatest change we had to make.  Motif
 * widgets use a "compound string" notion. So whenever you feed
 * text to the Motif widgets it must be in compound string form.
 * To do that you can use one of the mechanisms provided to do
 * that. We use:
 *        XmStringCreate(str,XmSTRING_DEFAULT_CHARSET)
 *
 */
   cstr = XmStringCreate(scratch,XmSTRING_DEFAULT_CHARSET);
```

```
/*
 * Notice the new resource names.  There are a few changes: the
 * first, we use XmN not XtN, and the second, the Motif widgets
 * define their own resources and we cannot assume that they would
 * have selected the same names that were in the Athena set.
 */
    n = 0;
    XtSetArg(arg[n],XmNleftAttachment,XmATTACH_FORM); n++;
    XtSetArg(arg[n],XmNlabelString,cstr); n++;
    hr = XtCreateManagedWidget("hour",xmPushButtonWidgetClass,
                    button_container,arg,n);
    XtAddCallback(hr,XmNactivateCallback,set_hour,NULL);
    XtFree(cstr);
/*
 * You'll first notice that the Athena Command widget is replaced
 * by the Motif PushB.  The Motif Command widget is for actually
 * entering in commands while the Athena Command widget is a
 * button.
 *
 * The next thing to notice is that the callback is placed on the
 * XmNactivateCallback list, not XtNcallback.  You will find that
 * many of the Motif widgets have a variety of callbacks that are
 * invoked by particular actions.  This one happens when the mouse
 * button is pressed.  Recalling the discussion in Chapter 5 we
 * know exactly what is going on.  Essentially, an action proc is
 * kicking off the callback.  As in the case of the Athena List
 * widget, the action proc could be filling in some data to pass
 * to the callback.
 *
 * The last thing to notice is the "freeing" of the cstr.  The
 * reason we do that is because the XmCreateString() function gives
 * XtMalloc() some space, so since we are good clients we give back
 * the resource.
 */
    memset(scratch,'\0',sizeof(scratch));
    if (alarmData.min <= 9)
        sprintf(scratch,"0%1d",alarmData.min);
    else
        sprintf(scratch,"%2d",alarmData.min);
    cstr = XmStringCreate(scratch,XmSTRING_DEFAULT_CHARSET);
    n = 0;
    XtSetArg(arg[n],XmNleftWidget,hr); n++;
    XtSetArg(arg[n],XmNleftAttachment,XmATTACH_WIDGET); n++;
    XtSetArg(arg[n],XmNlabelString,cstr); n++;
```

```
    min= XtCreateManagedWidget("minute",xmPushButtonWidgetClass,
                    button_container,arg,n);
    XtAddCallback(min,XmNactivateCallback,set_minute,NULL);
    XtFree(cstr);

    memset(scratch,'\0',sizeof(scratch));
    sprintf(scratch,(alarmData.amOrpm == PM) ? "PM" : "AM");
        cstr = XmStringCreate(scratch,XmSTRING_DEFAULT_CHARSET);
    n = 0;
    XtSetArg(arg[n],XmNleftWidget,min); n++;
    XtSetArg(arg[n],XmNlabelString,cstr); n++;
    XtSetArg(arg[n],XmNleftAttachment,XmATTACH_WIDGET); n++;
    am_pm = XtCreateManagedWidget("am_pm",xmPushButtonWidgetClass,
                   button_container,arg,n);
    XtAddCallback(am_pm,XmNactivateCallback,set_ampm,NULL);
    XtFree(cstr);

    n = 0;
    XtSetArg(arg[n],XmNtopWidget,hr); n++;
    XtSetArg(arg[n],XmNtopAttachment,XmATTACH_WIDGET); n++;
    XtSetArg(arg[n],XmNbottomAttachment,XmATTACH_FORM); n++;
    set = XtCreateManagedWidget("set",xmPushButtonWidgetClass,
                    button_container,arg,n);

    XtAddCallback(set,XmNactivateCallback,set_alarm,NULL);

    n = 0;
        cstr = XmStringCreate(DISABLE,XmSTRING_DEFAULT_CHARSET);
    XtSetArg(arg[n],XmNlabelString,cstr); n++;
    XtSetArg(arg[n],XmNleftWidget,set); n++;
    XtSetArg(arg[n],XmNleftAttachment,XmATTACH_WIDGET); n++;
    XtSetArg(arg[n],XmNbottomAttachment,XmATTACH_FORM); n++;
    setLbl = XtCreateManagedWidget("setLabel",xmLabelWidgetClass,
                    button_container,arg,n);
    XtFree(cstr);

    XtRealizeWidget(top);

    XtMainLoop();
}
```

The remaining source code stays practically the same. The only change is to create compound strings prior to giving the labels any information. The process would be as follows:

```
cstr = XmStringCreate(scratch,XmSTRING_DEFAULT_CHARSET);
XtSetArg(arg[0],XmNlabelString,cstr);
XtSetValues(w,arg,(Cardinal)1);
XtFree(cstr);
```

You should take the time and make the changes yourself, it will be good practice.

The thing to notice about this client is that almost nothing major happened! This is extremely nice to see.

9.4.2. Changing xawlist to mlist

The next client is the "xawlist." If you recall, this widget contained a list and a label managed by a form. If you thought "alarm" was easy, take a look at this one (shown in Figure 9-4):

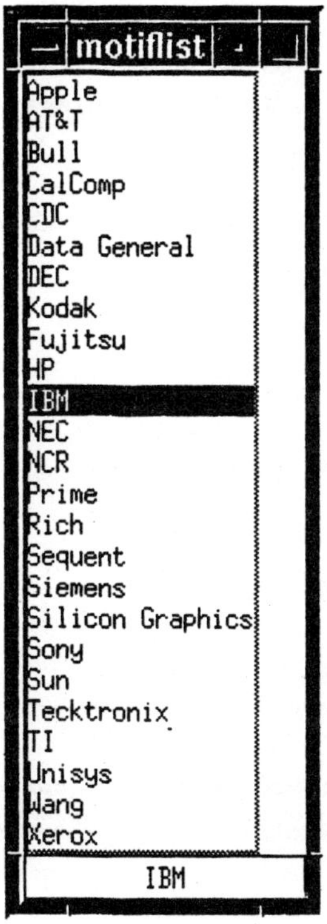

Figure 9-4 Mlist.

```
/* FILE:    mlist.c
 */

#include "XbkUtils.h"
#define XbkShellName     "mlist"
#define XbkApplClass     "Mlist"

#include <Xm/Xm.h>
#include <Xm/Form.h>
#include <Xm/List.h>
#include <Xm/Label.h>

static void selection_callback();

static char *str[] = {
    "Apple","AT&T","Bull","CalComp","CDC",
    "Data General","DEC","Kodak","Fujitsu",
    "HP","IBM","NEC","NCR","Prime","Rich",
    "Sequent","Siemens","Silicon Graphics",
    "Sony","Sun","Tecktronix","TI","Unisys",
    "Wang","Xerox"};

Widget lbl;    /* Need to make it global so the callback can
                * use it.
                */
main(argc,argv)
int argc; char *argv[];
{
    Widget    top,container,lst;
    int  i,n;
    Arg  args[10];
    XmString *lstr,*cstr;

    top =
XtInitialize(XbkShellName,XbkApplClass,NULL,0,&argc,argv);

    container = XtCreateManagedWidget("container",
              xmFormWidgetClass,top,NULL,(Cardinal)0);

/* Find out the number of items.  We need to make the text a
 * compound string for the Motif widgets.  If you don't, things
 * don't work just right.  If you don't believe me, try for
 * yourself!
 */
```

```
    cstr = (XmString *) XtMalloc(sizeof(XmString) * XtNumber(str));
    for (i=0;i < XtNumber(str); i++)
         cstr[i] = XmStringCreate(str[i],XmSTRING_DEFAULT_CHARSET);

/* Now set the list to the widget.
 * Notice the different resource names.
 */
    n = 0;
    XtSetArg(args[n],XmNitems,cstr);     n++;
    XtSetArg(args[n],XmNitemCount, XtNumber(str)); n++;
    XtSetArg(args[n],XmNtopAttachment,XmATTACH_FORM); n++;
    XtSetArg(args[n],XmNvisibleItemCount, XtNumber(str)); n++;
    lst = XtCreateManagedWidget("list",
              xmListWidgetClass,container,args,(Cardinal)n);
    XtAddCallback(lst,XmNbrowseSelectionCallback,
              selection_callback,  NULL);
/*
 * In this case our callback goes on the XmbrowseSelectionCallback
 * list. As we pointed out before, Motif widgets tend to use
 * callbacks quite heavily and often have a few connected to the
 * widget.
 */

    lstr = XmStringCreate("No selection yet !!",
            XmSTRING_DEFAULT_CHARSET);
    XtSetArg(args[n],XmNlabelString,lstr); n++;
    XtSetArg(args[n],XmNtopWidget,lst);     n++;
    XtSetArg(args[n],XmNtopAttachment,XmATTACH_WIDGET); n++;
    lbl = XtCreateManagedWidget("lbl",
              xmLabelWidgetClass,container,args,(Cardinal)n);
    XtRealizeWidget(top);
    XtMainLoop();
}
static void selection_callback(w,client_data,call_data)
    Widget w;
    caddr_t *client_data;
    XmListCallbackStruct *call_data;
{
/*
 * The only change here was different typedef for the call_data.
 */
    Arg args[1];
    XtSetArg(args[0],XmNlabelString,call_data->item);
    XtSetValues(lbl,args,(Cardinal)1);
```

Could it be any easier? These two clients demonstrate that Motif is truly an Intrinsics-based mechanism. You can use the standard Intrinsics mechanisms for creating the components without resorting to the convenience functions. This could give us the chance to perhaps move to another widget set should Motif not make the grade in the long haul, although I doubt this will be the case.

9.4.3. Mixing Athena and Motif Widgets

Many people believe that we can simply mix widgets from different sets. If they didn't like the Motif scrollbar, they think they would be able to use the Athena one. Or perhaps they decide the XWIN PushPin is neat, so they think they'll take it. Before you go off mixing and matching, let me sound a warning right here: **For the most part, widgets cannot be mixed from set to set.**

The reason for this inability to mix is simple: an Open Look slider has a set of superclasses that it needs to conduct its business, and these superclasses are not in the Motif set. If you wanted the slider, you would have to bring over the superclasses. Next, suppose you wanted to place the Open Look slider in the Motif scrolled window. (Talk about weird!) Could you do it? The MIT books say that if you write widgets according to specifications, they should work without a problem. Let me tell you now: they may work with the Intrinsics, but they won't interact with the other Motif widgets. Why? Well, to start, the Motif widgets probably do not have a clue what resources the Open Look widgets use. Next, most complex widgets "toy" with the instance structure directly. Now then, if this is the case, the Motif scrolled window might try something on the Open Look slider that the slider wouldn't like. In fact, the slider may get mad enough to kill the client, or perhaps crash the machine. (The old pointer gremlin again!).

When can you take widgets from other sets and use them with yours. The answer is when they are direct descendants of the Core class, or when they can be used so that they require no widget interaction, only application interaction. To demonstrate this "grafting," let's create an application that displays the Athena ClockWidget in a Motif client (see Figure 9-5). To give the clock a 3D visual appearance, it will be inserted into an XmFrame.

This client was created as a result of a friend's (Vincent Alonzi) desire to have international clocks displayed on the foreign exchange traders workstations. The result is shown in Figure 9-6. The entire source is as follows:

```
/* FILE: mclk.c
 */
/* Most of the XrmOptionDescRec was borrowed from xclock.c
 */

#include <X11/StringDefs.h>
#include <Xm/Xm.h>
#include <Xm/RowColumn.h>
```

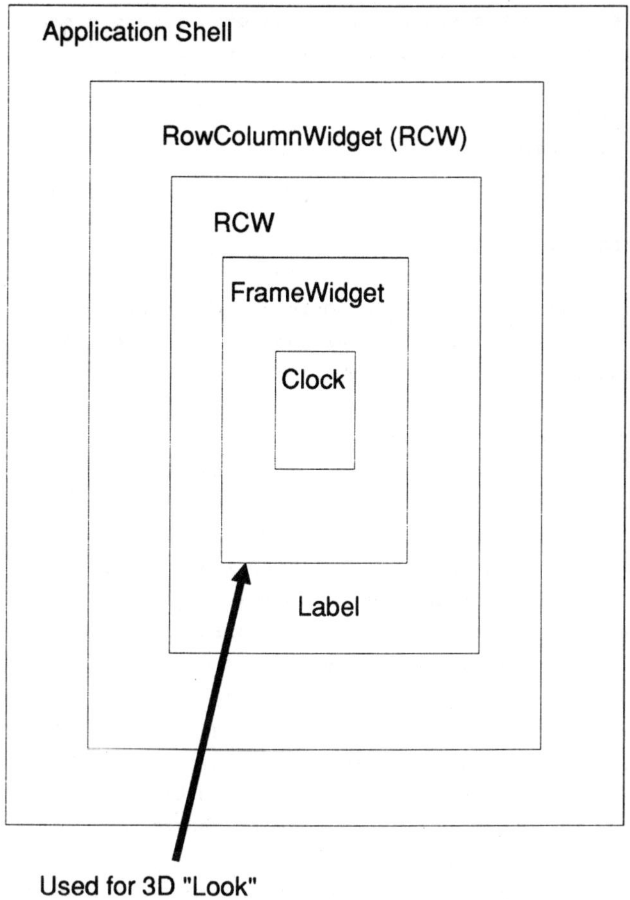

Figure 9-5 Adding Motif 3D.

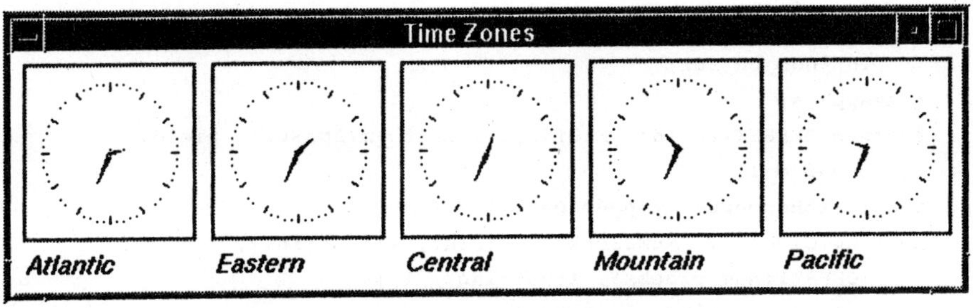

Figure 9-6 Mclk client.

```
/* This is really the Athena Clock widget.  I made a small change
 * to add the capability of having a time zone.
 */
#include "IClock.h"
#include <Xm/Frame.h>
#include <Xm/Label.h>

extern void exit();

/* Command line options table.  Only resources are entered here.
There is a pass  * over the remaining options after XtParseCommand
is let loose. */

static XrmOptionDescRec options[] = {
{"-chime",    "*chime",         XrmoptionNoArg,          "TRUE"},
{"-hd",       "*hands",         XrmoptionSepArg,    NULL},
{"-hands",    "*hands",         XrmoptionSepArg,    NULL},
{"-hl",       "*highlight", XrmoptionSepArg,    NULL},
{"-highlight",    "*highlight", XrmoptionSepArg,    NULL},
{"-update",   "*update",    XrmoptionSepArg,    NULL},
{"-padding",  "*padding",   XrmoptionSepArg,    NULL},
{"-d",        "*analog",    XrmoptionNoArg,          "FALSE"},
{"-digital",  "*analog",    XrmoptionNoArg,          "FALSE"},
{"-analog",   "*analog",    XrmoptionNoArg,          "TRUE"},
{"-clkHgt",   "*clkHgt",         XrmoptionSepArg,    NULL},
{"-clkWth",   "*clkWth",         XrmoptionSepArg,    NULL},
{"-numClocks",    "*numClocks",       XrmoptionSepArg,    NULL},
{"-numOnRow",   "*numOnRow",    XrmoptionSepArg,    NULL},
};

struct _myAppRes {
     int num_clocks;
     int hgt;
     int wth;
     int num_on_row;
{ myAppRes;
#define OFFSET(field)  XtOffset(struct _myAppRes*, field)
int myDef = 1;
static XtResource myAppResOpts[] = {
   {"numClocks", "NumClocks", XtRInt, sizeof(int),
     OFFSET(num_clocks), XtRString, "1"},
   {"clkHgt", "ClkHgt", XtRInt, sizeof(int),
     OFFSET(hgt), XtRString, "50"},
   {"clkWth", "ClkWth", XtRInt, sizeof(int),
     OFFSET(wth), XtRString, "50"},
```

```
};
#undef OFFSET
/*
 * We will limit the number of clocks to six.
*/

#define NUMCLKS 6
/*
 * This macro will help create a class name in our loop.
 */
#define SET_CLASS_NAME(name,holder,incr)\
{memset(holder,'\0',sizeof(holder));\
              sprintf(holder,"%s%d",name,incr);}
void main(argc, argv)
     int argc;
     char **argv;
{
     Widget toplevel,container,clkBox[NUMCLKS],
            clkLbl[NUMCLKS],clk[NUMCLKS],clkFrame[NUMCLKS];
     char cname[6];

     int n,j;
     Arg args[20];


     toplevel = XtInitialize("mclks", "MClks", options,
                  XtNumber(options), &argc, argv);

     XtGetApplicationResources(toplevel, &myAppRes, myAppResOpts,
                          XtNumber(myAppResOpts),NULL, 0);
     if (myAppRes.num_clocks > NUMCLKS) {
     printf("Sorry too many clocks !!!\n");
     XtCloseDisplay(XtDisplay(toplevel));
     exit(-1);
     }

/* We employ the RowColumn Container from the Motif set.
 */
   container =
    XtCreateManagedWidget("container",
        xmRowColumnWidgetClass, toplevel, NULL,0);
/* Notice the use of XtN resource settings.  The reason for doing
 * this is, we are now creating an Athena widget, and those widgets
 * know about XtN, not XmN.
 */
```

```
  n = 0;
  XtSetArg(args[n],XtNwidth,myAppRes.wth); n++;
  XtSetArg(args[n],XtNheight,myAppRes.hgt); n++;
  XtSetArg(args[n],XtNborderWidth, 0); n++;

  for(j=0;j<myAppRes.num_clocks;j++) {
/*
 * This will keep the clock and label together no matter how the
 * resizing occurs.  We could have used the XmForm and given a few
 * constraints.  I thought that would be harder to do and this
 * seems to be straightforward.
 */

  SET_CLASS_NAME("clkBox",cname,j);
  clkBox[j] = XtCreateWidget(cname,xmRowColumnWidgetClass,
           container,NULL,0);
/* We make clk and clkLbl managed children of clkBox.  We use
 * clkBox, since we want the layout to be in a vertical fashion
 * and this is easier than using the Form widget.  Also, the
 * children will be resized to the column width.
 */
   SET_CLASS_NAME("clkFrm",cname,j);
/*
 * Notice the use of XmFrame, this gives the Athena widget a
 * 3D look.
 */
   clkFrame[j] = XtCreateManagedWidget(cname, xmFrameWidgetClass,
           clkBox[j],NULL,0);
   SET_CLASS_NAME("clk",cname,j);

/* The Athena Widget is created */
   clk[j] = XtCreateManagedWidget (cname, clockWidgetClass,
                   clkFrame[j], args, (Cardinal)n);
   SET_CLASS_NAME("clkLbl",cname,j);

/* Now a Motif Label */
   clkLbl[j] = XtCreateManagedWidget(cname,xmLabelWidgetClass,
               clkBox[j],NULL,0);
   }
/* This "batching" gives the manager widget a break and makes
 * creation a bit faster.
 */
   XtManageChildren(clkBox,myAppRes.num_clocks);
   XtRealizeWidget (toplevel);
   XtMainLoop();
}
```

Now that wasn't so bad at all. As you can tell, Athena and Motif were perfect together. Actually, this exercise is quite nice because it points out the fact that you can look (with care) to other widget sets for components that are not currently available in your widget set. In this case, you didn't have to re-create a clock since it existed and was very, very easy to integrate with Motif.

10

A Sample Application: Motif Version

In Chapter 8 you created a client that demonstrated quite a few interface components. The focus of that chapter was to teach how things got done when programming Intrinsics-based clients. This chapter revisits that program and converts it to a Motif client so you can see how the same application would look using Motif.

10.1. Client Components

This "new" client, "mwtrade" (shown in Figure 10-1), showcases the following components from the Motif Widget Set:

MainWindow
MessageBox
ListWidget
BulletinBoard
PushButtonWidget
CascadeButtonWidget
FormWidget
TextWidget
LabelWidget

In addition, "FieldEdWidget" from Chapter 6 will be subclassed off of the Motif TextWidget.

After reading the source for this client you will know how to create a client based on MainWindow layout, use the FormWidget, create field-level help, create a pull-down menu, create pop-up scrolled help, and create a pop-up option list.

10.2. Building the Client

The best way to get a handle on what it takes to construct a Motif client is to dive right into one. With that, the source for mwtrade.c is as follows:

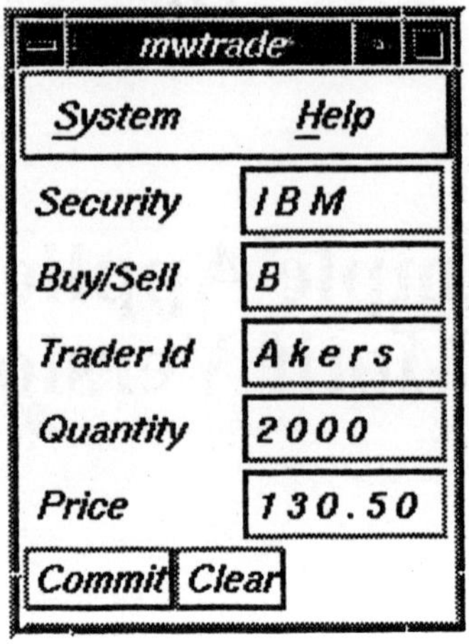

Figure 10-1 Mwtrade.

```
/* FILE:    mwtrade.c
 */

/* Use our standard header file */
#include "XbkUtil.h"

/* These are needed to check on file status */
#include <sys/types.h>
#include <sys/stat.h>
/* Include the Motif headers */
#include <Xm/Xm.h>
#include <Xm/MainW.h>
#include <Xm/MessageB.h>
#include <Xm/Label.h>
#include <Xm/List.h>
#include <Xm/BulletinB.h>
#include <Xm/PushB.h>
#include <Xm/CascadeB.h>
#include <Xm/RowColumn.h>
#include <Xm/Form.h>
#include <Xm/Text.h>

/* Include our Motif version of the field editor.  The major
 * changes were, subclass off of the Motif Text Widget and provide
 * our own insert position management.
 */
```

```
#include "MwFieldE.h"

#define TRADESTRSIZE            80
#define SECURITY_SIZE           8
#define TRADER_SIZE             5
/*
 * This macro is used to clear the field...
 */
#define CLEAR_FIELD(w)\
    {char     junk[TRADESTRSIZE];\
    XmTextPosition lastPos = XmTextGetMaxLength(w);\
    memset(junk,' ',lastPos);junk[lastPos] = '\0';\
    XmTextReplace(w,0,lastPos,junk);\
   }
/*
 * This is a handy macro for creating a compound string...
 */
#define XbkString(A)
XmStringCreateLtoR(A,XmSTRING_DEFAULT_CHARSET)

#define XbkShellName    "mwtrade"
#define XbkApplClass    "MwTrade"

/*
 * Forward Declarations...
 * Notice, the different naming used.  These functions use a
 * suffix of CB to denote a Callback.
 *
 */
XtCallbackProc      CommitCB(),ExitCB(),ClearCB(),MenuCB(),
         HelpOkayCB(),FieldHelpCB(),HelpCB(),SelectionCB();
XtActionProc   MakeNxtFldActive(),MakePrvFldActive(),PopList();
FwProc         CheckBuySell();

Widget         create_the_menuBar(),create_the_entryForm(),
               create_the_mainHelp(),create_the_optionList();
/*
 * Action and Translation Tables...
 */

static String fldAxns =
        "Shift<Key>Tab:              MakePrvFldActive() \n\
         <Key>Tab:                   MakeNxtFldActive() ";
```

```
/* We will use F2 for the pop-up in place of F1.  F1 is used to
 * trigger help in Motif.
 */

static String popListAxns = "<Key>F2:   PopList()";

XtActionsRec    appAxnsTbl[] = {
        {"MakePrvFldActive", MakePrvFldActive},
        {"MakeNxtFldActive", MakeNxtFldActive},
        {"PopList",     PopList},
        {NULL, NULL},
};
XtTranslations  fldTrans,popListTrans;
/*
 * Field/Form definitions...
 */
typedef struct _FIELDINIT {
        char    *label;       /* Label string    */
        int     editor_type;  /* Kind of editor  */
        int     flen;         /* Length of field */
        Widget  fe;           /* Widget id of editor */
        Widget  fl;           /* Widget id of label */
        FwProc  editor;       /* Ptr to editor proc */
        FwProc  enter_window;
        FwProc  focus_out;
        FwProc  focus_in;
        FwProc  field_axn;
        Widget  help;         /* Help widget id */
        char    *helptxt;     /* Ptr to help text */
} FIELDINIT;

/* You will notice that we have added "help" to this structure.
 * This gives us field-level help.  There are many ways of doing
 * this; however, it is a good idea to keep your code organized,
 * hence, the inclusion here.
 */
FIELDINIT Fields[] = {
{"Security ",FE_ALPHA, SECURITY_SIZE,
      0,0,NULL,NULL,NULL,NULL,MakeNxtFldActive,0,
"Enter the security name for the trade.  Use ALPHA characters
 only \n\ since the field will reject any other character.
  To invoke the \n\ selection list press F2."},
  {"Buy/Sell ",FE_ALPHA,1, 0,0,NULL,NULL,NULL,NULL,CheckBuySell,0,
```

```
"The Buy/Sell Indicator requires the input of
  a 'B','b','S', or 's'\n\ any other character will be rejected."},
  {"Trader Id",FE_ALPHANUMERIC,TRADER_SIZE,
        0,0,NULL,NULL,NULL,NULL,MakeNxtFldActive,0,
"Enter a trader name or id.  You may use ALPHA
  or NUMERIC characters."  }, {"Quantity ",FE_INT,7,
  0,0,NULL,NULL, NULL,NULL,MakeNxtFldActive,0,
"Enter the quantity of shares being traded.
  Field accepts only whole\n\ numbers (i.e., 10000)."},
  {"Price    ",FE_FLOAT, 8,
    0,0,NULL,NULL, NULL,NULL,MakeNxtFldActive,0,
"Enter the price of the shares being traded."},
};
/*
 * Pop-up menu...
 */
#define    MENU_HELP    100
#define MENU_UNPOP    101

typedef struct _MENUBODY {
        String          label;
        XtCallbackProc  cbProc;
        int         cbData;
/* This is new.  When defining Motif Menus, we can add a mnemonic
 * that the user may use when kicking off a menu item.
 */
        char        mnemonic;
} MENUBODY;

MENUBODY pmenu [] = {
        {"Help",        MenuCB,MENU_HELP,'H'},
        {"UnPop",       MenuCB,MENU_UNPOP,'U'},
        {"Exit",        ExitCB,NULL,'E'},
};
/*
 * Define the application resource gathering parts...
 */
struct _myAppRes {
        Boolean useMenuBar;
        String  filename;
        String  helpFile;
        String  listFile;
} myAppRes;
```

```
/*
 * Rather then "fixing" the list in the code, we will provide a
list
 * name and use it to create the pop up.
 */
XrmOptionDescRec myCmdOpts[] = {
{ "-useMenuBar", "*useMenuBar", XrmoptionNoArg, "TRUE" },
{"-filename","*fileName",XrmoptionSepArg,NULL},
{"-helpFile","*helpFile",XrmoptionSepArg,NULL},
{"-listFile","*listFile",XrmoptionSepArg,NULL},
};
#define OFFSET(field)  XtOffset(struct _myAppRes*, field)
static XtResource myAppResOpts[] = {
   {"useMenuBar", "UseMenuBar", XtRBoolean, sizeof(Boolean),
         OFFSET(useMenuBar), XtRString, "False"},
   {"fileName", "FileName", XtRString, sizeof(String),
         OFFSET(filename), XtRString, "trade.dat"},
   {"helpFile", "HelpFile", XtRString, sizeof(String),
         OFFSET(helpFile), XtRString, "trade.hlp"},
   {"listFile", "ListFile", XtRString, sizeof(String),
         OFFSET(listFile), XtRString, "trade.lst"},
};
#undef OFFSET

/*
 * Set up the character set used in the Motif functions...
 */
XmStringCharSet charset = (XmStringCharSet)
XmSTRING_DEFAULT_CHARSET;
/*
 * Widgets in the client...
 */

/* One thing to notice right away, the number of variables for the
 * widgets has decreased dramatically.  In the previous version we
 * too could have paid less attention to storing the names but we
 * didn't.  This client is more representative of the way you
 * would tend to write a client.
 */
Widget   topShell; /* Top level of application */
Widget   mainWindow;     /* Main Window */
Widget   menuBar;  /* Menu Bar */
Widget   mainHelp; /* Overall Help */
```

```
Widget   optionList;    /* Popup List for options */
Widget   entryForm;     /* Entry Form        */

FILE    *fout;          /* file for output of trade record */

main (int argc,char **argv)
{

    Display   *dpy;
    Arg  arglist[MAXARGS];
    int  argcnt = 0;

/*
 * Initialize the Toolkit...
 */
    XtToolkitInitialize();
/*
 * Open a connection to the X server...
 */
    dpy = XtOpenDisplay(NULL,NULL,XbkShellName,XbkApplClass,
         myCmdOpts,XtNumber(myCmdOpts),&argc,argv);
    if (!dpy) {
         printf("Sorry ... Couldn't open display !\n");
         exit(-1);
    }
/*
 * Create a top level application shell...
 */
    topShell = XtAppCreateShell(XbkShellName,XbkApplClass,
              applicationShellWidgetClass,dpy,NULL,0);
/*
 * Include the client specific action procedures...
 */
        XtAddActions(appAxnsTbl, XtNumber(appAxnsTbl));
        fldTrans     = XtParseTranslationTable(fldAxns);
        popListTrans = XtParseTranslationTable(popListAxns);
/*
 * Get application resources from the databases...
 */
        XtGetApplicationResources(topShell, &myAppRes,
                                  myAppResOpts,
                                  XtNumber(myAppResOpts),NULL, 0);
/*
```

```
 * Open the file for output...
 */
    if ((fout = fopen(myAppRes.filename,"w+")) == NULL) {
         printf("ERROR: Could not open file !!!");
         XtCloseDisplay(XtDisplay(topShell));
         exit(-1);
    }
/*
 * Create a Motif Main Window...
 */
        mainWindow = XmCreateMainWindow (topShell, "main",
          NULL, 0);
        XtManageChild (mainWindow);
/*
 * Create the Menu Bar for the Main Window...
 */
    menuBar = create_the_menuBar(mainWindow);
    XtManageChild(menuBar);
/*
 * Create the Entry Form...
 */
   entryForm = create_the_entryForm(mainWindow);
   XtManageChild(entryForm);
/*
 * Create the Main Help...
 */
mainHelp  = create_the_mainHelp(mainWindow);
/*
 * Set the Main Window Areas...
 */
    XmMainWindowSetAreas (mainWindow, menuBar, NULL, NULL, NULL,
                                    entryForm);
/*
 * Realize the Widgets...
 */
    XtRealizeWidget(topShell);
/*
 * Process X Events...
 */
    XtMainLoop();
}
```

10.2.1. Creating a Menu Bar

Creating a menu bar in Motif is a four-step process:

1. Use XmCreateMenuBar( ) to set up the correct container.
2. Create the pull-down menus using XmCreatePullDownMenu( ).
3. Insert the panes into the menus by using XmCreatePushButton( ) for regular panes or XmCreateCascadeButton( ) for panes with submenus.
4. Connect the filled-in pull-down menu to a cascade button using

```
XtSetArg (arglist[argcnt], XmNsubMenuId, menu_pane);
cascade = XmCreateCascadeButton (menu_bar, "System", arglist,
          argcnt);
XtManageChild (cascade);
```

where menu_pane is the widget returned from the XmCreatePullDownMenu( );

The source for the client is as follows:

```
/*
 * Functions for MenuBar...
 */
Widget    create_the_menuBar(parent)
  Widget parent;
{
        Widget      menu_bar;       /*  RowColumnWidget              */
        Widget      menu_pane;      /*  RowColumnWidget              */
        Widget      cascade;
        Widget      button;         /*  PushButtonWidget             */
        Arg         arglist[10];
        int         argcnt,i;
        XmString  strA;
/*
 * Create the Menu Bar...
 */
        menu_bar = XmCreateMenuBar (parent, "menuBar", NULL, 0);
/*
 * Create the Pulldown Menu...
 */
        menu_pane = XmCreatePulldownMenu (menu_bar, "menuBody",
                                                  NULL,  0);
/*
```

```
 * Create the Panes...
 */
    for(i=0; i<XtNumber (pmenu); i++) {
          argcnt = 0;
          XtSetArg(arglist[argcnt], XmNlabelString,
               XmStringCreateLtoR(pmenu[i].label,charset));
argcnt++;
          XtSetArg(arglist[argcnt], XmNmnemonic, pmenu[i].mnemonic);
          argcnt++;
          button = XmCreatePushButton (menu_pane, pmenu[i].label,
               arglist,argcnt);
          if (pmenu[i].cbProc != NULL)
                    XtAddCallback (button, XmNactivateCallback,
                    pmenu[i].cbProc, pmenu[i].cbData);
          XtManageChild (button);
    }
/*
 * Now add "PullDown" to a button...
 */
    argcnt = 0;
    XtSetArg (arglist[argcnt], XmNsubMenuId, menu_pane);  argcnt++;
    XtSetArg(arglist[argcnt], XmNlabelString,
          XmStringCreateLtoR("System", charset)); argcnt++;
    XtSetArg(arglist[argcnt], XmNmnemonic, 'S'); argcnt++;
    cascade = XmCreateCascadeButton (menu_bar, "System", arglist,
              argcnt);
    XtManageChild (cascade);

/*     Create "Help" button.
 */
    argcnt = 0;
    XtSetArg(arglist[argcnt], XmNmnemonic, 'H'); argcnt++;
    cascade = XmCreateCascadeButton (menu_bar, "Help", arglist,
                argcnt);
    XtAddCallback (cascade, XmNactivateCallback, MenuCB,
                 MENU_HELP);
    XtManageChild (cascade);

    argcnt = 0;
    XtSetArg (arglist[argcnt], XmNmenuHelpWidget, cascade);
              argcnt++;
    XtSetValues (menu_bar, arglist, argcnt);

    return menu_bar;
}
```

10.2.2. Creating an Entry Form

The entry form in this application will have two parts: the field entry area and the action buttons. The container used for the entire form is none other than XmForm. For the field entry area the XmRowColumnWidget is used. RowColumn is perfect for the job since you want to have two columns per field and the remaining laid out below. By setting the RowColumn widget to a horizontal orientation and setting the number of columns to two, the desired effect is produced.

The last part are the buttons, which are managed by a form. The source is as follows:

```
/*
 * Function for the Entry Form...
 */
Widget create_the_entryForm(parent)
  Widget parent;
{
        Widget      container;      /*  FormWidget                */
        Widget      form;           /*  RowColumnWidget           */
        Widget      box;            /*  FormWidget            */
        Widget      button;         /*  PushButtonWidget          */
        Arg         arglist[10],farg[MAXARGS];
        int         argcnt,i,fcnt,marker;
        XmString    strA;
/*
 * Create the container...
 */
    argcnt = 0;
    container = XmCreateForm(parent,"entryForm",arglist,argcnt);
/*
 * Create the entry manager...
 *
 */
    argcnt = 0;
    XtSetArg(arglist[argcnt],XmNtopAttachment,XmATTACH_FORM);
            argcnt++;
    XtSetArg(arglist[argcnt],XmNorientation,XmHORIZONTAL);
            argcnt++;
    XtSetArg(arglist[argcnt],XmNnumColumns,XtNumber(Fields));
            argcnt++;
   form = XmCreateRowColumn(container,"entry_form",
                               arglist,argcnt);
   XtManageChild(form);
/*
```

```
 * Create the option list for the field editor...
 */
    optionList = create_the_optionList(form);
/*
 * Insert the fields...
 */
    fcnt = 0;
    XtSetArg(farg[fcnt],XmNeditMode,XmSINGLE_LINE_EDIT);   fcnt++;
    XtSetArg(farg[fcnt],XmNeditable,True); fcnt++;
    marker = fcnt;

    for (i=0;i< XtNumber(Fields); i++) {
/*
 * Create the field label...
 */
    argcnt = 0;
    strA = XbkString(Fields[i].label);
    XtSetArg(arglist[argcnt], XmNlabelString,strA);argcnt++;
    Fields[i].fl = XtCreateManagedWidget("field_label",
            xmLabelWidgetClass,form,arglist,argcnt);
    XmStringFree(strA);
/*
 * Create the field editor...
 *
 * Install the editor-type procs that will be invoked whenever we
 * are asking to perform character insertion or deletion.
 */
        XtSetArg(farg[fcnt],XmwNeditorType,Fields[i].editor_type);
        fcnt++;
        XtSetArg(farg[fcnt],XmNcolumns,Fields[i].flen);fcnt++;
        XtSetArg(farg[fcnt],XmNmaxLength,Fields[i].flen);fcnt++;
        if (Fields[i].enter_window !=NULL){
                XtSetArg(farg[fcnt],XmwNenterWindowProc,
                        Fields[i].enter_window); fcnt++;
        }
        if (Fields[i].focus_in !=NULL) {
                XtSetArg(farg[fcnt],XmwNfocusInProc,
                        Fields[i].focus_in); fcnt++;
        }
        if (Fields[i].focus_out !=NULL){
                XtSetArg(farg[fcnt],XmwNfocusOutProc,
                        Fields[i].focus_out); fcnt++;
        }
        if (Fields[i].field_axn !=NULL) {
                XtSetArg(farg[fcnt],XmwNfieldAxnProc,
                        Fields[i].field_axn); fcnt++;
```

```
        }
/*
 * We will use our "modified" field editor.  The changes needed
 * were fairly straightforward.  They are:
 *        1. subclass off of XmTextWidget
 *        2. remove the method of creating the source and the sink
 *        3. replace all Xt with Xm
 *  That's it.
 */
        Fields[i].fe = XtCreateManagedWidget("field_editor",
                     mwFieldEdWidgetClass,form,farg,fcnt);
        XtOverrideTranslations(Fields[i].fe,fldTrans);
         fcnt = marker;
```

10.2.2.1. Creating Field-Level Help To create field-level help (see Figure 10-2), you will use the XmMessageDialog. This component gives a text string and a few buttons. A few of the buttons will be unmanaged so that one remains. Off of the remaining button will be a callback that will "unpop" the help dialog. The source fragment is as follows:

```
/*
 * Create the field help widget...
 *
 */
        if (Fields[i].helptxt != NULL) {
             /* Add a help callback */
             XtAddCallback(Fields[i].fe,XmNhelpCallback,
                       FieldHelpCB,NULL);
             argcnt = 0;
             XtSetArg(arglist[argcnt],
                  XmNautoUnmanage, FALSE);argcnt++;
             XtSetArg(arglist[argcnt],XmNmessageString,
                  XbkString(Fields[i].helptxt));argcnt++;
             XtSetArg(arglist[argcnt],XmNokLabelString,
                  XbkString("Done")); argcnt++;
             Fields[i].help = XmCreateMessageDialog(Fields[i].fe,
                     "FieldHelp",arglist,argcnt);
             XtUnmanageChild(XmMessageBoxGetChild(Fields[i].help,
                  XmDIALOG_CANCEL_BUTTON));
             XtUnmanageChild(XmMessageBoxGetChild(Fields[i].help,
                  XmDIALOG_HELP_BUTTON));
             XtAddCallback(Fields[i].help,XmNokCallback,
                  HelpOkayCB,NULL);
        }
    }
```

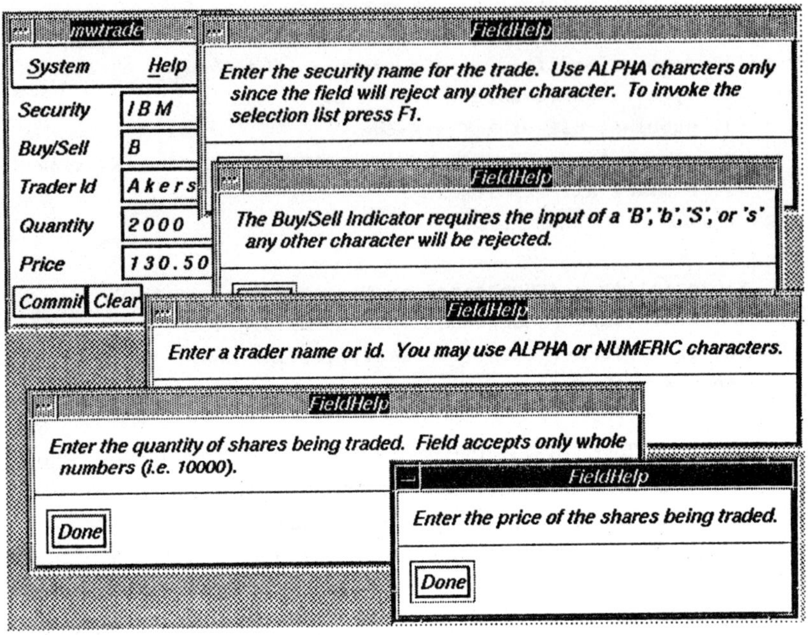

Figure 10-2 Helps.

```
/*
 * Add Pop-up List translation...
 */
    XtOverrideTranslations(Fields[0].fe,popListTrans);
/*
 * Create the action button box...
 */
    argcnt = 0;
    XtSetArg(arglist[argcnt],XmNtopAttachment,
             XmATTACH_WIDGET);argcnt++;
    XtSetArg(arglist[argcnt],XmNtopWidget,form); argcnt++;
    box = XmCreateForm(container,"BtnBox",arglist,argcnt);
    XtManageChild(box);
/*
 * Create the commit button...
 */
    argcnt= 0;
    XtSetArg(arglist[argcnt],XmNtopAttachment,
         XmATTACH_FORM);argcnt++;
    XtSetArg(arglist[argcnt],XmNleftAttachment,
         XmATTACH_FORM);argcnt++;
```

```
    button = XmCreatePushButton(box,"Commit",arglist,argcnt);
    XtAddCallback(button,XmNactivateCallback,CommitCB,NULL);
    XtManageChild(button);
/*
 * Install the commit button accelerators onto the entry fields...
 */
    for(i=0;i<XtNumber(Fields);i++)
         XtInstallAccelerators(Fields[i].fe,button);
    argcnt= 0;
    XtSetArg(arglist[argcnt],XmNtopAttachment,
         XmATTACH_FORM);argcnt++;
    XtSetArg(arglist[argcnt],XmNleftAttachment,
         XmATTACH_WIDGET);argcnt++;
    XtSetArg(arglist[argcnt],XmNleftWidget,button);argcnt++;
    button = XmCreatePushButton(box,"Clear",arglist,argcnt);
    XtAddCallback(button,XmNactivateCallback,ClearCB,NULL);
    XtManageChild(button);

return container;
}
```

10.2.2.2. Creating an Option List The option list shown in Figure 10-3 is very easy to do. In this case you read in a file of options. For each record, you create a compound string as part of an array of items. When you have finished with the file, it is closed. Then a dialog container is created. Once that is done, you set up the widget resources and create a scrolled list using the Motif convenience routine:

```
Widget create_the_optionList(parent)
    Widget parent;
{
    Widget     container;
    Widget     scroller;
    XmString   *cpstr;
    char       rec[20];
    Arg        arg[10];
    int        n,i,status;
    FILE       *infile;

    if ((infile = fopen(myAppRes.listFile,"r")) == NULL) {
            XtWarning("Couldn't open file !!");
            return NULL;
    }
    cpstr = (XmString *) XtMalloc(sizeof(XmString) * 100);
    i = 0;
```

```
    while(i < 100) {
            memset(rec,'\0',sizeof(rec));
            status = fscanf(infile,"%s",rec);
            if (status == EOF) break;
            cpstr[i] = XmStringCreate(rec,
                            XmSTRING_DEFAULT_CHARSET);
            i++;
    }
    fclose(infile);
/*
 * Create the container...
 */
    n = 0;
    container = XmCreateBulletinBoardDialog(parent,
                "optionShell",arg,n);
/*
 * Create the scrolled list...
 */
    n = 0;
    XtSetArg(arg[n],XmNitems, cpstr);         n++;
    XtSetArg(arg[n],XmNitemCount, i - 1);     n++;
    XtSetArg(arg[n],XmNvisibleItemCount,10); n++;
    XtSetArg(arg[n],XmNselectionPolicy,XmSINGLE_SELECT);n++;
    scroller = XmCreateScrolledList(container,"optionList",arg,n);
    XtAddCallback(scroller,XmNbrowseSelectionCallback,
```

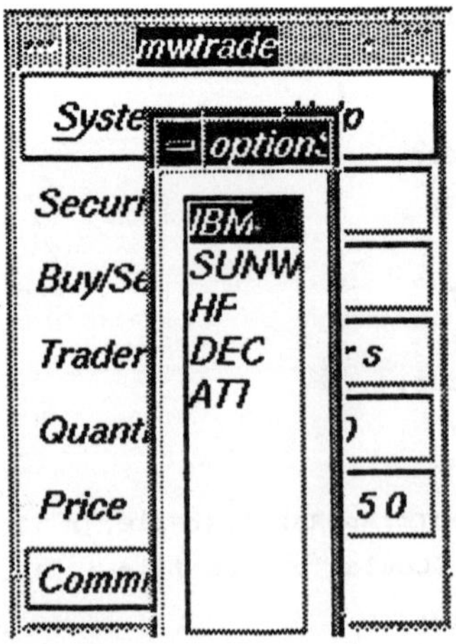

Figure 10-3 Mwtrade option list.

```
        SelectionCB,NULL);
    XtManageChild(scroller);

    return container;
}
```

10.2.3. Scrolled Text: MainHelp

In the previous section the MessageDialog was used to provide field-level help. It is a pretty good candidate for that job since the nature of the help is fairly small. For a larger amount of textual help (as in Figure 10-4), the XmText widget in a scrolled window works wonders:

```
/*
 * Function for the Main Help...
 */
Widget create_the_mainHelp(parent)
  Widget parent;
{
    Widget    container;
    Widget    text;
    struct  stat     statbuf;          /* Information on a file. */
    int          file_length;      /* Length of file.        */
    unsigned char      *file_string;  /* Contents of file.       */
    FILE               *fp = NULL;     /* Pointer to open file.   */
    Arg      arglist[MAXARGS];
    int      argcnt;
    if ((fp = fopen(myAppRes.helpFile, "r")) == NULL) {
    XtWarning("Couldn't get helpfile ... ");
    return NULL;
    }
/*
 * Create the space for the file, then read it in.
 */
    if (stat(myAppRes.helpFile, &statbuf) == 0)
         file_length = statbuf.st_size;
    else
         file_length = 1024; /* Assume it is only 1k then */
    file_string = (unsigned char *)
                   XtMalloc((unsigned)file_length);
    fread(file_string, sizeof(char), file_length, fp);
/* close up the file */
      if (fclose(fp) != NULL)
        XtWarning("Problem closing helpFile !!");
```

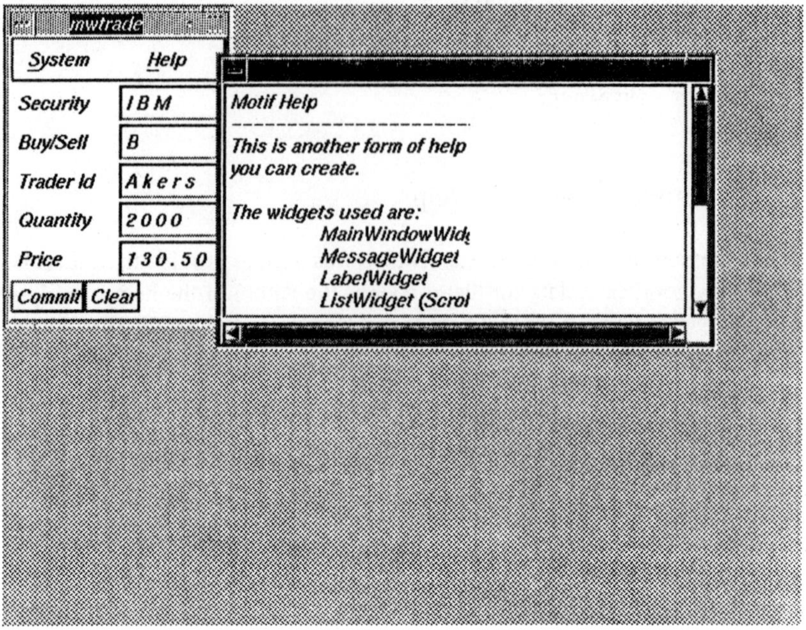

Figure 10-4 Mwtrade main help.

```
/*
 * Create the container...
 *
 * Since we are creating our own dialog we employ one of the
 * creation mechanisms that allow us to do that.  In this case, we
 * use the FormDialog
 */

    argcnt = 0;
    XtSetArg(arglist[argcnt],XmNdialogTitle,"Main Help");argcnt++;
    container = XmCreateFormDialog(parent,"helpShell",
                arglist,argcnt);
/*
 * Create the text widget...
 *
 * We tell XmText to be 40 cols by 10 rows, it is not resizable,
 * always has a vertical scrollbar, and it is a multi-line
 * instance.
 */
```

```
    argcnt = 0;
    XtSetArg (arglist[argcnt], XmNrows, 10);  argcnt++;
    XtSetArg (arglist[argcnt], XmNcolumns, 40);  argcnt++;
    XtSetArg (arglist[argcnt], XmNresizeWidth, False);  argcnt++;
    XtSetArg (arglist[argcnt], XmNresizeHeight, False);  argcnt++;
    XtSetArg (arglist[argcnt], XmNscrollVertical, True);  argcnt++;
    XtSetArg (arglist[argcnt], XmNeditMode, XmMULTI_LINE_EDIT);
             argcnt++;
    text = XmCreateScrolledText(container,"mainHelp",
                                 arglist,argcnt);
    XmTextSetString(text,file_string);
    XtManageChild(text);

    return container;
}
```

10.2.4. Supporting Functions

The remaining part of the source provides all of the supporting functions. The first part is the field action routine from the previous client. It is followed by the traversal routines, then the application callbacks.

The biggest change between trade to mwtrade is that the "pop ups" are brought to life by managing them, not popping them. The same is true for bringing them down, except they are unmanaged. The code is as follows:

```
/*
 * Field action routine...
 */
FwProc CheckBuySell(w)
        Widget w;
{
        Arg arg[1];
        char *sval;

        XtSetArg(arg[0],XmwNstringVal,&sval);
        XtGetValues(w,arg,(Cardinal)1);
        if (((sval == NULL) || strlen(sval)) &&
            (strcmp(sval,"B") == 0) || (strcmp(sval,"b") == 0) ||
            (strcmp(sval,"s") == 0) || (strcmp(sval,"S") == 0))
                MakeNxtFldActive(w,NULL,NULL,NULL);
        else
                XBell(XtDisplay(w), 50);
}
```

```
/*
 * Action Procedures used in the client...
 */
XtActionProc PopList(w,event,param,num_params)
  Widget w; XEvent *event; String *param; Cardinal num_params;
{
        Arg arg[MAXARGS];
        int width  = 0, x = 0,y = 0;
        int rx,ry;
        int cnt;
/*
 * If no option list created, return
 */
    if (optionList == NULL) return;
/*
 * Find out where the widget that "popped us" is...
 */
         XtSetArg(arg[0],XtNwidth,&width);
         XtGetValues(w,arg,1);
         XtTranslateCoords(w, 0, 0, &rx, &ry);
         rx = rx + width;
/*
 * Reset our position so we are next to it...
 */
         cnt = 0;
         XtSetArg(arg[cnt],XtNx,rx);                        cnt++;
         XtSetArg(arg[cnt],XtNy,ry);                        cnt++;
         XtSetValues(optionList,arg,cnt);

         XtManageChild(optionList);
}
XtActionProc MakeNxtFldActive(w,event,param,num_params)
  Widget w; XEvent *event; String *param; Cardinal num_params;
{
         Widget ww;
         int i,numFlds = XtNumber(Fields);
         for(i=0;i<numFlds;i++)
                 if (Fields[i].fe == w){
              ww = (i == (numFlds-1)) ?
                   Fields[0].fe : Fields[i+1].fe;
                        XSetInputFocus(XtDisplay(ww), XtWindow(ww),
                                  RevertToPointerRoot,
                                  CurrentTime);
                        break;
                 }
}
```

```
XtActionProc MakePrvFldActive(w,event,param,num_params)
  Widget w; XEvent *event; String *param; Cardinal num_params;
{
        Widget ww;
        int i,numFlds = XtNumber(Fields);
        for(i=0;i<numFlds;i++)
                if (Fields[i].fe == w){
              ww = (i == 0) ?
                   Fields[numFlds-1].fe : Fields[i-1].fe;
                        XSetInputFocus(XtDisplay(ww), XtWindow(ww),
                                  RevertToPointerRoot,
                                  CurrentTime);
                        break;
              }
}
/*
 * Callbacks...
 */

XtCallbackProc  SelectionCB(w,client_data,call_data)
  Widget w;
  caddr_t *client_data;
  XmListCallbackStruct *call_data;
{
    char *txt;
    XmStringGetLtoR(call_data->item,XmSTRING_DEFAULT_CHARSET,&txt);
    XmTextSetString(Fields[0].fe,txt);
    XtFree(txt);
    XtUnmanageChild(optionList);
}
XtCallbackProc
FieldHelpCB(whoCalledMe,dataFromClient,dataToGiveClient)
  Widget whoCalledMe;
  caddr_t dataFromClient;
  caddr_t dataToGiveClient;
{
    int i = 0;
/* Find the field asking for help, then manage the help if
   available */
    for(i=0;i<XtNumber (Fields);i++)
         if (Fields[i].fe == whoCalledMe){
              if (Fields[i].help != NULL)
                   XtManageChild(Fields[i].help);
              break;
         }
}
```

```
XtCallbackProc  HelpCB(whoCalledMe,dataFromClient,dataToGiveClient)
  Widget whoCalledMe;
  caddr_t dataFromClient;
  caddr_t dataToGiveClient;
{
/*
 * This is for the MainHelp...
 */
    XtManageChild(mainHelp);
}
XtCallbackProc  HelpOkayCB(whoCalledMe,dataFromClient,
                dataToGiveClient)
  Widget whoCalledMe;
  caddr_t dataFromClient;
  caddr_t dataToGiveClient;
{
/*
 * This is for the help dialog's fields
 */
    XtUnmanageChild(whoCalledMe);
}
XtCallbackProc  MenuCB(whoCalledMe,dataFromClient,dataToGiveClient)
  Widget whoCalledMe;
  caddr_t dataFromClient;
  caddr_t dataToGiveClient;
{
/*
 * Our menu callback has two functions: help or unpop.
 * Help should manage the MainHelp.
 */
        switch((int)dataFromClient){
        case MENU_HELP:
                  XtManageChild(mainHelp);
                break;
        case MENU_UNPOP:
                break;
        }
}

XtCallbackProc  CommitCB(whoCalledMe,dataFromClient,
                         dataToGiveClient)
        Widget whoCalledMe;
        caddr_t dataFromClient;
        caddr_t dataToGiveClient;
{
```

```
        int ival; float fval; char *sval;
        Arg arg[1]; int i,numFlds = XtNumber(Fields);
        char out_rec[TRADESTRSIZE];
/*
 * Write the trade data to the file
 */
    memset(out_rec,'\0',sizeof(out_rec));
    sprintf(out_rec+strlen(out_rec), "From File: ");

    for(i=0;i<numFlds;i++)
          switch(Fields[i].editor_type) {
          case FE_ALPHA:
          case FE_ALPHANUMERIC:
          case FE_APPL:
               XtSetArg(arg[0],XmwNstringVal,&sval);
               XtGetValues(Fields[i].fe,arg,1);
          if (sval != NULL)
               sprintf(out_rec+strlen(out_rec),
               "%s ",sval);
          break;
          case FE_INT:
                XtSetArg(arg[0],XmwNintVal, &ival);
                XtGetValues(Fields[i].fe,arg,(Cardinal)1);
                     sprintf(out_rec+strlen(out_rec),
                     "%i ",ival);
                break;
          case FE_FLOAT:
                XtSetArg(arg[0],XmwNfloatVal, &fval);
                XtGetValues(Fields[i].fe,arg,(Cardinal)1);
                     sprintf(out_rec+strlen(out_rec),
                     "%.3f ",fval);
                break;
          }
    fprintf(fout,"%s\n",out_rec);
    fflush(fout);    /* So it gets to the file */
}
XtCallbackProc
ClearCB(whoCalledMe,dataFromClient,dataToGiveClient)
  Widget whoCalledMe;
  caddr_t dataFromClient;
  caddr_t dataToGiveClient;
{
    int i,numFlds = XtNumber(Fields);
    for(i = 0; i < numFlds; i++){
```

```
            char junk[TRADESTRSIZE];
            XmTextPosition lastPos = XmTextGetMaxLength(Fields[i].fe);
            memset(junk,' ',lastPos);junk[lastPos] = '\0';
            XmTextReplace(Fields[i].fe,0,lastPos,junk);
            XmTextSetInsertionPosition(Fields[i].fe,0);
    }
}
XtCallbackProc
ExitCB(whoCalledMe,dataFromClient,dataToGiveClient)
  Widget whoCalledMe;
  caddr_t dataFromClient;
  caddr_t dataToGiveClient;
{
    XtUnmapWidget(topShell);
    XtDestroyWidget(topShell);
    XtCloseDisplay(XtDisplay(topShell));
    fclose(fout);
    exit(0);
}
```

10.3. Summing Up

As you can see, this client was much easier to create with the Motif set. By employing the convenience mechanisms for creating the different components, you can reduce the amount of labor it takes to craft the application. I guess they weren't kidding when they called those "convenience" functions!

Appendix C contains details regarding the routines used in this chapter. If you have further questions, you should consult the OSF/Motif documentation.

11

Application Development: Advanced Topics

The first part of this book has explored several areas related to day-to-day programming with the Intrinsics. As a last subject, this chapter examines two advanced topics: inter-client communication (ICC) and managing multiple displays.

11.1. Inter-Client Communication

Inter-client communication refers to the exchange of information between two or more X clients. This information could be notification of creation of a window, the update of shared data, or perhaps the death of a client. In the UNIX domain, there exists a whole set of inter-process communication (IPC) facilities that can accomplish these tasks. These facilities include semaphores ("event flags"), shared memory segments, message queues, and signals. In X, the facilities used are properties and client messages.

Perhaps the question, "If I can use UNIX IPC facilities why would I bother using X ICC facilities?" has come to mind. The answer is fairly straightforward. To start, X is a network-based windowing system, and as such may have clients running on any number of machines running different operating systems. If that is the case, then the UNIX facilities are no longer valid.

Additionally, since the clients may be running on different machines, the exchange of data is much harder using the UNIX facilities (if you could) than X (you will see what I mean). Another point is that when you are writing X clients, you know that there will be at least one common denominator: the X server. With that, why not exploit any of the advantages this common ground gives us?

Before going any further, it is worth noting that this area of ICC has been an interesting subject of conversation. Many people have spent a large amount of time concerning themselves with how clients "chat" with each other. This topic has been such a concern that the X Consortium has adopted a manual that details how this dialog should be done. The manual is titled *Inter-Client Communications Conventions Manual* (ICCCM, pronounced "I-triple C-M") and is available on the release tape distributed by MIT.

This chapter simply demonstrates how to perform ICC, and does not pretend to present policies. If you, as an application writer, really care about such things, then reading the ICCCM is a must. (Since we are talking about Intrinsics applications, most of the ICCCM compatibility issues are taken care of by the widget sets. However, topics such as ICCCM compliance are things you should be aware of.)

11.1.1. What's an Atom?

The first thing that is needed for client communication is the creation of a thing called an *atom*. An atom is nothing more than shorthand for identifying a string. By using a unique number, programs (namely the X server) can get to the information quickly, since it is far easier and faster to ask if a number equals another number than whether one string "matches" another string.

The process of creating or accessing an atom is referred to as *interning* the atom. The function for doing this is as follows:

```
Atom MYATOM = XInternAtom(dpy,"A STRING",True);
```

This will obtain a unique id for the character sequence "A STRING." The second argument says, "Give me an atom whether one exists or not." If one did not, the return value of the function would be false and MYATOM would equal "None."

The lifetime of an atom is quite long. When an atom is interned, the X server creates it and never lets it go. The only time an atom can be destroyed is when the server is restarted.

Caution: Since atoms don't go away, client writers need to be careful of excessive use. Simply put, if you find that you need 200 atoms for your client, there is most likely a better approach to the problem.

11.1.2. What's a Property?

Now that you can intern atoms, the second piece of the ICC puzzle is needed. This piece is referred to as a *property* and can be viewed as a collection of named, typed data connected to a window. This is to say, it is an area of memory that is referenced by name with an associated type. Clients need to agree on the physical layout of the property and what type it is.

You can think of properties as shared memory. If you've ever used shared memory, you are well aware of how processes must cooperate in what the segment looks like and what type the data is. If they don't, unexpected things may happen. As an example, suppose you had two clients. One provides real-time data while the other interprets the data. The layout of the shared data according to the provider is:

```
struct {
	char	name_of_data[10];
	float	data_value;
} provider_version;
```

where "name_of_data" is a tag to be used in displaying the information, and "data_value" is the actual information. Now the interpreter views the data as

```
struct {
     float     data_value;
     char      name_of_data[10];
} interpreter_version;
```

As you can see, provider and interpreter do not agree!

One thing to be aware of when getting involved with ICC mechanisms is that X has a few predefined atoms and property names. For instance, the way clients talk with window managers is through properties. If you have explored the Intrinsics code or have written an Xlib client, you would have come across a function XSetStandardProperties(). That function changes properties that the window manager knows about. Those properties are quite obviously predefined. The point is, just like you need to look up the predefined resources in StringDefs.h (or Xm.h if you are using OSF/Motif), you must look up atoms and property names. The following is a table of commonly used atoms for property names:

Table 11-1
Commonly Used Property Names

XA_CUT_BUFFER0	XA_CUT_BUFFER1	XA_CUT_BUFFER2
XA_CUT_BUFFER3	XA_CUT_BUFFER4	XA_CUT_BUFFER5
XA_CUT_BUFFER6	XA_CUT_BUFFER7	XA_RGB_GREEN_MAP
XA_RGB_RED_MAP	XA_RGB_BLUE_MAP	XA_RGB_GRAY_MAP
XA_RGB_BEST_MAP	XA_RGB_DEFAULT_MAP	XA_RESOURCE_MANAGER
XA_WM_CLASS	XA_WM_CLIENT_MACHINE	XA_WM_COMMAND
XA_WM_HINTS	XA_WM_ICON_NAME	XA_WM_ICON_SIZE
XA_WM_NAME	XA_WM_NORMAL_HINTS	XA_WM_TRANSIENT_FOR
XA_WM_ZOOM_HINTS		

A property is really a continuous chunk of bytes. From the server's perspective it doesn't matter what the contents of those bytes are. However, from the client's perspective, the sequence of bytes has some meaning. That meaning is derived from the type part of a property, which also has an atom associated with it. The following is a table of predefined atoms used for types:

Table 11-2
Predefined Atoms

XA_ARC	XA_ATOM	XA_BITMAP	XA_CARDINAL
XA_COLORMAP	XA_CURSOR	XA_DRAWABLE	XA_FONT
XA_INTEGER	XA_PIXMAP	XA_POINT	XA_RGB_COLOR_MAP
XA_RECTANGLE	XA_STRING	XA_VISUALID	XA_WINDOW
XA_WM_HINTS	XA_WM_SIZE_HINTS		

11.1.3. Handling Properties: Changing, Getting, and Deleting

Properties are created and set using the same function call:

```
XChangeProperty(dpy,wdw,pname,ptype,format,mode,&data,dsize)
```

where "dpy" is the display that the property is on, "wdw" is the window id that the property is associated with, "pname" is the atom associated with the property name, "ptype" is the atom associated with the property type, "format" is the size in bits of the data elements (8, 16, or 32), "mode" is the nature of the change (PropModeReplace, PropModePrepend, or PropModeAppend), "&data" is the address of the data used in the change, and "dsize" is the number of "format"-sized elements in data. If the property does not exist, it is created and the data applied.

The confusing part of the function call is the "dsize" argument, which needs to be the number of "format" elements in "data." It is the number of *n*-bit elements in data. The *n* represents the number of 8-, 16-, or 32-bit elements in the block of bytes being passed. So, if the data to share looked like this:

```
struct {
      char name[10];
      int  value;
} data;
```

The dsize argument would be 11 on a 32-bit machine. The reason is that there are 10 32-bit elements in the char array, and one 32-bit element for the int.

When a client receives a property-notify event or is just interested in what (if anything) is stored in the property, the function for getting the data associated with the property is

```
XGetWindowProperty(dpy,wdw,pname,offset,len,action,rtype,&atype,
&aformat,&nitems,&bytes_left,&data)
```

where "dpy" is the display the property is on, "wdw" is the window the property is associated with, "pname" is the atom associated with the property, "offset" is the place to start the return in the data, "len" is the number of elements to return, "action" informs the server to delete (True) or leave the data alone (False), "rtype" is an atom for the data type of the property or the constant AnyPropertyType, "atype" is the actual type returned (if the property does not exist, the value would be None), "aformat" is the actual format of the data (the value 0 if the property does not exist, otherwise 8, 16, or 32), "nitems" is the number of atoms returned, "bytes_left" is the number of bytes remaining, and "data" is the data returned.

Properties, unlike atoms, can be deleted by clients. They live for as long as the window they are associated with exists or until they are deleted by the client. The function for deleting a property is

```
XDeleteProperty(dpy,wdw,pname)
```

where “dpy” is the display the property is on, “wdw” is the window id that the property is associated with, and “pname” is the atom associated with the property.

11.1.4. Talking to Other Clients with Properties

If you recall, Chapter 5 discussed the many events that can be watched by clients. The property-notify event was one of them. This implies that the only addition to the client is to add some processing to handle the detection of a property event. You can go about that in many ways, using translation tables, event handlers, or checking the event yourself. (You will do this shortly.)

As was pointed out, properties are associated with a window id. The nice thing about that is, if you know the id of a window, you can check the property list for that window. Additionally, you can register for property notification events on that window. For most clients, the window ids are private and therefore other clients do not have any clue that other clients are running on the server. There is one window that *all* clients know about: the root window. The root window is therefore an ideal candidate for ICC mechanisms of the form of property notification events.

There are some important details to be aware of when attempting this kind of communication. To start, the Intrinsics will not know about the root window in the client's widget tree. Therefore, you will have to check each event for property-notify on the root window *before* giving the event off to the dispatch mechanism. Next, when registering for property notification on the root window, the client will get *every* property notification event on the root window. This makes a lot of sense, but suppose there are several clients using the same technique for ICC. That means your clients get to find out about, and have a few CPU cycles devoted to rejecting, the “spurious” events. Always think about what is actually going on before “running” in a direction.

Now, to communicate through the root window, clients need only perform the following steps:

1. Intern atoms.
2. Inform the X server of desire for property notification events on the root window (use XSelectInput()).
3. Check for the property notification event on the root window and process the information.

To demonstrate, the “trade” client from Chapter 8 will have the changing of a property added to it. To show that the property has been set, the “watch” client of Chapter 5 will have the necessary processing for getting a value from a property added to it.

The new "trade" client will need a new header file containing the ICC items (i.e., atoms, string names, data structure), a function to intern the atoms used, and a function to set the property. The header file used is as follows:

```
/* FILE:   XbkICC.h
 * PURPOSE:     Set up the shareable information that clients
 *              will be using to do Inter-Client Communication.
 *
 * Since multiple clients will be using a "string" to intern atoms
 * it is a good idea to create a #define for them to use.  By doing
 * this, the chance of errors is greatly reduced since clients will
 * use the #define, not the actual string.
 */
#define XbkAtomTradeInfo      "Trade Info"
#define XbkAtomTradeType      "Trade Type"
#define XbkAtomTradeDone      "Trade Done"
#define XbkAtomWatcher        "Watcher"
/*
 * Some messages and sizes to be used in the clients.
 */
#define PROPERTY_FAILED       "Could not get the property !!"
#define TRADESTRSIZE          80
#define SECURITY_SIZE         8
#define TRADER_SIZE           5
/*
 * These are the atoms that will be used for setting and getting
 * properties.
 */
Atom      TRADE_INFO,TRADE_TYPE,TRADE_EXITED,WATCH_WINDOW;
/*
 * This is the data that will be exchanged.
 */
typedef  struct _trade_data {
    char      security[SECURITY_SIZE];
    char      buyOrSell;
    char      trader[TRADER_SIZE];
    int       quantity;
    float     price;
} trade_data;
```

After including the new header file, a function to intern the atoms that will be used for property-handling is created as follows:

```
/*
 * This routine interns the atoms for the "shared" information to
 * be placed on the root window. Note, there is no window
 * associated with an atom, just the "display id" which happens to
 * be the server the client is running on.
 */
int init_icc(w)
    Widget w;
{
    TRADE_INFO     = XInternAtom(XtDisplay(w),XbkAtomTradeInfo,
                         FALSE);
    TRADE_TYPE     = XInternAtom(XtDisplay(w),XbkAtomTradeType,
                         FALSE);
}
```

Lastly, the function for "changing" (setting) the property is:

```
int send_trade(w)
    Widget w;
{
/*
 * This is a little hackish!  We will fill in the trade_data
 * for each field by using the field index.  This is by no means
 * a nice generic way!
 */
    trade_data     *tData;
    int ival; float fval; char *sval;
    Arg arg[1];

/* Recall that the FieldEdWidget GetValues() method will return
 * a string, int, or float value.  Given that, we use the
 * "standard" Intrinsics mechanism for getting widget data and let
 * GetValues() handle the conversion for us.
 */
    XtSetArg(arg[0],XtNstringVal,&sval);
    XtGetValues(Fields[0].fe,arg,1);
    if (sval != NULL)
         strncpy(tData->security,sval,7);
    else
         strncpy(tData->security,"-------",7);

    XtSetArg(arg[0],XtNstringVal,&sval);
    XtGetValues(Fields[1].fe,arg,1);
    if (sval != NULL)
```

```
            tData->buyOrSell = sval[0];
        else
            tData->buyOrSell = '-';
        XtSetArg(arg[0],XtNstringVal,&sval);
        XtGetValues(Fields[2].fe,arg,1);
        if (sval != NULL)
            strncpy(tData->trader,sval,5);
        else
            strncpy(tData->trader,"-----",5);
        XtSetArg(arg[0],XtNintVal,&ival);
        XtGetValues(Fields[3].fe,arg,1);
        tData->quantity = ival;

        XtSetArg(arg[0],XtNfloatVal,&fval);
        XtGetValues(Fields[4].fe,arg,1);
        tData->price = fval;
/*
 * With the data filled in, we can "change" the property on the
 * root window, providing it our data.
 */
        XChangeProperty(XtDisplay(w),DefaultRootWindow(XtDisplay(w)),
                    TRADE_INFO,TRADE_TYPE,
                    32,PropModeReplace,
                    (unsigned char *)tData,
                    SECURITY_SIZE + TRADER_SIZE + 1 + 1 + 2);
/*
 * The line (SECURITY_SIZE + TRADER_SIZE + 1 + 1 + 2) tells us how
 * many 32 bit items are in the data.  Since we are on a 32 bit
 * machine and int = 1 32 bit item, char = 1 32 bit item, and
 * float = 2 32  bit items we can add up all those things in the
 * tData structure.
 */
}
```

To fold these new functions into the original “trade" client requires the following steps:

1. Include XbkICC.h as a header file.
2. Add the call init_icc() in the main program after at least one widget has been created.
3. Add the send_trade() function in the callback that is off of the Commit button.

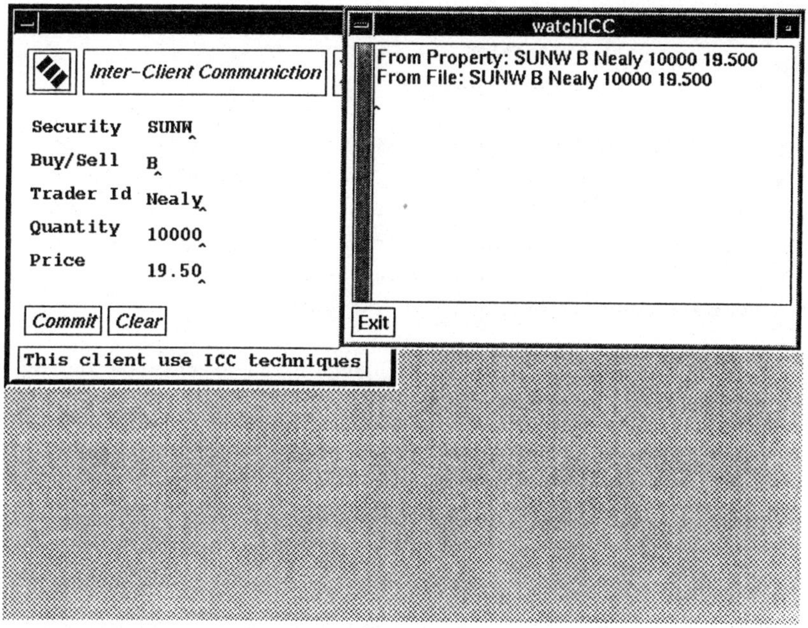

Figure 11-1 Property notify.

Now, the additions to the "watch" client include adding XbkICC.h as a header file, the function init_icc(), a request for property notification events on the root window (Figure 11-1 shows the property-notify window), logic for event checking, and a function to process the trade notification. The header file and init_icc() is the same as above. The following are the changes needed in the "watch" client:

```
/*
 * This code would be in the main program of the Watch client...
 *
 * To pull off the property notification magic we must do a
 * few  things.  First, we must tell the server to tell us when
 * property notifications happen to the root window.  Notice,
 * this is NOT our 'top' window.  Rather, it is the root window of
 * the display we are connected to. You will notice the use of an
 * Xlib primitive and macro.  The primitive is XSelectInput() which
 * is the way all clients inform the server of the events it
 * cares about.  Xt simply hides the details through the use
 * of the XtAddEventHandler() and Translation Manager mechanisms.
 * You should also notice DefaultRootWindow().  This is a macro
 * that knows how to get the window id for the root via the
 * display id.
 */
```

```
    XSelectInput(XtDisplay(top),
            DefaultRootWindow(XtDisplay(top)),
            PropertyChangeMask);
/*
 * Since we are children of the root, the Xt Dispatch mechanism
 * will not inform us of what is happening to the root.  The
 * reason is, none of the widgets will have the root window id as
 * its window id.  So, in order to recognize the fact that a
 * property notification happened on the root, we need to check
 * BEFORE we give the events to the Xt Dispatcher.
 *
 * To do this, we break apart XtMainLoop() and place some logic
 * in.
 */
    for(;;) {
        XtNextEvent(&event); /* get the event from the queue */
/*
 * Check the event type if it is a PropertyNotify event
 * (which maps to the PropertyChangeMask), then check if it was on
 * the root window.  If it was and the atom of the property that
 * changed was TRADE_INFO, then we should process it.  Otherwise,
 * give it to the Dispatcher.
 *
 * If the event type was not property-notify, then just give it
 * to the Dispatcher.
 */
        switch(event.type){
        case PropertyNotify:
            if((event.xproperty.window ==
               DefaultRootWindow(XtDisplay(top)))
               && (event.xproperty.atom == TRADE_INFO))
                   process_trade_notification(fileOutput);
            else
                XtDispatchEvent(&event);
            break;
        default:
            XtDispatchEvent(&event);
            break;
        }
    }
```

The function to process "trade" is as follows:

```
int process_trade_notification(displayWidget)
    Widget displayWidget;
{
    int type,format,nItems,remainder;
    trade_data     *tData;
    char dpyStr[TRADESTRSIZE];

    if (XGetWindowProperty(XtDisplay(displayWidget),
            DefaultRootWindow(XtDisplay(displayWidget)),
            TRADE_INFO, 0, sizeof(trade_data),
            FALSE, TRADE_TYPE,
            &type,&format,&nItems,&remainder,
            &tData) == Success) {
        memset(dpyStr,'\0',sizeof(dpyStr));
        sprintf(dpyStr+strlen(dpyStr),
            "From Property: ");
        sprintf(dpyStr+strlen(dpyStr),
            "%s ",tData->security);
        sprintf(dpyStr+strlen(dpyStr),
            "%c ",tData->buyOrSell);
        sprintf(dpyStr+strlen(dpyStr),
            "%s ",tData->trader);
        sprintf(dpyStr+strlen(dpyStr),
            "%d ",tData->quantity);
        sprintf(dpyStr+strlen(dpyStr),
            "%.3f\n",tData->price);
        XtxuTextInsertString(displayWidget,dpyStr);
        XtTextSetInsertionPoint(fileOutput,0);
        XFree(tData);  /* Don't forget to give back malloc space !
*/
  } else {
        XtxuTextInsertString(displayWidget,PROPERTY_FAILED);
        XtTextSetInsertionPoint(fileOutput,0);
  }
}
```

11.1.5. Communicating with Client Events

Up to now, it has been assumed that events simply occurred due to some situation taking place (i.e., the visibility of a window, a keypress, a mouse movement). There is, however, a mechanism for clients to exchange events. Essentially, a client could redirect an event that it received to another client. This is accomplished through the use of the id of the window to be sent the event. The function for sending an event is as follows:

```
XSendEvent(dpy,wdw,propagate,mask,&event)
```

where "dpy" is the display the client to receive the event, "wdw" is the window to be informed of the event, "propagate" tells the server to redirect the event to ancestors if the wdw is not interested in the event, "mask" is the event mask for the event being sent, and "event" is the actual event structure.

One use of XSendEvent() is for sending client messages. A client message does not go through the server, and is used mainly to provide a form of ICC. You could consider a client message as a semaphore or signal that a client might use to inform other clients that certain kinds of things were happening. The client message can contain data, but it is limited to 20 bytes as defined by the XClientMessageEvent structure in Xlib.h. Additionally, a client message is a non-maskable event type, so clients interested in receiving client messages must specify NoEventMask as the mask argument of XSelectInput() or XtAddEventHandler().

To demonstrate client messages, let's again add some code to "trade" and "watch." What you want to do is simply inform the "watch" client that the "trade" client has been exited (see Figure 11-2). The "watch" client will display a message in its window informing the user that "trade" has existed. To do this, you must create a property that will contain the window id of the watch window so you can send a client message to "watch" which will be understood as a signal that "trade" has been exited. Calling on the previous section discussion, this simply means interning an atom for this property and setting the value in the property. The code for "trade" is as follows:

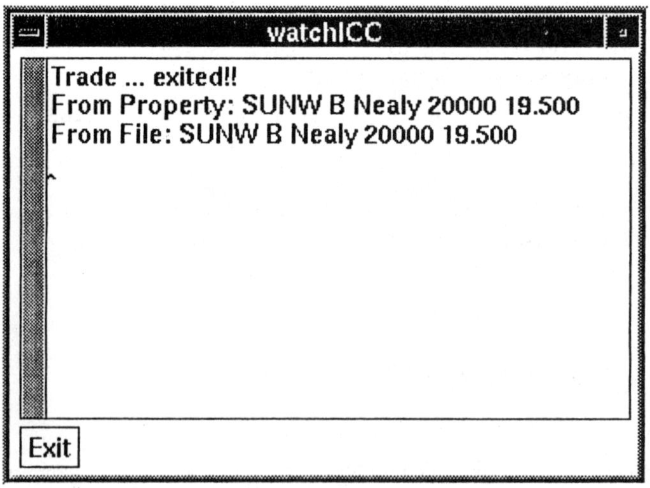

Figure 11-2 Watch with trade-exited message.

```
XtCallbackProc
Chow(whoCalledMe,dataFromClient,dataToGiveClient)
    Widget whoCalledMe;
    caddr_t dataFromClient;
    caddr_t dataToGiveClient;
{
    XClientMessageEvent event;
    Window    *watch_window;
    int type,format,nItems,remainder;
/*
 * We will be using client messages to tell the watcher window
 * that we are going away.
 *
 * First see if the atom exists.  If it does (!=None), then
 * get the window id for the watcher.  If we got it okay,
 * send an event telling it that we are going away.
 * Otherwise, pass over this code.
 */
    WATCH_WINDOW = XInternAtom(XtDisplay(top),XbkAtomWatcher,TRUE);
    if (WATCH_WINDOW != None) {
         if (XGetWindowProperty(XtDisplay(top),
              DefaultRootWindow(XtDisplay(top)),
              WATCH_WINDOW,0,4,FALSE,XA_WINDOW,
              &type,&format,&nItems,&remainder,&watch_window)
         == Success) {
/*
 * Since we are simply telling Watch that we've been asked to
 * exit we do not need to fill in any data.
 *
 * If we had to pass data, we would set the event.format field
 * to 8, 16, or 32, then provide the data in the 20 byte data part
 * of this message type.
 */
         if (*watch_window != NULL) {
              event.display     = XtDisplay(top);
              event.window      = *watch_window;
              event.type   = ClientMessage;
              event.message_type = TRADE_INFO;
              XSendEvent(event.display,event.window,
                 TRUE,XtAllEvents,&event);
              XFlush(event.display);
         }
         }
    }
```

```
    XtUnmapWidget(top);
    XtDestroyWidget(top);
    XtCloseDisplay(XtDisplay(top));
    fclose(fout);
    exit(0);
}
```

The "watch" client needs to set the property to hold its window id so "trade" can send it an event, install an event handler to handle the client message, and provide the event handler to handle the client message event. The following are the code additions needed to "watch":

```
int init_icc(w)
    Widget w;
{
    Window wdw        = XtWindow(w);
    Display *disPLAY = XtDisplay(w);
/*
 * We are setting up our window id on the root window so that
 * other clients may send messages to us.  With the window id
 * they can actually do more than that, but we are an "open"
 * world and have client agreements that they will do no more
 * than send us client events.
 */
    WATCH_WINDOW     = XInternAtom(disPLAY,XbkAtomWatcher,FALSE);
    XChangeProperty(disPLAY,DefaultRootWindow(disPLAY),
                         WATCH_WINDOW,XA_WINDOW,
                         32,PropModeAppend,&wdw,1);
    TRADE_INFO       = XInternAtom(disPLAY,XbkAtomTradeInfo,FALSE);
    TRADE_TYPE       = XInternAtom(disPLAY,XbkAtomTradeType,FALSE);
/*
 * We use the XInternAtom call that will either create or return a
 * value for the requested atom.
 */
}

XtCallbackProc      Xit(w,call_data,client_data)
    Widget w;
    caddr_t    call_data,client_data;
{
    Display *disPLAY = XtDisplay(w);
/*
 * We should remove the property for watch_window so
 * that anyone trying to send us a message will know we are
 * dead.
 */
```

```
    XDeleteProperty(disPLAY,DefaultRootWindow(disPLAY),
                    WATCH_WINDOW);
    XtUnmapWidget(w);
    XtCloseDisplay(disPLAY);
    exit(0);
}
```

The following code fragment would be in the main program:

```
/*
 * We install an event handler to keep an eye out for client
 * messages.  Since they are non-maskable events we use the
 * NoEventMask and set the third argument to TRUE to tell the
 * dispatcher that the event we are looking
 * for is a non-maskable event.
 */
    XtAddEventHandler(fileOutput,NoEventMask, TRUE,
         Handle_ClientMessages, fileOutput);
```

Lastly, you need to code the event handler used for the client message event:

```
XtEventHandler Handle_ClientMessages(w,clientData,event)
        Widget  w;
        caddr_t clientData;
        XEvent  *event;
{
/*
 * The tradeICC client will send us the message_type as trade_info
 * to tell us it died.  We do it this way so we do not have to
 * create a separate atom for this information.  If you are
 * setting up your own private protocol you might need more
 * message_type entries so you understand what the event was all
 * about.
 */
    if (event->xclient.message_type == TRADE_INFO)
    XtxuTextInsertString((Widget)clientData,"Trade ...
exited!!\n");
}
```

11.1.6. Cutting and Pasting: The Xt Selection Mechanism

The last ICC technique is a provision built into the X server. It is referred to as the *selection mechanism*, and is used to transfer data from client to client. The most common use of this technique is when text is cut from one client and pasted into another. Text is not the only thing that may be transferred; images and bitmaps could also be transferred, provided that both clients understood what was being transferred.

The Intrinsics provides a function that installs functions to handle three things that occur for selections: convert, lose, and done. The function is as follows:

```
XtOwnSelection(wdg, selection, time, cvtProc, loseProc, doneProc)
```

where "wdg" is the widget that wants ownership of the selection, "selection" is an atom for the selection to own (usually xa_primary or xa_secondary), "time" is the current server time (use CurrentTime), "cvtProc" is a pointer to a procedure to handle conversion of the selection, "loseProc" is a pointer to a procedure to lose the selection, and "doneProc" is used to finish off the selection.

Since most application writers use the standard widgets from one of the widget sets, the details of the selection mechanism are hidden within the widget. As an example, both the Athena and OSF/Motif TextWidgets have built-in mechanisms for handling selections. Given that, the details of selections are better left to a widget implementation, and from a practical point of view, not something covered in this book. If you are still interested in the "how," read through the Athena TextWidget for how it goes about doing selections. This is a far better way to understand a practical application than working through some bogus example that would be application-based.

11.2. Using Multiple Displays

The last topic to discuss is the management through a single client of multiple displays. This is an interesting topic since it is fairly easy to do and may be a good way to implement some display-only real-time update programs, such as "tickerstrips" (a scrolling display of security prices). To discuss how to do this, you must first be introduced to the notion of an *application context*. This is simply the information pertaining to an application, its context. The information would be the windows under management, the display to be connected to, etc.

Essentially, the application context is all the information needed for an application to run. You could think of it as the environment that each UNIX process runs under. The environment is like a context in that it contains the environment variables (i.e., HOME, SHELL) that the process may use to perform some task. An application context allows for multiple main loops used to manage a client.

The procedure for managing multiple displays is quite simple, and is as follows:

1. Initialize the toolkit.
2. Create *n* application shells (one for each server).
3. If you have a multithreaded OS, create a separate application context to run the main loop on the different threads.
4. Open the connection to the server.

5. Realize each top-level widget.
6. If you have a multithreaded OS, send each main loop on its own thread.

To demonstrate this, let's examine a very trivial client called "multidpys" (shown in Figure 11-3). This client simply has a command button that, when clicked, toggles the foreground/background of each command button on the different displays. Since this client was developed on an IBM PS/2 under AIX 1.1 in a non-networked environment, I started multiple X servers and toggled between each. If it was extended to a multi-host network, each host would have to allow the other machine access to its display. This would be done by adding the host id to the server access list through xhost. The client is defined as follows:

```
/* FILE:        multidpys.c
 * PURPOSE:     Using a single client to manage multiple
 *              application shells on multiple displays.
 *
 */

#include "XbkUtil.h"

#define XbkShellName    "multidpys"
#define XbkApplClass    "Multidpys"
```

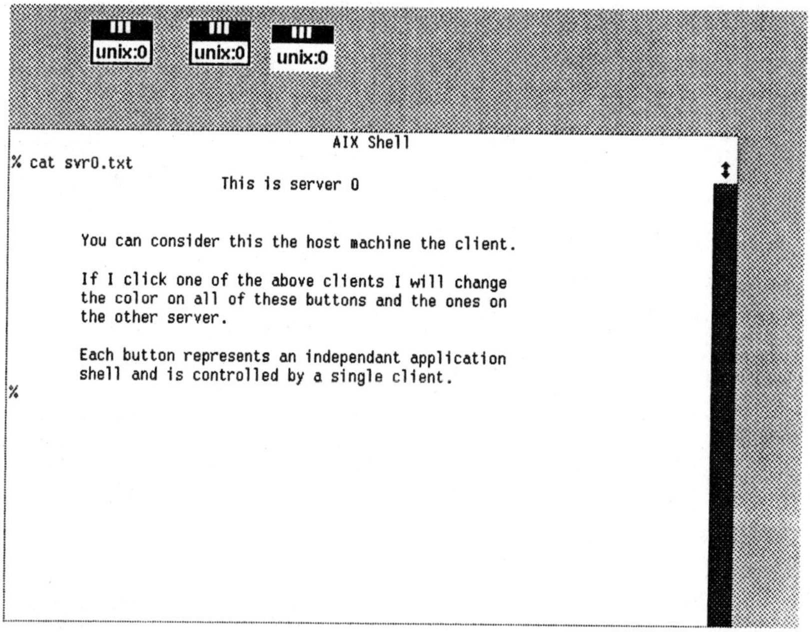

Figure 11-3a Multiple displays.

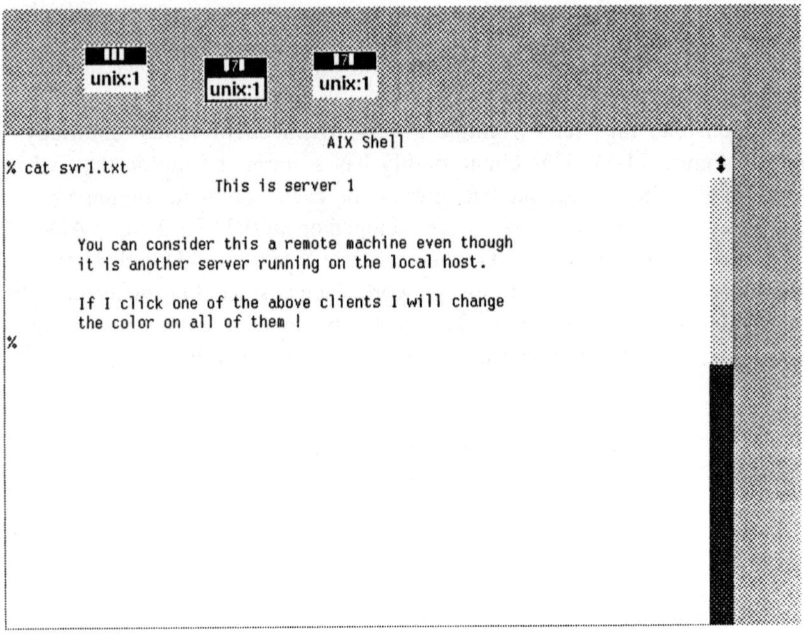

Figure 11-3b Multiple displays.

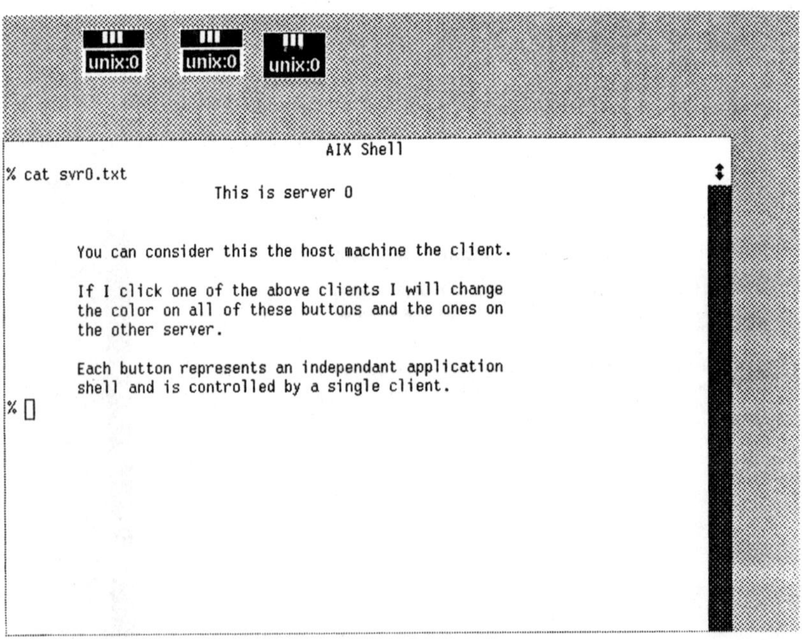

Figure 11-3c Multiple displays.

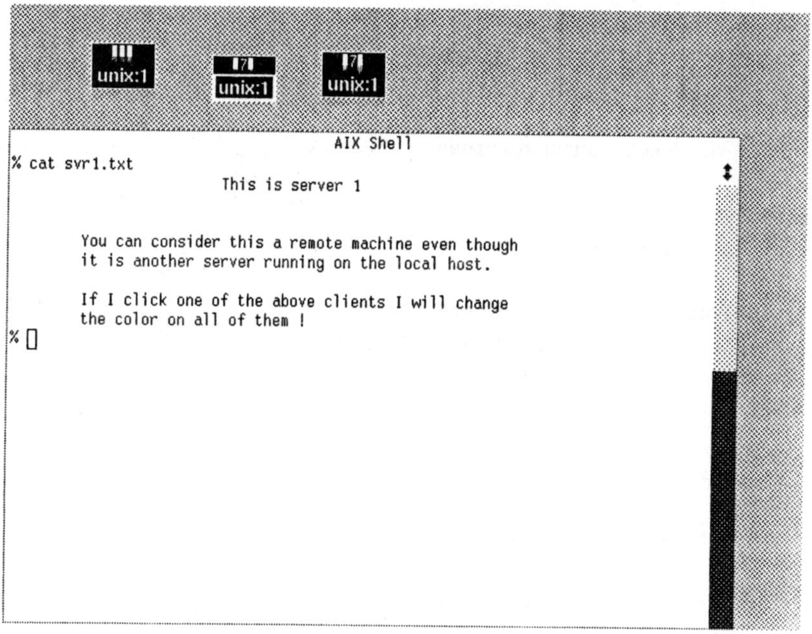

Figure 11-3d Multiple displays.

```
/* Add the widget headers */

#ifdef X11R3
#include <X11/Command.h>
#else
#include <X11/Xaw/Command.h>
#endif

/* We can define the list of X servers to connect to.  In this case
 * I'll be running two on my machine.  You could of course add
 * several machines in the list.
 */

static char *connections[] = {
    "unix:0",
    "unix:0",
    "unix:0",
    "unix:1",
    "unix:1",
    "unix:1",
    NULL};

#define NUMCONNECTIONS    10
```

```
/* The callback in this example will toggle the colors for each of
 * the command buttons under control by this client.  To do this
 * we make the cmb array external so the callback can use it.
 */
Widget        cmb[NUMCONNECTIONS];

main(argc, argv)
int argc; char **argv;
{
    XtAppContext    appC[NUMCONNECTIONS];
    Display         *dpy[NUMCONNECTIONS];
    Widget          top[NUMCONNECTIONS];
    int             i;

    XtCallbackProc     change_colors();

    XtToolkitInitialize();

    for(i = 0; i < XtNumber(connections); i++) {

/* Since we're not really multithreaded, create one application
 * context. When the day comes for multithreaded, simply remove
 * the logic.
 */
          appC[i] = (i == 0) ? XtCreateApplicationContext() :
                     appC[i-1];
          dpy[i]  = XtOpenDisplay(appC[i], connections[i],
                     XbkShellName,XbkApplClass,NULL, 0, &argc, argv);
          top[i]  = XtAppCreateShell(appC[i],XbkApplClass,
                applicationShellWidgetClass, dpy[i], NULL, 0);
          cmb[i]  = XtCreateManagedWidget(connections[i],
                     commandWidgetClass,
                     top[i],NULL,0);
          XtAddCallback(cmb[i],XtNcallback,change_colors,NULL);
          XtRealizeWidget(top[i]);
/* Now, if we had a multithreaded OS, we could send each shell off
 * on a different thread.

          XtAppMainLoop(appC[i]);
 */
    }
/* Since we don't we'll simply manage the single context.
 */
    XtAppMainLoop(appC[0]);
/* actually all would do the trick */
}
```

```
XtCallbackProc      change_colors(w,junk,more_junk)
    Widget w; caddr_t junk,more_junk;
{
    Pixel fg,bg;
    int i;
    Arg gargs[2],sargs[2];

    XtSetArg(gargs[0],XtNforeground,&fg);
    XtSetArg(gargs[1],XtNbackground,&bg);
    XtSetArg(sargs[0],XtNbackground,fg);
    XtSetArg(sargs[1],XtNforeground,bg);

    for(i=0;i<XtNumber(connections);i++) {
         XtGetValues(cmb[i],gargs,(Cardinal)2);
         XtSetValues(cmb[i],sargs,(Cardinal)2);
    }
}
```

11.3. Summing Up

As you can see, the Intrinsics provides a great deal of flexibility to develop clients. ICC is a powerful feature and should be well thought out prior to its implementation. Managing a client that updates multiple displays is fairly easy, and is an interesting subject to explore.

Appendix A

Widgets, Classing, and Exported Functions OSF/Motif and Athena XAW (R4 and R3)

This appendix identifies all of the widgets (and gadgets for Motif) in the widget sets. Additionally, the classing is identified along with the widget exported functions.

A.1. Motif Widgets

Header File	**Widget Class Name**
ArrowB.h	xmArrowButtonWidgetClass;
ArrowBG.h	xmArrowButtonGadgetClass;
BulletinB.h	xmBulletinBoardWidgetClass;
CascadeB.h	xmCascadeButtonWidgetClass;
CascadeBG.h	xmCascadeButtonGadgetClass;
Command.h	xmCommandWidgetClass;
DialogS.h	xmDialogShellWidgetClass;
DrawingA.h	xmDrawingAreaWidgetClass;
DrawnB.h	xmDrawnButtonWidgetClass;
FileSB.h	xmFileSelectionBoxWidgetClass;
Form.h	xmFormWidgetClass;
Frame.h	xmFrameWidgetClass;
Label.h	xmLabelWidgetClass;
LabelG.h	xmLabelGadgetClass;
List.h	xmListWidgetClass;
MainW.h	xmMainWindowWidgetClass;
MenuShell.h	xmMenuShellWidgetClass;
MessageB.h	xmMessageBoxWidgetClass;
PanedW.h	xmPanedWindowWidgetClass;

Header File	Widget Class Name
PushB.h	xmPushButtonWidgetClass;
PushBG.h	xmPushButtonGadgetClass;
RowColumn.h	xmRowColumnWidgetClass;
SashP.h	xmSashWidgetClass;
Scale.h	xmScaleWidgetClass;
ScrollBar.h	xmScrollBarWidgetClass;
ScrolledW.h	xmScrolledWindowWidgetClass;
SelectioB.h	xmSelectionBoxWidgetClass;
SeparatoG.h	xmSeparatorGadgetClass;
Separator.h	xmSeparatorWidgetClass;
Text.h	xmTextWidgetClass;
ToggleB.h	xmToggleButtonWidgetClass;
ToggleBG.h	xmToggleButtonGadgetClass;
Xm.h	xmPrimitiveWidgetClass;
Xm.h	xmGadgetClass;
Xm.h	xmManagerWidgetClass;

A.2. Motif Widget Classing

```
typedef struct _XmArrowButtonGadgetClassRec
   RectObjClassPart               rect_class;
   XmGadgetClassPart              gadget_class;
   XmArrowButtonGadgetClassPart arrow_button_class;
} XmArrowButtonGadgetClassRec;
typedef struct _XmArrowButtonClassRec
   CoreClassPart          core_class;
   XmPrimitiveClassPart  primitive_class;
   XmArrowButtonClassPart      arrowbutton_class;
} XmArrowButtonClassRec;
typedef struct _XmBulletinBoardClassRec
     CoreClassPart          core_class;
     CompositeClassPart     composite_class;
     ConstraintClassPart    constraint_class;
     XmManagerClassPart     manager_class;
     XmBulletinBoardClassPart     bulletin_board_class;
} XmBulletinBoardClassRec;
typedef struct _XmCascadeButtonGadgetClassRec
    RectObjClassPart                 rect_class;
    XmGadgetClassPart                gadget_class;
    XmLabelGadgetClassPart           label_class;
    XmCascadeButtonGadgetClassPart cascade_button_class;
} XmCascadeButtonGadgetClassRec;
```

```
typedef struct _XmCascadeButtonClassRec
    CoreClassPart          core_class;
    XmPrimitiveClassPart    primitive_class;
    XmLabelClassPart        label_class;
    XmCascadeButtonClassPart cascade_button_class;
} XmCascadeButtonClassRec;
typedef struct _XmCommandClassRec
   CoreClassPart            core_class;
   CompositeClassPart       composite_class;
   ConstraintClassPart      constraint_class;
   XmManagerClassPart       manager_class;
   XmBulletinBoardClassPart bulletin_board_class;
   XmSelectionBoxClassPart  selection_box_class;
   XmCommandClassPart       command_class;
} XmCommandClassRec;
typedef struct _XmDialogShellClassRec
    CoreClassPart           core_class;
    CompositeClassPart          composite_class;
    ShellClassPart              shell_class;
    WMShellClassPart               wm_shell_class;
    VendorShellClassPart        vendor_shell_class;
    TransientShellClassPart        transient_shell_class;
    XmDialogShellClassPart      dialog_shell_part;
} XmDialogShellClassRec;
typedef struct _XmDrawingAreaClassRec
     CoreClassPart          core_class;
     CompositeClassPart     composite_class;
     ConstraintClassPart    constraint_class;
     XmManagerClassPart     manager_class;
     XmDrawingAreaClassPart     drawing_area_class;
} XmDrawingAreaClassRec;
typedef struct _XmDrawnButtonClassRec {
    CoreClassPart     core_class;
    XmPrimitiveClassPart  primitive_class;
    XmLabelClassPart      label_class;
    XmDrawnButtonClassPart drawnbutton_class;
} XmDrawnButtonClassRec;
typedef struct _XmFileSelectionBoxClassRec
   CoreClassPart        core_class;
   CompositeClassPart  composite_class;
   ConstraintClassPart constraint_class;
   XmManagerClassPart  manager_class;
   XmBulletinBoardClassPart    bulletin_board_class;
   XmSelectionBoxClassPart    selection_box_class;
   XmFileSelectionBoxClassPart    file_selection_box_class;
} XmFileSelectionBoxClassRec;
```

```
typedef struct _XmFormClassRec
   CoreClassPart        core_class;
   CompositeClassPart   composite_class;
   ConstraintClassPart  constraint_class;
   XmManagerClassPart   manager_class;
   XmBulletinBoardClassPart  bulletin_board_class;
   XmFormClassPart      form_class;
} XmFormClassRec;
typedef struct _XmFrameClassRec
   CoreClassPart        core_class;
   CompositeClassPart   composite_class;
   ConstraintClassPart  constraint_class;
   XmManagerClassPart   manager_class;
   XmFrameClassPart     frame_class;
} XmFrameClassRec;
typedef struct _XmLabelGadgetClassRec
    RectObjClassPart        rect_class;
    XmGadgetClassPart       gadget_class;
    XmLabelGadgetClassPart  label_class;
} XmLabelGadgetClassRec;
typedef struct _XmLabelClassRec
    CoreClassPart        core_class;
    XmPrimitiveClassPart primitive_class;
    XmLabelClassPart     label_class;
} XmLabelClassRec;
typedef struct _XmListClassRec
   CoreClassPart        core_class;
   XmPrimitiveClassPart primitive_class;
   XmListClassPart      list_class;
} XmListClassRec;
typedef struct _XmMainWindowClassRec {
    CoreClassPart  core_class;
    CompositeClassPart  composite_class;
    ConstraintClassPart constraint_class;
    XmManagerClassPart  manager_class;
    XmScrolledWindowClassPart     swindow_class;
    XmMainWindowClassPart     mwindow_class;
} XmMainWindowClassRec;
typedef struct _XmMenuShellClassRec
    CoreClassPart       core_class;
    CompositeClassPart          composite_class;
    ShellClassPart       shell_class;
    OverrideShellClassPart  override_shell_class;
    XmMenuShellClassPart    menu_shell_class;
} XmMenuShellClassRec;
```

```
typedef struct _XmMessageBoxClassRec
   CoreClassPart              core_class;
   CompositeClassPart         composite_class;
   ConstraintClassPart        constraint_class;
   XmManagerClassPart         manager_class;
   XmBulletinBoardClassPart   bulletin_board_class;
   XmMessageBoxClassPart      message_box_class;
} XmMessageBoxClassRec;
typedef struct _XmPanedWindowClassRec {
    CoreClassPart        core_class;
    CompositeClassPart   composite_class;
    ConstraintClassPart  constraint_class;
    XmManagerClassPart   manager_class;
    XmPanedWindowClassPart     vpaned_class;
} XmPanedWindowClassRec;
typedef struct _XmPushButtonGadgetClassRec
   RectObjClassPart               rect_class;
   XmGadgetClassPart              gadget_class;
   XmLabelGadgetClassPart         label_class;
   XmPushButtonGadgetClassPart    pushbutton_class;
} XmPushButtonGadgetClassRec;
typedef struct _XmPushButtonClassRec {
    CoreClassPart     core_class;
    XmPrimitiveClassPart   primitive_class;
    XmLabelClassPart       label_class;
    XmPushButtonClassPart  pushbutton_class;
} XmPushButtonClassRec;
typedef struct _XmRowColumnClassRec
    CoreClassPart        core_class;
    CompositeClassPart        composite_class;
    ConstraintClassPart       constraint_class;
    XmManagerClassPart        manager_class;
    XmRowColumnClassPart      row_column_class;
} XmRowColumnClassRec;
typedef struct _XmSashClassRec {
    CoreClassPart          core_class;
    XmPrimitiveClassPart   primitive_class;
    XmSashClassPart     sash_class;
} XmSashClassRec;
typedef struct _XmScaleClassRec
   CoreClassPart        core_class;
   CompositeClassPart   composite_class;
   ConstraintClassPart  constraint_class;
   XmManagerClassPart   manager_class;
   XmScaleClassPart     scale_class;
} XmScaleClassRec;
```

```
typedef struct _XmScrollBarClassRec
   CoreClassPart        core_class;
   XmPrimitiveClassPart primitive_class;
   XmScrollBarClassPart scrollBar_class;
} XmScrollBarClassRec;
typedef struct _XmScrolledWindowClassRec {
    CoreClassPart  core_class;
    CompositeClassPart  composite_class;
    ConstraintClassPart constraint_class;
    XmManagerClassPart  manager_class;
    XmScrolledWindowClassPart     swindow_class;
} XmScrolledWindowClassRec;
typedef struct _XmSelectionBoxClassRec
     CoreClassPart            core_class;
     CompositeClassPart       composite_class;
     ConstraintClassPart      constraint_class;
     XmManagerClassPart       manager_class;
     XmBulletinBoardClassPart bulletin_board_class;
     XmSelectionBoxClassPart       selection_box_class;
} XmSelectionBoxClassRec;
typedef struct _XmSeparatorGadgetClassRec
   RectObjClassPart            rect_class;
   XmGadgetClassPart           gadget_class;
   XmSeparatorGadgetClassPart  separator_class;
} XmSeparatorGadgetClassRec;
typedef struct _XmSeparatorClassRec
   CoreClassPart          core_class;
   XmPrimitiveClassPart   primitive_class;
   XmSeparatorClassPart   separator_class;
} XmSeparatorClassRec;
typedef struct _XmTextClassRec {
    CoreClassPart core_class;
    XmPrimitiveClassPart primitive_class;
    XmTextClassPart text_class;
} XmTextClassRec;
typedef struct _XmToggleButtonGadgetClassRec {
    RectObjClassPart             rect_class;
    XmGadgetClassPart            gadget_class;
    XmLabelGadgetClassPart           label_class;
    XmToggleButtonGadgetClassPart    toggle_class;
} XmToggleButtonGadgetClassRec;
```

```
typedef struct _XmToggleButtonClassRec {
    CoreClassPart          core_class;
    XmPrimitiveClassPart       primitive_class;
    XmLabelClassPart           label_class;
    XmToggleButtonClassPart    toggle_class;
} XmToggleButtonClassRec;
typedef struct _XmPrimitiveClassRec
    CoreClassPart          core_class;
    XmPrimitiveClassPart primitive_class;
} XmPrimitiveClassRec;
typedef struct _XmGadgetClassRec
   RectObjClassPart  rect_class;
   XmGadgetClassPart gadget_class;
} XmGadgetClassRec;
typedef struct _XmManagerClassRec
    CoreClassPart        core_class;
    CompositeClassPart   composite_class;
    ConstraintClassPart constraint_class;
    XmManagerClassPart   manager_class;
} XmManagerClassRec;
```

A.3. Motif Exported Functions

Header	Return Type	Function Name
ArrowB.h	Widget	XmCreateArrowButton();
ArrowBG.h	Widget	XmCreateArrowButtonGadget();
BulletinB.h	Widget	XmCreateBulletinBoard();
BulletinB.h	Widget	XmCreateBulletinBoardDialog();
CascadeB.h	Widget	XmCreateCascadeButton();
CascadeB.h	void	XmCascadeButtonHighlight();
CascadeBG.h	Widget	XmCreateCascadeButtonGadget();
CascadeBG.h	void	XmCascadeButtonHighlight();
Command.h	Widget	XmCreateCommand();
Command.h	Widget	XmCommandGetChild();
Command.h	void	XmCommandAppendValue();
Command.h	void	XmCommandSetValue();
Command.h	void	XmCommandError();
CutPaste.h	int	XmClipboardBeginCopy();
CutPaste.h	int	XmClipboardStartCopy();
CutPaste.h	int	XmClipboardCopy();
CutPaste.h	int	XmClipboardEndCopy();

Header	Return Type	Function Name
CutPaste.h	void	XmClipboardCancelCopy();
CutPaste.h	int	XmClipboardCopyByName();
CutPaste.h	int	XmClipboardUndoCopy();
CutPaste.h	int	XmClipboardLock();
CutPaste.h	int	XmClipboardUnlock();
CutPaste.h	int	XmClipboardStartRetrieve();
CutPaste.h	int	XmClipboardRetrieve();
CutPaste.h	int	XmClipboardEndRetrieve();
CutPaste.h	int	XmClipboardInquireCount();
CutPaste.h	int	XmClipboardInquireFormat();
CutPaste.h	int	XmClipboardInquireLength();
CutPaste.h	int	XmClipboardInquirePendingItems();
CutPaste.h	int	XmClipboardWithdrawFormat();
CutPaste.h	int	XmClipboardRegisterFormat();
DialogS.h	Widget	XmCreateDialogShell();
DrawingA.h	Widget	XmCreateDrawingArea();
DrawnB.h	Widget	XmCreateDrawnButton();
FileSB.h	Widget	XmCreateFileSelectionBox();
FileSB.h	Widget	XmCreateFileSelectionDialog();
FileSB.h	Widget	XmFileSelectionBoxGetChild();
Form.h	Widget	XmCreateForm();
Form.h	Widget	XmCreateFormDialog();
Frame.h	Widget	XmCreateFrame();
Label.h	Widget	XmCreateLabel();
LabelG.h	Widget	XmCreateLabelGadget();
List.h	void	XmListAddItem();
List.h	void	XmListAddItemUnselected();
List.h	void	XmListDeleteItem();
List.h	void	XmListDeletePos();
List.h	void	XmListSelectItem();
List.h	void	XmListSelectPos();
List.h	void	XmListDeselectItem();
List.h	void	XmListDeselectPos();
List.h	void	XmListDeselectAllItems();
List.h	void	XmListSetPos();
List.h	void	XmListSetBottomPos();
List.h	void	XmListSetItem();
List.h	void	XmListSetBottomItem();
List.h	Boolean	XmListItemExists();
List.h	void	XmListSetHorizPos();
List.h	Widget	XmCreateList();
List.h	Widget	XmCreateScrolledList();
MainW.h	Widget	XmCreateMainWindow();

Header	Return Type	Function Name
MainW.h	Widget	XmMainWindowSep1();
MainW.h	Widget	XmMainWindowSep2();
MainW.h	void	XmMainWindowSetAreas();
MenuShell.h	Widget	XmCreateMenuShell();
MessageB.h	Widget	XmCreateMessageBox();
MessageB.h	Widget	XmCreateMessageDialog();
MessageB.h	Widget	XmCreateErrorDialog();
MessageB.h	Widget	XmCreateInformationDialog();
MessageB.h	Widget	XmCreateQuestionDialog();
MessageB.h	Widget	XmCreateWarningDialog();
MessageB.h	Widget	XmCreateWorkingDialog();
MessageB.h	Widget	XmMessageBoxGetChild();
PanedW.h	Widget	XmCreatePanedWindow();
PushB.h	Widget	XmCreatePushButton();
PushBG.h	Widget	XmCreatePushButtonGadget();
PushBG.h	Widget	XmCreatePushButtonGadget();
RowColumn.h	Widget	XmCreateRadioBox();
RowColumn.h	Widget	XmCreateRowColumn();
RowColumn.h	Widget	XmCreatePopupMenu();
RowColumn.h	Widget	XmCreatePulldownMenu();
RowColumn.h	Widget	XmCreateOptionMenu();
RowColumn.h	Widget	XmCreateMenuBar();
RowColumn.h	void	XmMenuPosition();
RowColumn.h	Widget	XmOptionLabelGadget();
RowColumn.h	Widget	XmOptionButtonGadget();
Scale.h	Widget	XmCreateScale();
Scale.h	void	XmScaleSetValue();
Scale.h	void	XmScaleGetValue();
ScrollBar.h	Widget	XmCreateScrollBar();
ScrollBar.h	void	XmScrollBarGetValues();
ScrollBar.h	void	XmScrollBarSetValues();
ScrolledW.h	Widget	XmCreateScrolledWindow();
ScrolledW.h	void	XmScrolledWindowSetAreas();
SelectioB.h	Widget	XmCreateSelectionBox();
SelectioB.h	Widget	XmCreateSelectionDialog();
SelectioB.h	Widget	XmCreatePromptDialog();
SelectioB.h	Widget	XmSelectionBoxGetChild();
SeparatoG.h	Widget	XmCreateSeparatorGadget();
Separator.h	Widget	XmCreateSeparator();
StringSrcP.h	XmTextSource	XmStringSourceCreate();
StringSrcP.h	void	XmStringSourceDestroy();
StringSrcP.h	char	*XmStringSourceGetValue();
StringSrcP.h	void	XmStringSourceSetValue();

Header	Return Type	Function Name
StringSrcP.h	Boolean	XmStringSourceGetEditable();
StringSrcP.h	void	XmStringSourceSetEditable();
StringSrcP.h	int	XmStringSourceGetMaxLength();
StringSrcP.h	void	XmStringSourceSetMaxLength();
Text.h	XmTextPosition	XmTextGetInsertionPosition();
Text.h	void	XmTextSetInsertionPosition();
Text.h	void	XmTextSetSource();
Text.h	void	XmTextShowPosition();
Text.h	void	XmTextDisableRedisplay();
Text.h	void	XmTextEnableRedisplay();
Text.h	Widget	XmCreateText();
Text.h	Widget	XmCreateScrolledText();
Text.h	void	XmTextClearSelection();
Text.h	char	*XmTextGetSelection();
Text.h	void	XmTextSetSelection();
Text.h	char	*XmTextGetString();
Text.h	void	XmTextSetString();
Text.h	void	XmTextReplace();
Text.h	Boolean	XmTextGetEditable();
Text.h	void	XmTextSetEditable();
Text.h	int	XmTextGetMaxLength();
Text.h	void	XmTextSetMaxLength();
TextOutP.h	LineNum	XmTextNumLines();
TextOutP.h	void	XmTextLineInfo();
TextOutP.h	LineNum	XmTextPosToLine();
TextOutP.h	void	XmTextMarkRedraw();
TextP.h	void	abort();
TextP.h	void	bcopy();
TextSrcP.h	void	XmTextInvalidate();
TextSrcP.h	void	XmTextSetHighlight();
ToggleB.h	unsigned int	XmToggleButtonGetState();
ToggleB.h	void	XmToggleButtonSetState();
ToggleB.h	Widget	XmCreateToggleButton();
ToggleBG.h	unsigned int	XmToggleButtonGadgetGetState();
ToggleBG.h	void	XmToggleButtonGadgetSetState();
ToggleBG.h	Widget	XmCreateToggleButtonGadget();
Xm.h	int	XmUseVersion;
Xm.h	void	XmCvtStringToUnitType();
Xm.h	void	XmSetFontUnit();
Xm.h	XmString	XmStringCreate();
Xm.h	XmString	XmStringDirectionCreate();
Xm.h	XmString	XmStringSeparatorCreate();
Xm.h	XmString	XmStringSegmentCreate();
Xm.h	XmString	XmStringLtoRCreate();

Header	Return Type	Function Name
Xm.h	XmString	XmStringCreateLtoR();
Xm.h	Boolean	XmStringInitContext();
Xm.h	void	XmStringFreeContext();
Xm.h	XmStringComponentType	XmStringGetNextComponent();
Xm.h	XmStringComponentType	XmStringPeekNextComponent();
Xm.h	Boolean	XmStringGetNextSegment();
Xm.h	Boolean	XmStringGetLtoR();
Xm.h	XmFontList	XmFontListCreate();
Xm.h	XmFontList	XmStringCreateFontList();
Xm.h	void	XmFontListFree();
Xm.h	XmFontList	XmFontListAdd();
Xm.h	XmFontList	XmFontListCopy();
Xm.h	XmString	XmStringConcat();
Xm.h	XmString	XmStringNConcat();
Xm.h	XmString	XmStringCopy();
Xm.h	XmString	XmStringNCopy();
Xm.h	Boolean	XmStringCompare();
Xm.h	Boolean	XmStringByteCompare();
Xm.h	int	XmStringLength();
Xm.h	Boolean	XmStringEmpty();
Xm.h	void	XmStringFree();
Xm.h	Dimension	XmStringWidth();
Xm.h	Dimension	XmStringHeight();
Xm.h	Dimension	XmStringBaseline();
Xm.h	void	XmStringExtent();
Xm.h	int	XmStringLineCount();
Xm.h	void	XmStringDraw();
Xm.h	void	XmStringDrawImage();
Xm.h	void	XmStringDrawUnderline();
Xm.h	char	*malloc();

A.4. XAW R4 Widgets

Header File	Widget Class Name
AsciiSink.h	asciiSinkObjectClass;
AsciiSrc.h	asciiSrcObjectClass;
AsciiText.h	asciiTextWidgetClass;
AsciiText.h	asciiStringWidgetClass;
AsciiText.h	asciiDiskWidgetClass;
Box.h	boxWidgetClass;
Clock.h	clockWidgetClass;
Command.h	commandWidgetClass;
Dialog.h	dialogWidgetClass;

Header File	Widget Class Name
Form.h	formWidgetClass;
Grip.h	gripWidgetClass;
Label.h	labelWidgetClass;
List.h	listWidgetClass;
Logo.h	logoWidgetClass;
Mailbox.h	mailboxWidgetClass;
MenuButton.h	menuButtonWidgetClass;
Paned.h	panedWidgetClass;
Paned.h	vPanedWidgetClass;
Scrollbar.h	scrollbarWidgetClass;
Simple.h	simpleWidgetClass;
SimpleMenu.h	simpleMenuWidgetClass;
Sme.h	smeObjectClass;
SmeBSB.h	smeBSBObjectClass;
SmeLine.h	smeLineObjectClass;
StripChart.h	stripChartWidgetClass;
Template.h	templateWidgetClass;
Text.h	textWidgetClass;
TextSink.h	textSinkObjectClass;
TextSrc.h	textSrcObjectClass;
Toggle.h	toggleWidgetClass;
Viewport.h	viewportWidgetClass;

A.5. XAW (R4) Classing

```
typedef struct _AsciiSinkClassRec {
    ObjectClassPart     object_class;
    TextSinkClassPart   text_sink_class;
    AsciiSinkClassPart  ascii_sink_class;
} AsciiSinkClassRec;
typedef struct _AsciiSrcClassRec {
    ObjectClassPart     object_class;
    TextSrcClassPart    text_src_class;
    AsciiSrcClassPart   ascii_src_class;
} AsciiSrcClassRec;
typedef struct _AsciiTextClassRec {
    CoreClassPart   core_class;
    SimpleClassPart      simple_class;
    TextClassPart   text_class;
    AsciiClassPart  ascii_class;
} AsciiTextClassRec;
```

```
typedef struct _AsciiStringClassRec {
    CoreClassPart  core_class;
    SimpleClassPart     simple_class;
    TextClassPart  text_class;
    AsciiClassPart ascii_class;
    AsciiStringClassPart string_class;
} AsciiStringClassRec;
typedef struct _AsciiDiskClassRec {
    CoreClassPart  core_class;
    SimpleClassPart     simple_class;
    TextClassPart  text_class;
    AsciiClassPart ascii_class;
    AsciiDiskClassPart  disk_class;
} AsciiDiskClassRec;
typedef struct _BoxClassRec {
    CoreClassPart  core_class;
    CompositeClassPart  composite_class;
    BoxClassPart   box_class;
} BoxClassRec;
typedef struct _ClockClassRec {
   CoreClassPart core_class;
   ClockClassPart clock_class;
   } ClockClassRec;
typedef struct _CommandClassRec {
    CoreClassPart  core_class;
    SimpleClassPart     simple_class;
    LabelClassPart label_class;
    CommandClassPart    command_class;
} CommandClassRec;
typedef struct _DialogClassRec {
    CoreClassPart  core_class;
    CompositeClassPart  composite_class;
    ConstraintClassPart constraint_class;
    FormClassPart  form_class;
    DialogClassPart     dialog_class;
} DialogClassRec;
typedef struct _FormClassRec {
    CoreClassPart  core_class;
    CompositeClassPart  composite_class;
    ConstraintClassPart constraint_class;
    FormClassPart  form_class;
} FormClassRec;
```

```
typedef struct _GripClassRec {
    CoreClassPart    core_class;
    SimpleClassPart  simple_class;
    GripClassPart    grip_class;
} GripClassRec;
typedef struct _LabelClassRec {
    CoreClassPart  core_class;
    SimpleClassPart     simple_class;
    LabelClassPart label_class;
} LabelClassRec;
typedef struct _ListClassRec {
    CoreClassPart   core_class;
    SimpleClassPart      simple_class;
    ListClassPart   list_class;
} ListClassRec;
typedef struct _LogoClassRec {
   CoreClassPart core_class;
   LogoClassPart logo_class;
   } LogoClassRec;
typedef struct _MailboxClassRec {
    CoreClassPart core_class;
    MailboxClassPart mailbox_class;
} MailboxClassRec;
typedef struct _MenuButtonClassRec {
  CoreClassPart         core_class;
  SimpleClassPart       simple_class;
  LabelClassPart        label_class;
  CommandClassPart      command_class;
  MenuButtonClassPart     menuButton_class;
} MenuButtonClassRec;
typedef struct _PanedClassRec {
    CoreClassPart       core_class;
    CompositeClassPart  composite_class;
    ConstraintClassPart constraint_class;
    PanedClassPart     paned_class;
} PanedClassRec;
typedef struct _ScrollbarClassRec {
    CoreClassPart          core_class;
    ScrollbarClassPart          scrollbar_class;
} ScrollbarClassRec;
typedef struct _SimpleMenuClassRec {
  CoreClassPart                core_class;
  CompositeClassPart      composite_class;
  ShellClassPart          shell_class;
  OverrideShellClassPart  override_shell_class;
  SimpleMenuClassPart     simpleMenu_class;
} SimpleMenuClassRec;
```

```
typedef struct _SimpleClassRec {
    CoreClassPart  core_class;
    SimpleClassPart     simple_class;
} SimpleClassRec;
typedef struct _SmeBSBClassRec {
    RectObjClassPart       rect_class;
    SmeClassPart     sme_class;
    SmeBSBClassPart  sme_bsb_class;
} SmeBSBClassRec;
typedef struct _SmeLineClassRec {
    RectObjClassPart    rect_class;
    SmeClassPart   sme_class;
    SmeLineClassPart    sme_line_class;
} SmeLineClassRec;
typedef struct _SmeClassRec {
    RectObjClassPart    rect_class;
    SmeClassPart   sme_class;
} SmeClassRec;
typedef struct _StripChartClassRec {
   CoreClassPart core_class;
   SimpleClassPart simple_class;
   StripChartClassPart strip_chart_class;
} StripChartClassRec;
typedef struct _TextClassRec {
    CoreClassPart   core_class;
    SimpleClassPart      simple_class;
    TextClassPart   text_class;
} TextClassRec;
typedef struct _TextSinkClassRec {
    ObjectClassPart     object_class;
    TextSinkClassPart   text_sink_class;
} TextSinkClassRec;
typedef struct _TextSrcClassRec {
    ObjectClassPart    object_class;
    TextSrcClassPart   textSrc_class;
} TextSrcClassRec;
typedef struct _ToggleClassRec {
    CoreClassPart  core_class;
    SimpleClassPart     simple_class;
    LabelClassPart label_class;
    CommandClassPart    command_class;
    ToggleClassPart     toggle_class;
} ToggleClassRec;
```

```
typedef struct _ViewportClassRec {
    CoreClassPart  core_class;
    CompositeClassPart  composite_class;
    ConstraintClassPart constraint_class;
    FormClassPart  form_class;
    ViewportClassPart   viewport_class;
} ViewportClassRec;
```

A..6 XAW R4 Exported Functions

Header File	Return Type	Function Name
AsciiSink.h	XawTextSink	XawAsciiSinkCreate();
Dialog.h	void	XawDialogAddButton();
Dialog.h	char	*XawDialogGetValueString();
Form.h	void	XawFormDoLayout();
List.h	void	XawListChange();
List.h	void	XawListUnhighlight();
List.h	void	XawListHighlight();
List.h	XawListReturnStruct	*XawListShowCurrent();
Paned.h	void	XawPanedSetMinMax();
Paned.h	void	XawPanedGetMinMax();
Paned.h	void	XawPanedSetRefigureMode();
Paned.h	int	XawPanedGetNumSub();
Paned.h	void	XawPanedAllowResize();
Scrollbar.h	void	XawScrollbarSetThumb();
Text.h	void	XawTextChangeOptions();
Text.h	int	XawTextGetOptions();
Text.h	void	XawTextSetLastPos();
Text.h	void	XawTextDisplay();
Text.h	void	XawTextEnableRedisplay();
Text.h	void	XawTextDisableRedisplay();
Text.h	void	XawTextSetSelectionArray();
Text.h	void	XawTextGetSelectionPos();
Text.h	void	XawTextSetSource();
Text.h	int	XawTextReplace();
Text.h	XawTextPosition	XawTextTopPosition();
Text.h	void	XawTextSetInsertionPoint();
Text.h	XawTextPosition	XawTextGetInsertionPoint();
Text.h	void	XawTextUnsetSelection();
Text.h	void	XawTextSetSelection();
Text.h	void	XawTextInvalidate();
Text.h	Widget	XawTextGetSource()
Text.h	XawTextPosition	XawTextSearch()
XawInit.h	void	XawInitializeWidgetSet();

A.7. XAW R3 Widgets

Header File	Widget Class Name
AsciiText.h	asciiStringWidgetClass;
AsciiText.h	asciiDiskWidgetClass;
Box.h	boxWidgetClass;
Clock.h	clockWidgetClass;
Command.h	commandWidgetClass;
Dialog.h	dialogWidgetClass;
Form.h	formWidgetClass;
Grip.h	gripWidgetClass;
Label.h	labelWidgetClass;
List.h	listWidgetClass;
Load.h	loadWidgetClass;
Logo.h	logoWidgetClass;
Mailbox.h	mailboxWidgetClass;
Scroll.h	scrollbarWidgetClass;
Simple.h	simpleWidgetClass;
Text.h	textWidgetClass;
VPaned.h	vPanedWidgetClass;
Viewport.h	viewportWidgetClass;

A.8. XAW R3 Classing

```
typedef struct _AsciiStringClassRec {
    CoreClassPart  core_class;
    SimpleClassPart     simple_class;
    TextClassPart  text_class;
    AsciiStringClassPart ascii_string_class;
} AsciiStringClassRec;
typedef struct _AsciiDiskClassRec {
    CoreClassPart  core_class;
    SimpleClassPart     simple_class;
    TextClassPart  text_class;
    AsciiDiskClassPart  ascii_disk_class;
} AsciiDiskClassRec;
typedef struct _BoxClassRec {
    CoreClassPart  core_class;
    CompositeClassPart  composite_class;
    BoxClassPart   box_class;
} BoxClassRec;
```

```
typedef struct _ClockClassRec {
   CoreClassPart core_class;
   ClockClassPart clock_class;
   } ClockClassRec;
typedef struct _CommandClassRec {
    CoreClassPart  core_class;
    SimpleClassPart     simple_class;
    LabelClassPart label_class;
    CommandClassPart    command_class;
} CommandClassRec;
typedef struct _DialogClassRec {
    CoreClassPart  core_class;
    CompositeClassPart  composite_class;
    ConstraintClassPart constraint_class;
    FormClassPart  form_class;
    DialogClassPart     dialog_class;
} DialogClassRec;
typedef struct _FormClassRec {
    CoreClassPart     core_class;
    CompositeClassPart     composite_class;
    ConstraintClassPart    constraint_class;
    FormClassPart     form_class;
} FormClassRec;
typedef struct _GripClassRec {
    CoreClassPart    core_class;
    SimpleClassPart  simple_class;
    GripClassPart    grip_class;
} GripClassRec;
typedef struct _LabelClassRec {
    CoreClassPart  core_class;
    SimpleClassPart     simple_class;
    LabelClassPart label_class;
} LabelClassRec;
typedef struct _ListClassRec {
    CoreClassPart     core_class;
    SimpleClassPart     simple_class;
    ListClassPart     list_class;
} ListClassRec;
typedef struct _LoadClassRec {
   CoreClassPart core_class;
   LoadClassPart load_class;
   } LoadClassRec;
```

```
typedef struct _LogoClassRec {
   CoreClassPart core_class;
   LogoClassPart logo_class;
   } LogoClassRec;
typedef struct _MailboxClassRec {
    CoreClassPart core_class;
    MailboxClassPart mailbox_class;
} MailboxClassRec;
typedef struct _ScrollbarClassRec {
    CoreClassPart        core_class;
    ScrollbarClassPart       scrollbar_class;
} ScrollbarClassRec;
typedef struct _SimpleClassRec {
    CoreClassPart  core_class;
    SimpleClassPart     simple_class;
} SimpleClassRec;
typedef struct _TextClassRec {
    CoreClassPart  core_class;
    SimpleClassPart     simple_class;
    TextClassPart  text_class;
} TextClassRec;
typedef struct _VPanedClassRec {
    CoreClassPart        core_class;
    CompositeClassPart   composite_class;
    ConstraintClassPart  constraint_class;
    VPanedClassPart      vpaned_class;
} VPanedClassRec;
typedef struct _ViewportClassRec {
    CoreClassPart  core_class;
    CompositeClassPart   composite_class;
    ConstraintClassPart  constraint_class;
    FormClassPart  form_class;
    ViewportClassPart   viewport_class;
} ViewportClassRec;
```

A.9. XAW R3 Exported Functions

Header	Return Type	Function Name
Dialog.h	void	XtDialogAddButton();
Dialog.h	char	*XtDialogGetValueString();
List.h	void	XtListChange();
List.h	void	XtListUnhighlight();
List.h	void	XtListHighlight();
List.h	XtListReturnStruct	*XtListShowCurrent();

Header	Return Type	Function Name
Scroll.h	void	XtScrollBarSetThumb();
Text.h	void	XtTextDisplay();
Text.h	void	XtTextSetSelectionArray();
Text.h	void	XtTextSetLastPos();
Text.h	void	XtTextGetSelectionPos();
Text.h	void	XtTextSetSource();
Text.h	int	XtTextReplace();
Text.h	XtTextPosition	XtTextTopPosition();
Text.h	void	XtTextSetInsertionPoint();
Text.h	XtTextPosition	XtTextGetInsertionPoint();
Text.h	void	XtTextUnsetSelection();
Text.h	void	XtTextChangeOptions();
Text.h	int	XtTextGetOptions();
Text.h	void	XtTextSetSelection();
Text.h	void	XtTextInvalidate();
Text.h	XtTextSource	XtTextGetSource()
Text.h	XtTextSink	XtAsciiSinkCreate();
Text.h	void	XtAsciiSinkDestroy();
Text.h	XtTextSource	XtDiskSourceCreate();
Text.h	void	XtDiskSourceDestroy();
Text.h	XtTextSource	XtStringSourceCreate();
Text.h	void	XtStringSourceDestroy();
VPaned.h	void	XtPanedSetMinMax();
VPaned.h	void	XtPanedRefigureMode();
VPaned.h	void	XtPanedGetMinMax();
VPaned.h	int	XtPanedGetNumSub();

Appendix B

Quick Xt Reference Guide X11R4

This appendix lists all the typedefs, function types, and function definitions for the X11R4 Intrinsics. Full descriptions of the functions can be found in the manuals provided on the MIT release tapes.

The following was compiled by using the various header files:

```
<X11/Intrinsic.h>
<X11/Core.h>
<X11/Composite.h>
<X11/Constraint.h>
<X11/Object.h>
<X11/RectObj.h>
```

```
#define XtNumber(arr)         ((Cardinal) (sizeof(arr) / sizeof(arr[0])))
```

B.1. Typedefs

```
typedef char *String;
typedef struct _WidgetRec *Widget;
typedef Widget *WidgetList;
typedef struct _WidgetClassRec *WidgetClass;
typedef struct _CompositeRec *CompositeWidget;
typedef struct _XtActionsRec *XtActionList;
typedef struct _XtEventRec *XtEventTable;
typedef struct _XtBoundAccActionRec *XtBoundAccActions;
typedef struct _XtAppStruct *XtAppContext;
typedef unsigned long   XtValueMask;
typedef unsigned long   XtIntervalId;
typedef unsigned long   XtInputId;
typedef unsigned long   XtWorkProcId;
typedef unsigned int    XtGeometryMask;
```

```
typedef unsigned long   XtGCMask;    /* Mask of values that are
                                        used by widget*/
typedef unsigned long   Pixel;       /* Index into colormap        */
typedef char        Boolean;
typedef long        XtArgVal;
typedef unsigned char   XtEnum;
typedef unsigned int    Cardinal;
typedef unsigned short  Dimension;   /* Size in pixels             */
typedef short       Position;    /* Offset from 0 coordinate       */
typedef char*       XtPointer;
typedef XtPointer    Opaque;
```

B.2. BASE Widget Typedefs

```
typedef struct _WidgetClassRec *CoreWidgetClass;
typedef struct _WidgetRec *CoreWidget;
typedef struct _CompositeClassRec *CompositeWidgetClass;
typedef struct _ConstraintClassRec *ConstraintWidgetClass;
typedef struct _ObjectRec *Object;
typedef struct _ObjectClassRec *ObjectClass;
typedef struct _RectObjRec *RectObj;
typedef struct _RectObjClassRec *RectObjClass;
```

B.3. Translation Management Typedefs

```
typedef struct _TranslationData *XtTranslations;
typedef struct _TranslationData *XtAccelerators;
typedef unsigned int Modifiers;
```

B.4. Intrinsic Specific Procedure Typedefs

```
typedef void (*XtActionProc)(
    Widget          /* widget */,
    XEvent*         /* event */,
    String*         /* params */,
    Cardinal*       /* num_params */
);

typedef XtActionProc* XtBoundActions;
```

```
typedef struct _XtActionsRec{
    String      string;
    XtActionProc proc;
} XtActionsRec;

typedef enum {
/* address mode          parameter representation    */
/* ------------          ------------------------    */
    XtAddress,           /* address              */
    XtBaseOffset,    /* offset           */
    XtImmediate,     /* constant              */
    XtResourceString,    /* resource name string        */
    XtResourceQuark,     /* resource name quark         */
    XtWidgetBaseOffset,  /* offset from ancestor        */
    XtProcedureArg  /* procedure to invoke       */
} XtAddressMode;

typedef struct {
    XtAddressMode   address_mode;
    XtPointer     address_id;
    Cardinal      size;
} XtConvertArgRec, *XtConvertArgList;

typedef void (*XtConvertArgProc)(
    Widget          /* widget */,
    Cardinal*       /* size */,
    XrmValue*       /* value */
);
typedef struct {
    XtGeometryMask request_mode;
    Position x, y;
    Dimension width, height, border_width;
    Widget sibling;
    int stack_mode;   /* Above, Below, TopIf, BottomIf, Opposite,
                         DontChange */
} XtWidgetGeometry;

/* Additions to Xlib geometry requests: ask what would happen,
   don't do it */
#define XtCWQueryOnly    (1 << 7)

/* Additions to Xlib stack modes: don't change stack order */
#define XtSMDontChange    5
```

```
typedef void (*XtConverter)(
    XrmValue*       /* args */,
    Cardinal*       /* num_args */,
    XrmValue*       /* from */,
    Xrmvalue*       /* to */
);

typedef Boolean (*XtTypeConverter)(
    Display*        /* dpy */,
    XrmValue*       /* args */,
    Cardinal*       /* num_args */,
    XrmValue*       /* from */,
    XrmValue*       /* to */,
    XtPointer*      /* converter_data */,
);

typedef void (*XtDestructor)(
    XtAppContext    /* app */,
    XrmValue*       /* to */,
    XtPointer           /* converter_data */,
    XrmValue*       /* args */,
    Cardinal*       /* num_args */
);

typedef Opaque XtCacheRef;
typedef Opaque XtActionHookId;

typedef void (*XtActionHookProc)(
    Widget          /* w */,
    XtPointer       /* client_data */,
    String          /* action_name */,
    XEvent*         /* event */,
    String*         /* params */,
    Cardinal*       /* num_params */
);

typedef void (*XtKeyProc)(
    Display*        /* dpy */,
    KeyCode*        /* keycode */,
    Modifiers*          /* modifiers */,
    Modifiers*          /* modifiers_return */,
    KeySym*         /* keysym_return */
);
```

```
typedef void (*XtCaseProc)(
    KeySym*          /* keysym */,
    KeySym*          /* lower_return */,
    KeySym*          /* upper_return */
);

typedef void (*XtEventHandler)(
    Widget           /* widget */,
    XtPointer        /* closure */,
    XEvent*          /* event */,
    Boolean*         /* continue_to_dispatch */
);
typedef unsigned long EventMask;

typedef enum {XtListHead, XtListTail } XtListPosition;

typedef unsigned long   XtInputMask;
#define XtInputNoneMask         0L
#define XtInputReadMask         (1L<<0)
#define XtInputWriteMask        (1L<<1)
#define XtInputExceptMask       (1L<<2)

typedef void (*XtTimerCallbackProc)(
    XtPointer        /* closure */,
    XtIntervalId*    /* id */
);

typedef void (*XtInputCallbackProc)(
    XtPointer             /* closure */,
    int*                  /* source */,
    XtInputId*            /* id */
);

typedef struct {
    String    name;
    XtArgVal  value;
} Arg, *ArgList;

typedef XtPointer    XtVarArgsList;

typedef void (*XtCallbackProc)(
    Widget     /* widget */,
    XtPointer  /* closure */, /* data the application registered */
    XtPointer  /* call_data */  /* callback specific data */
);
```

```
typedef struct _XtCallbackRec {
    XtCallbackProc  callback;
    XtPointer       closure;
} XtCallbackRec, *XtCallbackList;

typedef enum {
    XtCallbackNoList,
    XtCallbackHasNone,
    XtCallbackHasSome
} XtCallbackStatus;

typedef enum  {
    XtGeometryYes,      /* Request accepted. */
    XtGeometryNo,       /* Request denied. */
    XtGeometryAlmost,   /* Request denied, but willing to take
                           replyBox. */
    XtGeometryDone      /* Request accepted and done. */
} XtGeometryResult;

typedef enum {XtGrabNone, XtGrabNonexclusive, XtGrabExclusive}
             XtGrabKind;

typedef struct {
    Widget  shell_widget;
    Widget  enable_widget;
} XtPopdownIDRec, *XtPopdownID;

typedef struct _XtResource {
    String    resource_name; /* Resource name                    */
    String    resource_class;/* Resource class               */
    String    resource_type; /* Representation type desired      */
    Cardinal  resource_size; /* Size in bytes of representation  */
    Cardinal  resource_offset;/* Offset from base to put resource
                                 value    */
    String    default_type;  /* Representation type of specified
                                default */
    XtPointer default_addr;  /* Address of default resource
*/
} XtResource, *XtResourceList;
```

```
typedef void (*XtErrorMsgHandler)(
    String          /* name */,
    String          /* type */,
    String          /* class */,
    String          /* defaultp */,
    String*         /* params */,
    Cardinal*       /* num_params */
);

typedef void (*XtErrorHandler)(
  String      /* msg */
);

typedef Boolean (*XtWorkProc)(
    XtPointer           /* closure */    /* data the application
                                            registered */
);

typedef struct {
    char match;
    String substitution;
} SubstitutionRec, *Substitution;

typedef Boolean (*XtFilePredicate)( /* String filename */ );

typedef XtPointer XtRequestId;

/*
 * Routine to get the value of a selection as a given type.
 * Returns TRUE if it successfully got the value as requested,
 * FALSE otherwise. Selection is the atom describing the type of
 * selection (e.g., primary or secondary). Value is set to the
 * pointer of the converted value, with length elements of data,
 * each of size indicated by format. (This pointer will be freed
 * using XtFree when the selection has been delivered to the
 * requestor.)  Target is the type that the conversion should use
 * if possible; type is returned as the actual type returned.
 * Format should be either 8, 16, or 32, and specifies the word
 * size of the selection, so that Xlib and the server can convert
 * it between different machine types. */
```

```
typedef Boolean (*XtConvertSelectionProc)(
    Widget          /* widget */,
    Atom*           /* selection */,
    Atom*           /* target */,
    Atom*           /* type_return */,
    XtPointer*          /* value_return */,
    unsigned long* /* length_return */,
    int*      /* format_return */
);

/*
 * Routine to inform a widget that it no longer owns the given
 * selection.  */

typedef void (*XtLoseSelectionProc)(
    Widget          /* widget */,
    Atom*           /* selection */
);

/*
 * Routine to inform the selection owner when a selection requestor
 * has successfully retrieved the selection value.
 */

typedef void (*XtSelectionDoneProc)(
    Widget          /* widget */,
    Atom*           /* selection */,
    Atom*           /* target */
);

/*
 * Routine to call back when a requested value has been obtained
 * for a selection.
 */

typedef void (*XtSelectionCallbackProc)(
    Widget          /* widget */,
    XtPointer           /* closure */,
    Atom*           /* selection */,
    Atom*           /* type */,
    XtPointer           /* value */,
    unsigned long* /* length */,
    int*      /* format */
);
```

```
typedef void (*XtLoseSelectionIncrProc)(
    Widget          /* widget */,
    Atom*           /* selection */,
    XtPointer            /* client_data */
);

typedef void (*XtSelectionDoneIncrProc)(
    Widget          /* widget */,
    Atom*           /* selection */,
    Atom*           /* target */,
    XtRequestId*    /* receiver_id */,
    XtPointer            /* client_data */
);

typedef Boolean (*XtConvertSelectionIncrProc)(
    Widget          /* widget */,
    Atom*           /* selection */,
    Atom*           /* target */,
    Atom*           /* type */,
    XtPointer*           /* value */,
    unsigned long* /* length */,
    int*      /* format */,
    unsigned long* /* max_length */,
    XtPointer            /* client_data */,
    XtRequestId*    /* receiver_id */
);
typedef void (*XtCancelConvertSelectionProc)(
    Widget          /* widget */,
    Atom*           /* selection */,
    Atom*           /* target */,
    XtRequestId*    /* receiver_id */,
    XtPointer            /* client_data */
);
```

B.5. Container Routines

```
void XtManagechildren(
    WidgetList           /* children */,
    Cardinal        /* num_children */
);
void XtManageChild(
    Widget          /* child */
);
```

```
void XtUnmanageChildren(
    WidgetList          /* children */,
    Cardinal        /* num_children */
);
void XtUnmanageChild(
    Widget          /* child */
);
```

B.6. Resource Conversion

```
Boolean XtConvertAndStore(
    Widget          /* widget */,
    CONST String    /* from_type */,
    XrmValue*       /* from */,
    CONST String    /* to_type */,
    XrmValue*       /* to_in_out */
);

Boolean XtCallConverter(
    Display*        /* dpy */,
    XtTypeConverter     /* converter */,
    XrmValuePtr     /* args */,
    Cardinal        /* num_args */,
    XrmValuePtr     /* from */,
    XrmValue*       /* to_return */,
    XtCacheRef*         /* cache_ref_return */
);
```

B.7. Event Handling

```
Boolean XtDispatchEvent(
    XEvent*         /* event */
);

Boolean XtCallAcceptFocus(
    Widget          /* widget */,
    Time*           /* t */
);

Boolean XtPeekEvent(
    XEvent*         /* event */
);
```

```
Boolean XtAppPeekEvent(
    XtAppContext    /* appContext */,
    XEvent*         /* event */
);
```

B.8. Checking Routines

```
Boolean XtIsSubclass(
    Widget          /* widget */,
    WidgetClass     /* widgetClass */
);

Boolean XtIsObject(
    Widget          /* object */
);

Boolean _XtCheckSubclassFlag( /* implementation-private */
    Widget          /* object */,
    XtEnum          /* type_flag */
);

Boolean _XtIsSubclassOf( /* implementation-private */
    Widget          /* object */,
    WidgetClass         /* widget_class */,
    WidgetClass         /* flag_class */,
    XtEnum          /* type_flag */
);

Boolean XtIsManaged(
    Widget          /* rectobj */
);

Boolean XtIsRealized(
    Widget          /* widget */
);

Boolean XtIsSensitive(
    Widget          /* widget */
);
```

B.9. Selection Management

```
/*
 * Set the given widget to own the selection.  The convertProc
 * should be called when someone wants the current value of the
 * selection. If it is not null, the
 * losesSelection gets called whenever the window no longer owns
 * the selection (because someone else took it). If it is not
 * null, the doneProc gets called when the widget has provided the
 * current value of the selection to a requestor and the requestor
 * has indicated that it has succeeded in reading it by deleting
 * the property.
 */

Boolean XtOwnSelection(
    Widget              /* widget */,
    Atom                /* selection */,
    Time                /* time */,
    XtConvertSelectionProc  /* convert */,
    XtLoseSelectionProc /* lose */,
    XtSelectionDoneProc /* done */
);

/* incremental selection interface */

Boolean XtOwnSelectionIncremental(
    Widget              /* widget */,
    Atom                /* selection */,
    Time                /* time */,
    XtConvertSelectionIncrProc /* convert_callback */,
    XtLoseSelectionIncrProc /* lose_callback */,
    XtSelectionDoneIncrProc /* done_callback */,
    XtCancelSelectionCallbackProc /* cancel_callback */,
    XtPointer                /* client_data */
);
```

B.10. Geometry Management

```
XtGeometryResult XtMakeResizeRequest(
    Widget              /* widget */,
    Dimension           /* width */,
    Dimension                /* height */,
    Dimension*               /* replyWidth */,
    Dimension*               /* replyHeight */
);
```

```
void XtTransformCoords(
    Widget          /* widget */,
    Position        /* x */,
    Position        /* y */,
    Position*       /* rootx */,
    Position*       /* rooty */
);

void XtStringConversionWarning(
    CONST String  /* from */,  /* String attempted to convert.   */
    CONST String /* toType */ /* Type attempted to convert it to.*/
);

void XtDisplayStringConversionWarning(
    Display*        /* dpy */,
    CONST String    /* from */,  /* String attempted to convert.  */
    CONST String /* toType *//* Type attempted to convert it to. */
);

XtConvertArgRec colorConvertArgs[];
XtConvertArgRec screenConvertArg[];

void XtAppAddConverter( /* obsolete */
    XtAppContext    /* app */,
    CONST String    /* from_type */,
    CONST String    /* to_type */,
    XtConverter     /* converter */,
    XtConvertArgList    /* convert_args */,
    Cardinal        /* num_args */
);

void XtAddConverter( /* obsolete */
    CONST String    /* from_type */,
    CONST String    /* to_type */,
    XtConverter     /* converter */,
    XtConvertArgList    /* convert_args */,
    Cardinal        /* num_args */
);
```

```
void XtSetTypeConverter(
    CONST String    /* from_type */,
    CONST String    /* to_type */,
    XtTypeConverter      /* converter */,
    XtConvertArgList     /* convert_args */,
    Cardinal        /* num_args */,
    XtCacheType     /* cache_type */,
    XtDestructor    /* destructor */
);

void XtAppSetTypeConverter(
    XtAppContext    /* app_context */,
    CONST String    /* from_type */,
    CONST String    /* to_type */,
    XtTypeConverter      /* converter */,
    XtConvertArgList     /* convert_args */,
    Cardinal        /* num_args */,
    XtCacheType     /* cache_type */,
    XtDestructor    /* destructor */
);

void XtConvert(
    Widget          /* widget */,
    CONST String    /* from_type */,
    XrmValue*       /* from */,
    CONST String    /* to_type */,
    XrmValue*       /* to_return */
);

void XtDirectConvert(
    XtConverter     /* converter */,
    XrmValuePtr     /* args */,
    Cardinal        /* num_args */,
    XrmValuePtr     /* from */,
    XrmValue*       /* to_return */
);
```

B.11. Translation Management

```
XtTranslations XtParseTranslationTable(
    CONST String    /* source */
);
```

```
XtAccelerators XtParseAcceleratorTable(
    CONST String   /* source */
);

void XtOverrideTranslations(
    Widget        /* widget */,
    XtTranslations    /* new */
);

void XtAugmentTranslations(
    Widget          /* widget */,
    XtTranslations      /* new */
);

void XtInstallAccelerators(
    Widget          /* destination */,
    Widget          /* source */
);

void XtInstallAllAccelerators(
    Widget          /* destination */,
    Widget          /* source */
);

void XtUninstallTranslations(
    Widget          /* widget */
);

void XtAppAddActions(
    XtAppContext   /* app */,
    XtActionList   /* actions */,
    Cardinal       /* num_actions */
);

void XtAddActions(
    XtActionList   /* actions */,
    Cardinal       /* num_actions */
);

XtActionHookId XtAppAddActionHook(
    XtAppContext   /* app */,
    XtActionHookProc    /* proc */,
    XtPointer           /* client_data */
);
```

```
void XtRemoveActionHook(
    XtActionHookId      /* id */
);

void XtCallActionProc(
    Widget          /* widget */,
    CONST String    /* action */,
    XEvent*         /* event */,
    String*         /* params */,
    Cardinal        /* num_params */
);
void XtRegisterGrabAction(
    XtActionProc    /* action_proc */,
    Boolean         /* owner_events */,
    unsigned int    /* event_mask */,
    int             /* pointer_mode */,
    int             /* keyboard_mode */
);

void XtSetMultiClickTime(
    Display*        /* dpy */,
    int        /* milliseconds */
);


int XtGetMultiClickTime(
    Display*        /* dpy */
);

KeySym XtGetActionKeysym(
    XEvent*         /* event */,
    Modifiers*           /* modifiers_return */
);
```

B.12. Keycode and Keysym Procedures

```
void XtTranslateKeycode(
    Display*        /* dpy */,
    KeyCode         /* keycode */,
    Modifiers            /* modifiers */,
    Modifiers*           /* modifiers_return */,
    KeySym*         /* keysym_return */
);
```

```
void XtTranslateKey(
    Display*        /* dpy */,
    KeyCode*        /* keycode */,
    Modifiers*          /* modifiers */,
    Modifiers*          /* modifiers_return */,
    KeySym*         /* keysym_return */
);

void XtSetKeyTranslator(
    Display*        /* dpy */,
    XtKeyProc           /* proc */
);

void XtRegisterCaseConverter(
    Display*        /* dpy */,
    XtCaseProc          /* proc */,
    KeySym          /* start */,
    KeySym          /* stop */
);


void XtConvertCase(
    Display*        /* dpy */,
    KeySym          /* keysym */,
    KeySym*         /* lower_return */,
    KeySym*         /* upper_return */
);

KeySym* XtGetKeysymTable(
    Display*        /* dpy */,
    KeyCode*        /* min_keycode_return */,
    int*      /* keysyms_per_keycode_return */
);

void XtKeysymToKeycodeList(
    Display*        /* dpy */,
    KeySym          /* keysym */,
    KeyCode**       /* keycodes_return */,
    Cardinal*       /* keycount_return */
);
```

B.13. Event Management

```
#define XtAllEvents ((EventMask) -1L)

void XtInsertEventHandler(
    Widget          /* widget */,
    EventMask           /* eventMask */,
    Boolean         /* nonmaskable */,
    XtEventHandler      /* proc */,
    XtPointer           /* closure */,
    XtListPosition      /* position */
);

void XtInsertRawEventHandler(
    Widget                /* widget */,
    EventMask                 /* eventMask */,
    Boolean               /* nonmaskable */,
    XtEventHandler            /* proc */,
    XtPointer                 /* closure */,
    XtListPosition            /* position */
);

void XtAddEventHandler(
    Widget          /* widget */,
    EventMask           /* eventMask */,
    Boolean         /* nonmaskable */,
    XtEventHandler      /* proc */,
    XtPointer           /* closure */
);

void XtRemoveEventHandler(
    Widget          /* widget */,
    EventMask           /* eventMask */,
    Boolean         /* nonmaskable */,
    XtEventHandler      /* proc */,
    XtPointer           /* closure */
);

void XtAddRawEventHandler(
    Widget          /* widget */,
    EventMask           /* eventMask */,
    Boolean         /* nonmaskable */,
    XtEventHandler      /* proc */,
    XtPointer           /* closure */
);
```

```
void XtRemoveRawEventHandler(
    Widget          /* widget */,
    EventMask           /* eventMask */,
    Boolean         /* nonmaskable */,
    XtEventHandler      /* proc */,
    XtPointer           /* closure */
);

void XtInsertEventHandler(
    Widget          /* widget */,
    EventMask           /* eventMask */,
    Boolean         /* nonmaskable */,
    XtEventHandler      /* proc */,
    XtPointer           /* closure */,
    XtListPosition      /* position */
);

void XtInsertRawEventHandler(
    Widget          /* widget */,
    EventMask           /* eventMask */,
    Boolean         /* nonmaskable */,
    XtEventHandler      /* proc */,
    XtPointer           /* closure */,
    XtListPosition      /* position */
);

EventMask XtBuildEventMask(
    Widget          /* widget */
);

void XtAddGrab(
    Widget          /* widget */,
    Boolean         /* exclusive */,
    Boolean         /* spring_loaded */
);

void XtRemoveGrab(
    Widget          /* widget */
);

void XtProcessEvent(
    XtInputMask         /* mask */
);
```

```
void XtAppProcessEvent(
    XtAppContext          /* app */,
    XtInputMask           /* mask */
);

void XtMainLoop(
    void
);

void XtAppMainLoop(
    XtAppContext        /* app */
);

void XtAddExposureToRegion(
    XEvent*         /* event */,
    Region          /* region */
);

void XtSetKeyboardFocus(
    Widget          /* subtree */,
    Widget          /* descendent */
);

Time XtLastTimestampProcessed(
    Display*        /* dpy */
);
```

B.14. Event Gathering Routines

```
XtIntervalId XtAddTimeOut(
    unsigned long  /* interval */,
    XtTimerCallbackProc /* proc */,
    XtPointer           /* closure */
);

XtIntervalId XtAppAddTimeOut(
    XtAppContext   /* app */,
    unsigned long  /* interval */,
    XtTimerCallbackProc /* proc */,
    XtPointer           /* closure */
);
```

```
void XtRemoveTimeOut(
    XtIntervalId   /* timer */
);

XtInputId XtAddInput(
    int        /* source */,
    XtPointer            /* condition */,
    XtInputCallbackProc /* proc */,
    XtPointer            /* closure */
);

XtInputId XtAppAddInput(
    XtAppContext         /* app */,
    int        /* source */,
    XtPointer            /* condition */,
    XtInputCallbackProc /* proc */,
    XtPointer            /* closure */
);

void XtRemoveInput(
    XtInputId            /* id */
);

void XtNextEvent(
    XEvent*        /* event */
);

void XtAppNextEvent(
    XtAppContext   /* appContext */,
    XEvent*        /* event */
);

#define XtIMXEvent       1
#define XtIMTimer        2
#define XtIMAlternateInput   4
#define XtIMAll (XtIMXEvent | XtIMTimer | XtIMAlternateInput)

XtInputMask XtPending(
    void
);

XtInputMask XtAppPending(
    XtAppContext   /* appContext */
);
```

B.15. Logic Macros

```
#define XtIsRectObj(object)  (_XtCheckSubclassFlag(object,
(XtEnum)0x02))
#define XtIsWidget(object)   (_XtCheckSubclassFlag(object,
(XtEnum)0x04))
#define XtIsComposite(widget)     (_XtCheckSubclassFlag(widget,
(XtEnum)0x08))
#define XtIsConstraint(widget)    (_XtCheckSubclassFlag(widget,
(XtEnum)0x10))
#define XtIsShell(widget)    (_XtCheckSubclassFlag(widget,
(XtEnum)0x20))
#define XtIsOverrideShell(widget) \
    (_XtIsSubclassOf(widget,
(WidgetClass)overrideShellWidgetClass, \
                (WidgetClass)shellWidgetClass, (XtEnum)0x20))
#define XtIsWMShell(widget)  (_XtCheckSubclassFlag(widget,
(XtEnum)0x40))
#define XtIsVendorShell(widget)   \
    (_XtIsSubclassOf(widget, (WidgetClass)vendorShellWidgetClass, \
                (WidgetClass)wmShellWidgetClass, (XtEnum)0x40))
#define XtIsTransientShell(widget) \
    (_XtIsSubclassOf(widget,
                (WidgetClass)transientShellWidgetClass, \
                (WidgetClass)wmShellWidgetClass, (XtEnum)0x40))
#define XtIsTopLevelShell(widget)
                (_XtCheckSubclassFlag(widget, (XtEnum)0x80))
#define XtIsApplicationShell(widget) \
    (_XtIsSubclassOf(widget,
                (WidgetClass)applicationShellWidgetClass, \
                (WidgetClass)topLevelShellWidgetClass, (XtEnum)0x80))
```

B.16. Widget State

```
void XtRealizeWidget(
    Widget          /* widget */
);

void XtUnrealizeWidget(
    Widget          /* widget */
);
```

```
void XtDestroyWidget(
    Widget          /* widget */
);

void XtSetSensitive(
    Widget          /* widget */,
    Boolean         /* sensitive */
);

void XtSetMappedWhenManaged(
    Widget          /* widget */,
    Boolean         /* mappedWhenManaged */
);

Widget XtNameToWidget(
    Widget          /* root */,
    CONST String    /* name */
);

Widget XtWindowToWidget(
    Display*        /* display */,
    Window          /* window */
);
```

B.17. Argument List

```
#define XtSetArg(arg, n, d) \
    ((void)( (arg).name = (n), (arg).value = (XtArgVal)(d) ))

ArgList XtMergeArgLists(
    ArgList         /* args1 */,
    Cardinal        /* num_args1 */,
    ArgList         /* args2 */,
    Cardinal        /* num_args2 */
);

#define XtVaNestedList  "XtVaNestedList"
#define XtVaTypedArg    "XtVaTypedArg"

XtVarArgsList XtVaCreateArgsList(
    XtPointer       /*unused*/, ...
);
```

B.18. Information Gathering Routines

```
Display *XtDisplay(
            Widget          /* widget */
);

Display *XtDisplayOfObject(
            Widget          /* widget */
);

Screen *XtScreen(
    Widget          /* widget */
);

Screen *XtScreenOfObject(
    Widget          /* object */
);

Window XtWindow(
    Widget          /* widget */
);

Window XtWindowOfObject(
    Widget          /* object */
);

String XtName(
    Widget          /* object */
);

WidgetClass XtSuperclass(
    Widget          /* object */
);

WidgetClass XtClass(
    Widget          /* object */
);

Widget XtParent(
    Widget          /* widget */
);
```

B.19. Widget Mapping

```
#define XtMapWidget(widget)  XMapWindow(XtDisplay(widget),
                             XtWindow(widget))
#define XtUnmapWidget(widget)    \
        XUnmapWindow(XtDisplay(widget), XtWindow(widget))
```

B.20. Callbacks

```
void XtAddCallback(
    Widget          /* widget */,
    CONST String    /* callback_name */,
    XtCallbackProc      /* callback */,
    XtPointer           /* closure */
);

void XtRemoveCallback(
    Widget          /* widget */,
    CONST String    /* callback_name */,
    XtCallbackProc      /* callback */,
    XtPointer           /* closure */
);

void XtAddCallbacks(
    Widget          /* widget */,
    CONST String    /* callback_name */,
    XtCallbackList      /* callbacks */
);

void XtRemoveCallbacks(
    Widget          /* widget */,
    CONST String    /* callback_name */,
    XtCallbackList      /* callbacks */
);

void XtRemoveAllCallbacks(
    Widget          /* widget */,
    CONST String    /* callback_name */
);

void XtCallCallbacks(
    Widget          /* widget */,
    CONST String    /* callback_name */,
    XtPointer           /* call_data */
);
```

```
void XtCallCallbackList(
    Widget          /* widget */,
    XtCallbackList      /* callbacks */,
    XtPointer           /* call_data */
);

XtCallbackStatus XtHasCallbacks(
    Widget          /* widget */,
    CONST String    /* callback_name */
);
```

B.21. Geometry Management

```
XtGeometryResult XtMakeGeometryRequest(
    Widget          /* widget */,
    XtWidgetGeometry*   /* request */,
    XtWidgetGeometry*   /* reply_return */
);

XtGeometryResult XtQueryGeometry(
    Widget          /* widget */,
    XtWidgetGeometry*   /* intended */,
    XtWidgetGeometry*   /* reply_return */
);
```

B.22. Pop-ups

```
Widget XtCreatePopupShell(
    CONST String    /* name */,
    WidgetClass     /* widgetClass */,
    Widget          /* parent */,
    ArgList         /* args */,
    Cardinal        /* num_args */
);

Widget XtVaCreatePopupShell(
    CONST String     /* name */,
    WidgetClass          /* widgetClass */,
    Widget           /* parent */,
);
```

```
void XtPopup(
    Widget          /* widget */,
    XtGrabKind          /* grab_kind */
);

void XtPopupSpringLoaded(
    Widget          /* widget */
);

void XtCallbackNone(
    Widget          /* widget */,
    XtPointer           /* closure */,
    XtPointer           /* call_data */
);

void XtCallbackNonexclusive(
    Widget          /* widget */,
    XtPointer           /* closure */,
    XtPointer           /* call_data */
);

void XtCallbackExclusive(
    Widget          /* widget */,
    XtPointer           /* closure */,
    XtPointer           /* call_data */
);

void XtPopdown(
    Widget          /* widget */
);

void XtCallbackPopdown(
    Widget          /* widget */,
    XtPointer           /* closure */,
    XtPointer           /* call_data */
);

void XtMenuPopupAction(
    Widget          /* widget */,
    XEvent*         /* event */,
    String*         /* params */,
    Cardinal*       /* num_params */
);
```

B.23. Widget Creation

```
Widget XtCreateWidget(
    CONST String    /* name */,
    WidgetClass     /* widget_class */,
    Widget          /* parent */,
    ArgList         /* args */,
    Cardinal        /* num_args */
);

Widget XtCreateManagedWidget(
    CONST String    /* name */,
    WidgetClass     /* widget_class */,
    Widget          /* parent */,
    ArgList         /* args */,
    Cardinal        /* num_args */
);

Widget XtVaCreateWidget(
    CONST String     /* name */,
    WidgetClass            /* widget */,
    Widget           /* parent */,
);

Widget XtVaCreateManagedWidget(
    CONST String     /* name */,
    WidgetClass            /* widget_class */,
    Widget           /* parent */,
);

Widget XtCreateApplicationShell(
    CONST String    /* name */,
    WidgetClass     /* widget_class */,
    ArgList         /* args */,
    Cardinal        /* num_args */
);

Widget XtAppCreateShell(
    CONST String    /* name */,
    CONST String    /* class */,
    WidgetClass     /* widget_class */,
    Display*        /* display */,
    ArgList         /* args */,
    Cardinal        /* num_args */
);
```

```
Widget XtVaAppCreateShell(
    CONST String    /* name */,
    CONST String    /* class */,
    WidgetClass         /* widget_class */,
    Display*        /* display */,
    ...
);
```

B.24. Toolkit Initialization

```
void XtToolkitInitialize(
    void
);

void XtDisplayInitialize(
    XtAppContext    /* appContext */,
    Display*        /* dpy */,
    CONST String    /* name */,
    CONST String    /* class */,
    XrmOptionDescRec*   /* options */,
    Cardinal        /* num_options */,
    Cardinal*       /* argc */,
    char**          /* argv */
);

Widget XtAppInitialize(
    XtAppContext*  /* app_context_return */,
    CONST String        /* application_class */,
    XrmOptionDescList   /* options */,
    Cardinal        /* num_options */,
    Cardinal*       /* argc_in_out */,
    String*         /* argv_in_out */,
    CONST String*  /* fallback_resources */,
    ArgList         /* args */,
    Cardinal        /* num_args */
);

Widget XtVaAppInitialize(
    XtAppContext*  /* app_context_return */,
    CONST String   /* application_class */,
    XrmOptionDescList   /* options */,
    Cardinal       /* num_options */,
    Cardinal*      /* argc_in_out */,
    String*        /* argv_in_out */,
    CONST String*  /* fallback_resources */,
    ...
);
```

```
Widget XtInitialize(
    CONST String    /* name */,
    CONST String    /* class */,
    XrmOptionDescRec     /* options */,
    Cardinal        /* num_options */,
    Cardinal*       /* argc */,
    char**          /* argv */
);

Display *XtOpenDisplay(
    XtAppContext    /* appContext */,
    CONST String    /* displayName */,
    CONST String    /* applName */,
    CONST String    /* className */,
    XrmOptionDescRec*     /* urlist */,
    Cardinal        /* num_urs */,
    Cardinal*       /* argc */,
    char**          /* argv */
);

XtAppContext XtCreateApplicationContext(
    void
);

void XtAppSetFallbackResources(
    XtAppContext    /* app_context */,
    CONST String*   /* specification_list */
);

void XtDestroyApplicationContext(
    XtAppContext    /* appContext */
);

void XtInitializeWidgetClass(
    WidgetClass     /* widget_class */
);

XtAppContext XtWidgetToApplicationContext(
    Widget          /* widget */
);

XtAppContext XtDisplayToApplicationContext(
    Display*        /* dpy */
);
```

```
XrmDatabase XtDatabase(
    Display*        /* dpy */
);

void XtCloseDisplay(
    Display*        /* dpy */
);

void XtCopyFromParent(
    Widget          /* widget */,
    int             /* offset */,
    XrmValue*       /* value */
);

void XtCopyDefaultDepth(
    Widget          /* widget */,
    int             /* offset */,
    XrmValue*       /* value */
);

void XtCopyDefaultColormap(
    Widget          /* widget */,
    int             /* offset */,
    XrmValue*       /* value */
);

void XtCopyAncestorSensitive(
    Widget          /* widget */,
    int             /* offset */,
    XrmValue*       /* value */
);

void XtCopyScreen(
    Widget          /* widget */,
    int             /* offset */,
    XrmValue*       /* value */
);

void XrmCompileResourceList(
    XtResourceList        /* resources */,
    Cardinal        /* num_resources */
);
```

```
void XtGetApplicationResources(
    Widget          /* widget */,
    XtPointer           /* base */,
    XtResourceList      /* resources */,
    Cardinal        /* num_resources */,
    ArgList         /* args */,
    Cardinal        /* num_args */
);

void XtVaGetApplicationResources(
    Widget          /* widget */,
    XtPointer       /* base */,
    XtResourceList /* resources */,
    Cardinal        /* num_resources */,
    ...
);

void XtGetSubresources(
    Widget          /* widget */,
    XtPointer           /* base */,
    CONST String    /* name */,
    CONST String    /* class */,
    XtResourceList      /* resources */,
    Cardinal        /* num_resources */,
    ArgList         /* args */,
    Cardinal        /* num_args */
);

void XtVaGetSubresources(
    Widget          /* widget */,
    XtPointer       /* base */,
    CONST String    /* name */,
    CONST String    /* class */,
    XtResourceList /* resources */,
    Cardinal        /* num_resources */,
    ...
);

void XtSetValues(
    Widget          /* widget */,
    ArgList         /* args */,
    Cardinal        /* num_args */
);
```

```
void XtVaSetValues(
    Widget          /* widget */,
    ...
);

void XtGetValues(
    Widget          /* widget */,
    ArgList         /* args */,
    Cardinal        /* num_args */
);

void XtVaGetValues(
    Widget          /* widget */,
    ...
);

void XtSetSubvalues(
    XtPointer            /* base */,
    XtResourceList       /* resources */,
    Cardinal        /* num_resources */,
    ArgList         /* args */,
    Cardinal        /* num_args */
);

void XtVaSetSubvalues(
    XtPointer       /* base */,
    XtResourceList  /* resources */,
    Cardinal        /* num_resources */,
    ...
);

void XtGetSubvalues(
    XtPointer            /* base */,
    XtResourceList       /* resources */,
    Cardinal        /* num_resources */,
    ArgList         /* args */,
    Cardinal        /* num_args */
);

void XtVaGetSubvalues(
    XtPointer       /* base */,
    XtResourceList  /* resources */,
    Cardinal        /* num_resources */,
    ...
);
```

```
void XtGetResourceList(
    WidgetClass    /* widget_class */,
    XtResourceList*      /* resources_return */,
    Cardinal*      /* num_resources_return */
);

void XtGetConstraintResourceList(
    WidgetClass    /* widget_class */,
    XtResourceList*      /* resources_return */,
    Cardinal*      /* num_resources_return */
);

#define XtUnspecifiedPixmap    ((Pixmap)2)
#define XtUnspecifiedShellInt       (-1)
#define XtUnspecifiedWindow    ((Window)2)
#define XtUnspecifiedWindowGroup ((Window)3)
#define XtDefaultForeground  "XtDefaultForeground"
#define XtDefaultBackground  "XtDefaultBackground"
#define XtDefaultFont        "XtDefaultFont"

#define XtOffset(p_type,field) \
    ((Cardinal) (((char *) (&(((p_type)NULL)->field))) - ((char *)
NULL)))

#define XtOffsetOf(s_type,field) XtOffset(s_type*,field)
```

B.25. Error Handling

```
XtErrorMsgHandler XtAppSetErrorMsgHandler(
    XtAppContext   /* app */,
    XtErrorMsgHandler   /* handler */
);

void XtSetErrorMsgHandler(
    XtErrorMsgHandler   /* handler */
);

XtErrorMsgHandler XtAppSetWarningMsgHandler(
    XtAppContext   /* app */,
    XtErrorMsgHandler   /* handler */
);
```

```
void XtSetWarningMsgHandler(
    XtErrorMsgHandler    /* handler */
);

void XtAppErrorMsg(
    XtAppContext    /* app */,
    CONST String    /* name */,
    CONST String    /* type */,
    CONST String    /* class */,
    CONST String    /* defaultp */,
    String*         /* params */,
    Cardinal*       /* num_params */
);

void XtErrorMsg(
    CONST String    /* name */,
    CONST String    /* type */,
    CONST String    /* class */,
    CONST String    /* defaultp */,
    String*         /* params */,
    Cardinal*       /* num_params */
);

void XtAppWarningMsg(
    XtAppContext    /* app */,
    CONST String    /* name */,
    CONST String    /* type */,
    CONST String    /* class */,
    CONST String    /* defaultp */,
    String*         /* params */,
    Cardinal*       /* num_params */
);

void XtWarningMsg(
    CONST String    /* name */,
    CONST String    /* type */,
    CONST String    /* class */,
    CONST String    /* defaultp */,
    String*         /* params */,
    Cardinal*       /* num_params */
);
```

```
XtErrorHandler XtAppSetErrorHandler(
    XtAppContext   /* app */,
    XtErrorHandler      /* handler */
);

void XtSetErrorHandler(
    XtErrorHandler      /* handler */
);

XtErrorHandler XtAppSetWarningHandler(
    XtAppContext   /* app */,
    XtErrorHandler      /* handler */
);

void XtSetWarningHandler(
    XtErrorHandler      /* handler */
);

void XtAppError(
    XtAppContext   /* app */,
    CONST String   /* message */
);

void XtError(
    CONST String   /* message */
);

void XtAppWarning(
    XtAppContext   /* app */,
    CONST String   /* message */
);

void XtWarning(
    CONST String   /* message */
);

XrmDatabase *XtAppGetErrorDatabase(
    XtAppContext    /* app */
);

XrmDatabase *XtGetErrorDatabase(
    void
);
```

```
void XtAppGetErrorDatabaseText(
    XtAppContext    /* app */,
    CONST String    /* name */,
    CONST String    /* type */,
    CONST String    /* class */,
    CONST String    /* defaultp */,
    String          /* buffer */,
    int       /* nbytes */,
    XrmDatabase     /* database */
);

void XtGetErrorDatabaseText(
    CONST String    /* name */,
    CONST String    /* type */,
    CONST String    /* class */,
    CONST String    /* defaultp */,
    String          /* buffer */,
    int       /* nbytes */
);
```

B.26. Memory Management

```
#define XtNew(type) ((type *) XtMalloc((unsigned) sizeof(type)))
#define XtNewString(str) \
    ((str) == NULL ? NULL :
     (strcpy(XtMalloc((unsigned)strlen(str) + 1), str)))

char *XtMalloc(
    Cardinal        /* size */
);

char *XtCalloc(
    Cardinal        /* num */,
    Cardinal        /* size */
);

char *XtRealloc(
    char*           /* ptr */,
    Cardinal        /* num */
);

void XtFree(
    char*           /* ptr */
);
```

B.27. Work Procedures

```
XtWorkProcId XtAddWorkProc(
    XtWorkProc          /* proc */,
    XtPointer           /* closure */
);

XtWorkProcId XtAppAddWorkProc(
    XtAppContext   /* app */,
    XtWorkProc          /* proc */,
    XtPointer           /* closure */
);

void  XtRemoveWorkProc(
    XtWorkProcId   /* id */
);
```

B.28. Graphics Context

```
GC XtGetGC(
    Widget         /* widget */,
    XtGCMask       /* valueMask */,
    XGCValues*          /* values */
);

void XtDestroyGC(
    GC             /* gc */
);

void XtReleaseGC(
    Widget         /* object */,
    GC             /* gc */
);

void XtReleaseCacheRef(
    XtCacheRef*         /* cache_ref */
);

void XtCallbackReleaseCacheRef(
    Widget         /* widget */,
    XtPointer           /* closure */,    /* XtCacheRef */
    XtPointer           /* call_data */
);
```

```
void XtCallbackReleaseCacheRefList(
    Widget          /* widget */,
    XtPointer           /* closure */,    /* XtCacheRef* */
    XtPointer           /* call_data */
);

void XtSetWMColormapWindows(
    Widget          /* widget */,
    Widget*         /* list */,
    Cardinal        /* count */
);

String XtFindFile(
    CONST String    /* path */,
    Substitution    /* substitutions */,
    Cardinal        /* num_substitutions */,
    XtFilePredicate     /* predicate */
);

String XtResolvePathname(
    Display*        /* dpy */,
    CONST String    /* type */,
    CONST String    /* filename */,
    CONST String    /* suffix */,
    CONST String    /* path */,
    XtFilePredicate     /* predicate */
);
```

B.29. Selection Mechanisms

```
#define XT_CONVERT_FAIL (Atom)0x80000001

/*
 * The given widget no longer wants the selection.  If it still
 * owns it, then the selection owner is cleared, and the window's
 * losesSelection is called. */

void XtDisownSelection(
    Widget          /* widget */,
    Atom            /* selection */,
    Time            /* time */
);
```

```
/*
 * Get the value of the given selection.
 */

void XtGetSelectionValue(
    Widget          /* widget */,
    Atom            /* selection */,
    Atom            /* target */,
    XtSelectionCallbackProc /* callback */,
    XtPointer              /* closure */,
    Time            /* time */
);

void XtGetSelectionValues(
    Widget          /* widget */,
    Atom            /* selection */,
    Atom*           /* targets */,
    int        /* count */,
    XtSelectionCallbackProc /* callback */,
    XtPointer*             /* closures */,
    Time            /* time */
);

/* Set the selection timeout value, in units of milliseconds */

void XtAppSetSelectionTimeout(
    XtAppContext   /* app */,
    unsigned long  /* timeout */
);

void XtSetSelectionTimeout(
    unsigned long  /* timeout */
);

/* Return the selection timeout value, in units of milliseconds */

unsigned int XtAppGetSelectionTimeout(
    XtAppContext   /* app */
);

unsigned int XtGetSelectionTimeout(
    void
);
```

```
XSelectionRequestEvent *XtGetSelectionRequest(
    Widget          /* widget */,
    Atom            /* selection */,
    XtRequestId     /* request_id */
);

void XtGetSelectionValueIncremental(
    Widget          /* widget */,
    Atom            /* selection */,
    Atom            /* target */,
    XtSelectionCallbackProc /* selection_callback */,
    XtPointer            /* client_data */,
    Time            /* time */
);

void XtGetSelectionValuesIncremental(
    Widget          /* widget */,
    Atom            /* selection */,
    Atom*           /* targets */,
    int        /* count */,
    XtSelectionCallbackProc /* callback */,
    XtPointer*           /* client_data */,
    Time            /* time */
);
```

B.30. Grabs

```
void XtGrabKey(
    Widget          /* widget */,
    KeySym          /* keysym */,
    Modifiers       /* modifiers */,
    Boolean         /* owner_events */,
    int        /* pointer_mode */,
    int        /* keyboard_mode */
);

void XtUngrabKey(
    Widget          /* widget */,
    KeySym          /* keysym */,
    Modifiers       /* modifiers */
);
```

```
int XtGrabKeyboard(
    Widget          /* widget */,
    Boolean         /* owner_events */,
    int        /* pointer_mode */,
    int        /* keyboard_mode */,
    Time            /* time */
);

void XtUngrabKeyboard(
    Widget          /* widget */,
    Time            /* time */
);

void XtGrabButton(
    Widget          /* widget */,
    int        /* button */,
    Modifiers       /* modifiers */,
    Boolean         /* owner_events */,
    unsigned int    /* event_mask */,
    int        /* pointer_mode */,
    int        /* keyboard_mode */,
    Window          /* confine_to */,
    Cursor          /* cursor */
);

void XtUngrabButton(
    Widget          /* widget */,
    unsigned int    /* button */,
    Modifiers       /* modifiers */
);

int XtGrabPointer(
    Widget          /* widget */,
    Boolean         /* owner_events */,
    unsigned int    /* event_mask */,
    int        /* pointer_mode */,
    int        /* keyboard_mode */,
    Window          /* confine_to */,
    Cursor          /* cursor */,
    Time            /* time */
);

void XtUngrabPointer(
    Widget          /* widget */,
    Time            /* time */
);
```

B.31. Miscellaneous

```
void XtGetApplicationNameAndClass(
    Display*        /* dpy */,
    String*         /* name_return */,
    String*         /* class_return */
);
```

Appendix C

Quick Guide to the OSF/Motif Widget Set

This appendix details the important points of the OSF/Motif Widget Set. It can be used as a complete reference or a supplement to the OSF/Motif manuals.

C.1. OSF Widgets

Class Name	Pointer	Header	Type
XmArrowButton	xmArrowButtonWidgetClass	ArrowB.h	P
XmArrowButtonGadget	xmArrowButtonGadgetClass	ArrowBG.h	P
XmBulletinBoard	xmBulletinBoardWidgetClass	BulletinB.h	M
XmCascadeButton	xmCascadeButtonWidgetClass	CascadeB.h	P
XmCascadeButtonGadget	xmCascadeButtonGadgetClass	CascadeBG.h	P
XmCommand	xmCommandWidgetClass	Command.h	P
XmDialogShell	xmDialogShellWidgetClass	DialogS.h	M
XmDrawingArea	xmDrawingAreaWidgetClass	DrawingA.h	P
XmDrawnButton	xmDrawnButtonWidgetClass	DrawnB.h	P
XmFileSelectionBox	xmFileSelectionWidgetClass	FileSB.h	X
XmForm	xmFormWidget	Form.h	M
XmFrameWidget	xmFrameWidget	Frame.h	M
XmGadget	xmGadget	Gadget.h	P*
XmLabel	xmLabelWidgetClass	Label.h	P
XmLabelGadget	xmLabelGadgetClass	LabelG.h	P
XmList	xmListWidgetClass	List.h	P
XmMainWindow	xmMainWindowWidgetClass	MainW.h	X
XmManager	xmManagerWidgetClass		M*
XmMenuShell	xmMenuShellWidgetClass	MenuShell.h	M
XmMessageBox	xmMessageBoxWidgetClass	MessageB.h	X
XmPanedWindow	xmPanedWindowWidgetClass	PanedW.h	M
XmPrimitive	xmPrimitiveWidgetClass		P*

Class Name	Pointer	Header	Type
XmPushButton	xmPushButtonWidgetClass	PushB.h	P
XmRowColumn	xmRowColumnWidgetClass	RowColumn.h	M
XmSash	xmSashWidgetClass		PS
XmScale	xmScaleWidgetClass	Scale.h	X
XmScrollBar	xmScrollBarWidgetClass	ScrollBar.h	XPS
XmScrollWindow	xmScrollWindowWidgetClass	ScrolledW.h	X
XmSelectionBox	xmSelectionBoxWidgetClass	SelectioB.h	X
XmSeparator	xmSeparatorWidgetClass	Separator.h	PS
XmSeparatorGadget	xmSeparatorGadgetClass	SeparatoG.h	P
XmText	xmTextWidgetClass	Text.h	P
XmToggleButton	xmToggleButtonWidgetClass		P
XmToggleButtonGadget	xmToggleButtonGadgetClass		P

P represents a primitive widget/gadget.
M represents a manager widget (container).
X represents a widget composed with other widgets.
PS represents a primitive widget used to support other widgets.
* represents a meta widget.

C.2. Convenience Routines

The OSF/Motif Widget Set is quite complete. As a convenience to application writers, the developers have provided mechanisms for creating often-used display entities. The invocation is:

```
XmCreate[WhatYourCreating](parent,name,args,nargs)
```

where "parent" is the container this mechanism will belong to, "name" is the class name for this set of widgets, "args" is any Xm resources you would like to set, and "nargs" is the number of args.

The following convenience routines are available:

```
XmCreateErrorDialog( )
XmCreateFileSelectionDialog( )
XmCreateFormDialog( )
XmCreateInformationDialog( )
XmCreateMenuBar( )
XmCreateMessageDialog( )
XmCreateOptionMenu( )
XmCreatePopupMenu( )
XmCreatePromptDialog( )
XmCreatePulldownMenu( )
XmCreateQuestionDialog( )
```

```
XmCreateRadioBox( )
XmCreateScrolledList( )
XmCreateScrolledText( )
XmCreateSelectionDialog( )
XmCreateWarningDialog( )
XmCreateWorkingDialog( )
```

C.3. XmTextWidget Public Routines

The OSF/Motif Widget Set has a rather complex widget referred to as the "Text Widget." It is both a display and editing mechanism for text. Since it provides quite a bit of functionality, there are a few exported useful routines.

Return	Function and Description
char *	**XmTextGetString**(*XmTextWidget widget)* Retrieve the string from the widget.
void	**XmTextSetString**(*XmTextWidget widget, char *value)* Store a string to the widget.
void	**XmTextReplace**(*XmTextWidget widget, int frompos, int topos, char *value)* Replace/insert a string into the widget; to "replace," set frompos > topos, to "insert," set frompos = topos.
unsigned int	**XmTextGetEditable**(*XmTextWidget widget)* Determine if the text is editable.
void	**XmTextSetEditable**(*XmTextWidget widget, Boolean editable)* Tell the widget to be editable.
int	**XmTextGetMaxLength**(*XmTextWidget widget, int max_length)* Find out the maximum length for the string.
void	**XmTextSetMaxLength**(*XmTextWidget widget, int max_length)* Set the maximum length for the string.
char *	**XmTextGetSelection**(*XmTextWidget widget)* Extract the selection (highlighted area) from the widget.
void	**XmTextSetSelection**(*XmTextWidget widget, int frompos, int topos, Time time)* Set the selection in the widget.
void	**XmTextClearSelection**(*XmTextWidget widget, Time time)* Turn the selection off.

Return	Function and Description
XmTextPosition	**XmTextGetTopPosition***(XmTextWidget widget)* Find out the top line in the string that is displayed.
void	**XmTextSetTopPosition***(XmTextWidget widget, XmTextPosition top_positon)* Set the top line in the string to be displayed.
XmTextPosition	**XmTextGetInsertionPoint***(XmTextWidget widget)* Find out where the cursor is in the text.
void	**XmTextSetInsertionPoint***(XmTextWidget widget, XmTextPosition position)* Set the cursor to this position in the text.
Boolean	**XmTextGetSelectionPosition***(XmTextWidget widget, XmTextPosition *startpos, *endpos)* Determine the selection position.
XmTextPosition	**XmTextXYToPos***(XmTextWidget widget, Position x,y)* Given the x,y coordinates, find the position in the string.
Boolean	**XmTextPosToXY***(XmTextWidget widget, XmTextPosition position, Position *x, *y)* Given the position in the string, find the x,y coordinates.
void	**XmTextScroll***(XmTextWidget widget, int dir)* Scroll the text in the direction, where dir > 1 means scroll down, dir < 1 means scroll up.
void	**XmTextDisableRedisplay***(XmTextWidget widget, Boolean losesbackingstore)* Tell the widget not to make any more screen updates.
void	**XmTextEnableRedisplay***(XmTextWidget widget)* Tell the widget to continue making screen updates.

C.3.1. Compound Strings

Return	Function and Description
Boolean	**XmStringByteCompare***(XmString s1,s2)* Byte-by-byte compare of s1 and s2.
Boolean	**XmStringCompare***(XmString s1,s2)* Check if s1 and s2 are identical.
XmString	**XmStringConcat***(XmString s1,s2)* Just like strcat().
XmString	**XmStringCopy***(XmString s1)* Return a copy of s1.

Return	Function and Description
XmString	**XmStringCreate***(char *txt, XmStringCharSet charset)* Create a compound string out of txt using charset.
XmString	**XmStringCreateLtoR***(char *txt, XmStringCharSet charset)* Same as XmStringCreate except it converts \n to charset separators.
XmString	**XmStringDirectionCreate***(XmStringDirection direction)* Create a compound string with direction.
void	**XmStringDraw***(Display *d, Window w, XmFontList fontlist, XmString str, GC gc, Postion x,y, Dimension width, UChar align, lay_dir, XRectangle *clip)* Like XDrawString( ), but displays string with foreground only.
void	**XmStringDrawImage***(Display *d, Window w, XmFontList fontlist, XmString str, GC gc, Postion x,y, Dimension width, UChar align, lay_dir, XRectangle *clip)* Like XDrawImageString( ), but displays string with foreground and background.
void	**XmStringDrawUnderline***(Display *d, Window w, XmFontList fontlist,XmString str, GC gc, Postion x,y, Dimension width, UChar align, lay_dir, XRectangle *clip)* Draw an underlined compound string.
Boolean	**XmStringEmpty***(XmString str)* Check if str is empty.
void	**XmStringExtent***(XmFontList fontlist, XmString str, Dimension *width, *height)* Like XTextExtent( ), but returns the width and height of str.
XmFontList	**XmFontListAdd***(XmFontList old, XFontStruct *font, XmStringCharSet charset)* Add font to the font list destroying the old one.
XmFontList	**XmFontListCopy***(XmFontList fontlist)* Make a copy of fontlist.
XmFontList	**XmFontListCreate***(XFontStruct *font, XmStringCharSet charset)* Make a new font list using font.
void	**XmFontListFree***(XmFontList fontlist)* Free the storage used by fontlist.

Return	Function and Description
void	**XmStringFree**(*XmString str*) Free the storage used by str.
void	**XmStringFreeContext** (XmStringContext context) Free the storage used by context.
Boolean	**XmStringGetLtoR**(*XmString str, XmStringCharSet charset, char **txt*) Return the first component of the compound string found by searching left to right.
XmStringComponentType	**XmStringGetNextComponent**(*XmString context, char **txt, XmStringCharSet *charset, XmStringDirection *dir, XmStringComponentType *ctype, UShort *len, UChar **cval*) Get the next component of a compound string.
Boolean	**XmStringGetNextSegment**(*XmStringContext context, char **txt, XmStringCharSet *charset, XmStringDirection *dir, Boolean *separator*) Get the next segment of a compound string.
Dimension	**XmStringHeight**(*XmFontList fontlist, XmString str*) Get the height in pixels of a compound string.
Boolean	**XmStringInitContext**(*XmString *context, XmString str*) Create a string context used for XmStringGetNextComponent() or XmStringGetNextSegment().
int	**XmStringLength**(*XmString str*) Get the size (in bytes) of str.
int	**XmStringLineCount**(*XmString str*) Get the number of lines in str.
XmString	**XmStringCreateLtoR**(*char *txt, XmStringCharSet charset*) Same as XmStringCreateLtoR().
XmString	**XmStringNCopy**(*XmString s1, int n*) Return up to *n* chars of s1.
XmString	**XmStringNConcat**(*XmString s1,s2, int n*) Create a new string adding *n* bytes of s2 to s1.
XmString	**XmStringSegmentCreate**(*char *txt, XmStringCharSet charset, XmStringDirection dir, Boolean separator*) Create a segment using txt and charset in the direction dir adding a separator (when separator = TRUE).
voidXmString	**XmStringSeparatorCreate**() Get a string separator.
Dimension	**XmStringWidget**(*XmFontList fontlist, XmString str*) Get the width of str in pixels.

C.4. Resource Values

OSF/Motif widgets contain several resources that are specific to the widget set. For each of these resources there is a corresponding resource type that the resource represents. The following is a list of resource names, resource types, and the values for them:

XmNalignment (XmRAlignment)	XmALIGNMENT_CENTER XmALIGNMENT_END	XmALIGNMENT_BEGINNING
XmNarrowDirection (XmRArrowDirection)	XmARROW_UP XmARROW_LEFT	XmARROW_DOWN XmARROW_RIGHT
XmNattachment (XmRAttachment)	XmATTACH_NONE XmATTACH_OPPOSITE_FORM XmATTACH_OPPOSITE_WIDGET XmATTACH_SELF	XmATTACH_FORM XmATTACH_WIDGET XmATTACH_POSITION
XmNeditMode (XmREditMode)	XmMULTI_LINE_EDIT	XmSINGLE_LINE_EDIT
XmNdefaultButtonType (XmRDefaultButtonType)	XmDIALOG_OK_BUTTON XmDIALOG_HELP_BUTTON	XmDIALOG_CANCEL_BUTTON
XmNdialogStyle (XmRDialogStyle)	XmDIALOG_WORK_AREA XmDIALOG_APPLICATION_MODAL	XmDIALOG_MODELESS XmDIALOG_SYSTEM_MODAL
XmNdialogType (XmRDialogType)	XmDIALOG_ERROR XmDIALOG_MESSAGE XmDIALOG_WARNING XmDIALOG_PROMPT XmDIALOG_COMMAND	XmDIALOG_INFORMATION XmDIALOG_QUESTION XmDIALOG_WORKING XmDIALOG_SELECTION
XmNdisplayPolicy (XmRDisplayPolicy)	XmAS_NEEDED	XmSTATIC
XmNindicatorType (XmRIndicatorType)	XmN_OF_MANY	XmONE_OF_MANY
XmNlabelType (XmRLabelType)	XmSTRING	XmPIXMAP
XmNlistSizePolicy (XmRListSizePolicy)	XmCONSTANT XmRESIZE_IF_POSSIBLE	XmVARIABLE

XmNoreintation	XmVERTICAL	XmHORIZONTAL
(XmROreintation)		
XmNpacking	XmPACK_NONE	XmPACK_TIGHT
(XmRPacking)	XmPACK_COLUMN	
XmNrowColumnType	XmWORK_AREA	XmMENU_BAR
(XmRRowColumnType)	XmMENU_PULLDOWN	XmMENU_POPUP
	XmMENU_OPTION	
XmNsBPlacement	XmTOP_LEFT	XmTOP_RIGHT
(XmRSBPlacement)	XmBOTTOM_LEFT	XmBOTTOM_RIGHT
XmNprocessingDirection	XmMAX_ON_TOP	XmMAX_ON_BOTTOM
(XmRProcessingDirection)	XmMAX_ON_LEFT	XmMAN_ON_RIGHT
XmNresizePolicy	XmRESIZE_NONE	XmRESIZE_GROW
(XmRResizePolicy)	XmRESIZE_ANY	
XmNscrollPolicy	XmAUTOMATIC	XmAPPLICATION_DEFIND
(XmRScrollPolicy)		
XmNselectionPolicy	XmSINGLE_SELECT	XmMULTIPLE_SELECT
(XmRSelectionPolicy)	XmEXTENDED_SELECT	XmBROWSE_SELECT
XmNseparatorType	XmNO_LINE	XmSINGLE_LINE
(XmRSeparatorType)	XmDOUBLE_LINE	XmSINGLE_DASHED_LINE
	XmDOUBLE_DASHED_LINE	XmSHADOW_ETCHED_OUT
	XmSHADOW_ETCHED_IN	
XmNshadowType	XmSHADOW_ETCHED_IN	XmSHADOW_ETCHED_OUT
(XmRShadowType)	XmSHADOW_IN	XmSHADOW_OUT
XmNstringDirection	XmSTRING_DIRECTION_L_TO_R	
(XmRStringDirection)	XmSTRING_DIRECTION_R_TO_L	
XmNunitType	XmPIXELS	Xm100TH_MILLIMETERS
(XmRUnitType)	Xm100TH_INCHES	Xm100TH_POINTS
	Xm100TH_FONT_UNITS	
XmNvisualPolicy	XmVARIABLE	XmCONSTANT
(XmRVisualPolicy)		
XmNwhichButton	Button1	Button2
(XmRWhichButton)	Button3	Button4
	Button4	

C.5. Motif Callback Data Structures

The OSF/Motif Widget Set provides various callback procedures for the kinds of actions the widgets do. The following is a list of all the callback structures that are used by the various callback procedures used by OSF/Motif.

```
typedef struct {
    int         reason;
    XEvent      *event;
} XmAnyCallbackStruct;

typedef struct {
    int         reason;
    XEvent      *event;
    Window      window;
} XmDrawingAreaCallbackStruct;

typedef struct {
    int         reason;
    XEvent      *event;
    XmString    item;
    int         item_length;
    int         item_position;
    XmString    *selected_items;
    int         selected_item_count;
    int         selection_type;
} XmListCallbackStruct;

typedef struct{
    int         reason;
    XEvent      *event;
    int         value;
} XmScaleCallbackStruct;

typedef struct{
    int         reason;
    XEvent      *event;
    XmString    value;
    int         length;
} XmSelectionCallbackStruct;
```

```
typedef struct {
    int         reason;
    XEvent      *event;
    XmString    value;
    int         length;
    XmString    mask;
    int         mask_length;
} XmFileSelectionBoxCallbackStruct

typedef struct {
    int         reason;
    XEvent      *event;
    XmString    value;
    int         length;
} XmCommandCallbackStruct;

typedef struct {
    int         reason;
    XEvent      *event;
    Window      window;
} XmDrawnButtonCallbackStruct;

typedef struct {
    int         reason;
    XEvent      *event;
    Widget      widget;
    char        *data;
    char        *callbackstruct;
} XmRowColumnCallbackStruct;

typedef struct {
    int         reason;
    XEvent      *event;
    int         value;
} XmScrollBarCallbackStruct;

typedef struct {
    int         reason;
    XEvent      *event;
    int         set;
} XmToggleButtonCallbackStruct;
```

C.5.1. Possible Callback Reasons

XmCR_ACTIVATE	XmCR_ARM	XmCR_DISARM
XmCR_FOCUS	XmCR_MAP	XmCR_UNMAP
XmCR_CASCADING	XmCR_COMMAND_ENTERED	XmCR_RESIZE
XmCR_COMMAND_CHANGED	XmCR_EXPOSE	XmCR_INPUT
XmCR_HELP	XmCR_SINGLE_SELECT	XmCR_MULTIPLE_SELECT
XmCR_EXTENDED_SELECT	XmCR_BROWSE_SELECT	XmCR_DEFAULT_ACTION
XmCR_OK	XmCR_CANCEL	XmCR_VALUE_CHANGED
XmCR_DRAG	XmCR_INCREMENT	XmCR_DECREMENT
XmCR_PAGE_INCREMENT	XmCR_PAGE_DECREMENT	XmCR_TO_TOP
XmCR_TO_BOTTOM	XmCR_APPLY	XmCR_LOSING_FOCUS
XmCR_MODIFYING_TEXT_VALUE	XmCR_MOVING_INSERT_CURSOR	

The callback reasons are somewhat logical extensions of the resource names used by the widgets when specifying a callback. As you read through the next list, you will see that it is pretty simple to match the callback reason with the widget callback list.

C.5.2. Resources Used By Widget Classes

Widget	Resources	Type/Call Data Type
XmArrowButton	XtNarrowDirection	XmRArrowDirection
	XtNactivateCallback	XmNAnyCallbackStruct
	XtNarmCallback	XmNAnyCallbackStruct
	XtNdisarmCallback	XmNAnyCallbackStruct
XmArrowButtonGadget	XtNarrowDirection	XmRArrowDirection
	XtNactivateCallback	XmNAnyCallbackStruct
	XtNarmCallback	XmNAnyCallbackStruct
	XtNdisarmCallback	XmNAnyCallbackStruct
XmBulletinBoard	XmNshadowType	XmRShadowType
	XmNshadowThickness	XmRShort
	XmNmarginWidth	XmRShort
	XmNmarginHeight	XmRShort
	XmNdefaultButton	XmRWidget
	XmNcancelButton	XmRWidget
	XmNlabelFontList	XmRFontList
	XmNtextFontList	XmRFontList
	XmNtextTranslations	XmRTranslationTable
	XmNallowOverlap	XmRBoolean
	XmNautoUnmanage	XmRBoolean
	XmNdefaultPosition	XmRBoolean

Widget	Resources	Type/Call Data Type
	XmNresizePolicy	XmRResizePolicy
	XmNnoResize	XmRBoolean
	XmNdialogStyle	XmRDialogStyle
	XmNdialogTitle	XmRXmString
	XmNfocusCallback	XmAnyCallbackStruct
	XmNmapCallback	XmAnyCallbackStruct
	XmNunmapCallback	XmAnyCallbackStruct
XmCascadeButton	XmNsubMenuId	XmRMenuWidget
	XmNcascadePixmap	XmRPrimForegroundPixmap
	XmNmappingDelay	XmRInt
	XmNactivateCallback	XmAnyCallbackStruct
	XmNcascadingCallback	XmAnyCallbacksStruct
XmCascadeButtonGadget	XmNsubMenuId	XmRMenuWidget
	XmNcascadePixmap	XmRPrimForegroundPixmap
	XmNmappingDelay	XmRInt
	XmNactivateCallback	XmAnyCallbackStruct
	XmNcascadingCallback	XmAnyCallbacksStruct
XmCommand	XmNpromptString	XmRXmString
	XmNcommand	XmRXmString
	XmNhistoryItems	XmRXmStringTable
	XmNhistoryItemCount	XmRInt
	XmNhistoryMaxItems	XmRInt
	XmNhistoryVisibleItemCount	XmRInt
	XmNcommandEnteredCallback	XmCommandCallbackStruct
	XmNcommandChangedCallback	XmCommandCallbackStruct
XmDialogShell	XmNdeleteResponse	XmRDeleteResponse
XmDrawingArea	XmNmarginWidth	XmRShort
	XmNmarginHeight	XmRShort
	XmNresizePolicy	XmRResizePolicy
	XmNresizeCallback	XmDrawingAreaCallbackStruct
	XmNexposeCallback	XmDrawingAreaCallbackStruct
	XmNinputCallback	XmRDrawingAreaCallbackStruct
XmDrawnButton	XmNpushButtonEnabled	XmRBoolean
	XmNshadowType	XmRShadowType
	XmNactivateCallback	XmDrawnButtonCallbackStruct
	XmNarmCallback	XmDrawnButtonCallbackStruct
	XmNdisarmCallback	XmDrawnButtonCallbackStruct

Widget	Resources	Type/Call Data Type
	XmNexposeCallback	XmDrawnButtonCallbackStruct
	XmNresizeCallback	XmDrawnButtonCallbackStruct
XmFileSelectionBox	XmNdirSpec	XmRXmString
	XmNfilterLabelString	XmRXmString
	XmNdirMask	XmRXmString
	XmNfileSearchProc	XmRProc
	XmNlistUpdated	XmRBoolean
XmForm	XmNhorizontalSpacing	XmRInt
	XmNverticalSpacing	XmRInt
	XmNfractionBase	XmRInt
	XmNrubberPositioning	XmRBoolean
	Constraints	
	XmNtopAttachment	XmRAttachment
	XmNbottomAttachment	XmRAttachment
	XmNleftAttachment	XmRAttachment
	XmNrightAttachment	XmRAttachment
	XmNtopWidget	XmRWidget
	XmNbottomWidget	XmRWidget
	XmNleftWidget	XmRWidget
	XmNrightWidget	XmRWidget
	XmNtopPosition	XmRInt
	XmNbottomPosition	XmRInt
	XmNleftPosition	XmRInt
	XmNrightPosition	XmRInt
	XmNtopOffset	XmRInt
	XmNbottomOffset	XmRInt
	XmNleftOffset	XmRInt
	XmNrightOffset	XmRInt
	XmNresizeable	XmRBoolean
XmFrameWidget	XmNmarginWidth	XmRShort
	XmNmarginHeight	XmRShort
	XmNshadowType	XmRShadowType
XmGadget	XmNtraversalOn	XmRBoolean
	XmNhighlightOnEnter	XmRBoolean
	XmNhighlightThickness	XmRShort
	XmNshadowThickness	XmRShort
	XmNunitType	XmRUnitType
	XmNuserData	XmRPointer
	XmNhelpCallback	XmAnyCallbackStruct

Widget	Resources	Type/Call Data Type
XmLabel	XmNalignment	XmRAlignment
	XmNlabelType	XmRLabelType
	XmNlabelString	XmRXmString
	XmNmarginWidth	XmRShort
	XmNmarginHeight	XmRShort
	XmNmarginRight	XmRShort
	XmNmarginLeft	XmRShort
	XmNmarginBottom	XmRShort
	XmNmarginHeight	XmRShort
	XmNfontList	XmRFontList
	XmNlabelPixmap	XmRPrimForegroundPixmap
	XmNlabelInsensitivePixmap	XmRPixmap
	XmNstringDirection	XmRStringDirection
	XmNmnemonic	XmRChar
	XmNaccelerator	XmRString
	XmNacceleratorText	XmRXmString
	XmNrecomputeSize	XmRBoolean
XmLabelGadget	XmNalignment	XmRAlignment
	XmNlabelType	XmRLabelType
	XmNlabelString	XmRXmString
	XmNmarginWidth	XmRShort
	XmNmarginHeight	XmRShort
	XmNmarginRight	XmRShort
	XmNmarginLeft	XmRShort
	XmNmarginBottom	XmRShort
	XmNmarginHeight	XmRShort
	XmNfontList	XmRFontList
	XmNlabelPixmap	XmRPrimForegroundPixmap
	XmNlabelInsensitivePixmap	XmRPixmap
	XmNmnemonic	XmRChar
	XmNaccelerator	XmRString
	XmNacceleratorText	XmRXmString
	XmNrecomputeSize	XmRBoolean
	XmNstringDirection	XmRStringDirection
XmList	XmNlistSpacing	XmRShort
	XmNlistMarginWidth	XmRShort
	XmNlistMarginHeight	XmRShort
	XmNfontList	XmRFontList
	XmNitems	XmRXmStringTable
	XmNitemCount	XmRInt
	XmNselectedItems	XmRXmStringTable

Widget	Resources	Type/Call Data Type
	XmNselectedItemCount	XmRInt
	XmNvisibleItemCount	XmRInt
	XmNselectionPolicy	XmRSelectionPolicy
	XmNlistSizePolicy	XmRListSizePolicy
	XmNscrollBarDisplayPolicy	XmRScrollBarDisplayPolicy
	XmNautomaticSelection	XmRBoolean
	XmNhorizontalScrollBar	XmRWidget
	XmNverticalScrollBar	XmRWidget
	XmNsingleSelectionCallback	XmListCallbackStruct
	XmNmultipleSelectionCallback	XmListCallbackStruct
	XmNextendedSelectionCallback	XmListCallbackStruct
	XmNscrollBarPlacement	XmRScrollBarPlacement
	XmNscrolledWindowMarginHeight	XmRShort
	XmNscrolledWindowMarginWidth	XmRShort
	XmNbrowseSelectionCallback	XmListCallbackStruct
	XmNdefaultActionCallback	XmListCallbackStruct
XmMainWindow	XmNcommandWindow	XmRWidget
	XmNmenuBar	XmRWidget
	XmNmainWindowMarginWidth	XmRShort
	XmNmainWindowMarginHeight	XmRShort
	XmNshowSeparator	XmRBoolean
	XmNhighlightColor	XmRPixel
	XmNhighlightPixmap	XmRManHightlightPixmap
	XmNunitType	XmRUnitType
	XmNshadowThickness	XmRShort
	XmNtopShadowColor	XmRPixel
	XmNtopShadowPixmap	XmRManTopShadowPixmap
	XmNbottomShadowColor	XmRPixel
	XmNbottomShadowPixmap	XmRManBottomShadowPixmap
	XmNuserData	XmRPointer
	XmNUnitType	XmRUnitType
XmMenuShell	XmNsaveUnder	XmRBoolean
	XmNallowShellResize	XmRBoolean
XmMessageBox	XmNdialogType	XmRDialogType
	XmNminimizeButton	XmRBoolean
	XmNdefaultButtonType	XmRDefaultButtonType
	XmNmessageString	XmRXmString
	XmNmessageAlignment	XmRAlignment
	XmNsymbolPixmap	XmRManForegroundPixmap
	XmNokLabelString	XmRXmString

Widget	Resources	Type/Call Data Type
	XmNcancelLabelString	XmRXmString
	XmNhelpLabelString	XmRXmString
	XmNokCallback	XmAnyCallbackStruct
	XmNcancel	XmAnyCallbackStruct
XmPanedWindow	XmNmarginWidth	XmRShort
	XmNmarginHeight	XmRShort
	XmNspacing	XmRInt
	XmNrefigureMode	XmRBoolean
	XmNseparatorOn	XmRBoolean
	XmNsashIndent	XmRPosition
	XmNsashWidth	XmRDimension
	XmNsashHeight	XmRDimension
	XmNsashShadowThickness	XmRInt
	Constraints	
	XmNallowResize	XmRBoolean
	XmNminimum	XmRInt
	XmNmaximum	XmRInt
	XmNskipAdjust	XmRBoolean
XmPrimitive	XmNforeground	XmRPixel
	XmNbackgroundPixmap	XmRPixmap
	XmNborderWidth	XmRDimension
	XmNhighlightColor	XmRPixel
	XmNhighlightOnEnter	XmRBoolean
	XmNhighlightPixmap	XmRPrimHightlightPixmap
	XmNhighlightThickness	XmRShort
	XmNshadowThickness	XmRShort
	XmNtopShadowColor	XmRPixel
	XmNtopShadowPixmap	XmRPrimTopShadowPixmap
	XmNbottomShadowColor	XmRPixel
	XmNbottomShadowPixmap	XmRPrimBottomShadowPixmap
	XmNuserData	XmRPointer
	XmNhelpCallback	XmRCallback
	XmNtraverselOn	XmRBoolean
XmPushButton	XmNfillOnArm	XmRBoolean
	XmNarmColor	XmRPixel
	XmNarmPixmap	XmRPrimForegroundPixmap
	XmNshowAsDefault	XmRShort
	XmNshadowThickness	XmRShort
	XmNactivateCallback	XmAnyCallbackStruct
	XmNarmCallback	XmAnyCallbackStruct
	XmNdisarmCallback	XmAnyCallbackStruct

Widget	Resources	Type/Call Data Type
XmRowColumn	XmNresizeWidth	XmRBoolean
	XmNresizeHeight	XmRBoolean
	XmNadjustLast	XmRBoolean
	XmNmarginWidth	XmRDimension
	XmNmarginHeight	XmRDimension
	XmNspacing	XmRDimension
	XmNisAligned	XmRBoolean
	XmNadjustMargin	XmRBoolean
	XmNradioBehavior	XmRBoolean
	XmNradioAlwaysOne	XmRBoolean
	XmNisHomogeneous	XmRBoolean
	XmNentryClass	XmRInt
	XmNwhichButton	XmRButton
	XmNnowCursor	XmRPixmap
	XmNmenuHelpWidget	XmRMenuWidget
	XmNlabelString	XmRXmString
	XmNsubMenuId	XmRMenuWidget
	XmNmenuHistory	XmRMenuWidget
	XmNpopupEnabled	XmRBoolean
	XmNnumColumns	XmRShort
	XmNentryAlignment	XmRAlignment
	XmNrowColumnType	XmRRowColumnType
	XmNpacking	XmRPacking
	XmNmnemonic	XmRChar
	XmNorientation	XmROrientation
	XmNentryBorder	XmRDimension
	XmNmenuAccelerator	XmRString
	XmNentryCallback	XmRowColumnCallbackStruct
	XmNmapCallback	XmAnyCallbackStruct
	XmNunmapCallback	XmAnyCallbackStruct
XmSash	XmNborderWidth	XmRDimension
	XmNcallback	XmRCallback
XmScale	XmNvalue	XmRInt
	XmNmaximum	XmRInt
	XmNminimum	XmRint
	XmNorientation	XmROrientation
	XmNprocessingDirection	XmRProcessingDirection
	XmNtitleString	XmRXmString
	XmNfontList	XmRFontList
	XmNshowValue	XmRBoolean
	XmNdecimalPoints	XmRShort

Widget	Resources	Type/Call Data Type
	XmNscaleWidth	XmRDimension
	XmNscaleHeight	XmRDimension
	XmNhighlightOnEnter	XmRBoolean
	XmNhighlightThickness	XmRShort
	XmNvalueChangedCallback	XmScaleCallbackStruct
	XmNdragCallback	XmScaleCallbackStruct
XmScrollBar	XmNvalue	XmRInt
	XmNminimum	XmRInt
	XmNmaximum	XmRInt
	XmNsliderSize	XmRInt
	XmNshowArrows	XmRBoolean
	XmNorientation	XmROrientation
	XmNprocessingDirection	XmRProcessingDirection
	XmNincrement	XmRInt
	XmNpageIncrement	XmRInt
	XmNinitialDelay	XmRInt
	XmNrepeatDelay	XmRInt
	XmNvalueChangedCallback	XmScrollBarCallbackStruct
	XmNincrementCallback	XmScrollBarCallbackStruct
	XmNdecrementCallback	XmScrollBarCallbackStruct
	XmNpageIncrementCallback	XmScrollBarCallbackStruct
	XmNpageDecrementCallback	XmScrollBarCallbackStruct
	XmNtoTopCallback	XmScrollBarCallbackStruct
	XmNtoBottomCallback	XmScrollBarCallbackStruct
	XmdragCallback	XmScrollBarCallbackStruct
XmScrollWindow	XmNhorizontalScrollBar	XmRWidget
	XmNverticalScrollBar	XmRWidget
	XmNworkWindow	XmRWidget
	XmNclipWindow	XmRWidget
	XmNscrollingPolicy	XmRScrollingPolicy
	XmNvisualPolicy	XmRVisualPolicy
	XmNscrollBarDisplayPolicy	XmRScrollBarDisplayPolicy
	XmNscrollBarPlacement	XmRScrollBarPlacement
	XmNscrolledWindowMarginWidth	XmRShort
	XmNscrolledWindowMarginHeight	XmRShort
	XmNspacing	XmRInt
XmSelectionBox	XmNtextAccelerators	XmRAcceleratorTable
	XmNselectionLabelString	XmRXmString
	XmNlistLabelString	XmRXmString

Widget	Resources	Type/Call Data Type
	XmNtextColumns	XmRInt
	XmNtextString	XmRXmString
	XmNlistItems	XmRXmStringTable
	XmNlistItemCount	XmRInt
	XmNlistVisibleItemCount	XmRInt
	XmNokLabelString	XmRXmString
	XmNapplyLabelString	XmRXmString
	XmNcancelLabelString	XmRXmString
	XmNhelpLabelString	XmRXmString
	XmNmustMatch	XmRBoolean
	XmNminimizeButtons	XmRBoolean
	XmNdialogType	XmRDialogType
	XmNokCallback	XmAnyCallbackStruct
	XmNapplCallback	XmAnyCallbackStruct
	XmNcancelCallback	XmAnyCallbackStruct
	XmNnoMatchCallback	XmAnyCallbackStruct
XmSeparator	XmNseparatorType	XmRSeparatorType
	XmNmargin	XmRShort
	XmNorientation	XmROrientation
XmSeparatorGadget	XmNseparatorType	XmRSeparatorType
	XmNmargin	XmRShort
	XmNorientation	XmROrientation
XmToggleButton	XmNindicatorType	XmRIndicatorType
	XmNvisibleWhenOff	XmRBoolean
	XmNspacing	XmRShort
	XmNselectPixmap	XmRPixmap
	XmNselectInsenstivePixmap	XmRPixmap
	XmNset	XmRBoolean
	XmNindicatorOn	XmRBoolean
	XmNfillOnSelect	XmRBoolean
	XmNselectColor	XmRPixel
	XmNvalueChangedCallback	XmToggleButtonCallbackStruct
	XmNarmdCallback	XmToggleButtonCallbackStruct
	XmNdisarmdCallback	XmToggleButtonCallbackStruct
XmToggleButtonGadget	XmNindicatorType	XmRIndicatorType
	XmNvisibleWhenOff	XmRBoolean
	XmNspacing	XmRShort
	XmNselectPixmap	XmRPixmap
	XmNselectInsenstivePixmap	XmRPixmap

Widget	Resources	Type/Call Data Type
	XmNset	XmRBoolean
	XmNindicatorOn	XmRBoolean
	XmNfillOnSelect	XmRBoolean
	XmNselectColor	XmRPixel
	XmNvalueChangedCallback	XmToggleButtonCallbackStruct
	XmNarmedCallback	XmToggleButtonCallbackStruct
	XmNdisarmedCallback	XmToggleButtonCallbackStruct
XmText	XmNvalue	XmRString
	XmNmaxLength	XmRInt
	XmNmarginHeight	XmRShort
	XmNmarginWidth	XmRShort
	XmNoutputCreate	XmRFunction
	XmNinputCreate	XmRFunction
	XmNtopPosition	XmRInt
	XmNcursorPosition	XmRInt
	XmNeditMode	XmREditMode
	XmNautoShowCursorPosition	XmRBoolean
	XmNeditable	XmRBoolean
	XmNwordWrap	XmRBoolean
	XmNblinkRate	XmRShort
	XmNpendingDelete	XmRBoolean
	XmNselectThreshold	XmRInt
	XmNfontList	XmRFontList
	XmNcolumns	XmRShort
	XmNrows	XmRShort
	XmNresizeWidth	XmRBoolean
	XmNresizeHeight	XmRBoolean
	XmNscrollVertical	XmRBoolean
	XmNscrollHorizontal	XmRBoolean
	XmNscrollLeftSide	XmRBoolean
	XmNscrollRightSide	XmRBoolean
	XmNcursorPositionVisible	XmRBoolean
	XmNactivateCallback	XmAnyCallbackStruct
	XmNfocusCallback	XmAnyCallbackStruct
	XmNlosingFocusCallback	XmAnyCallbackStruct
	XmNvalueChangedCallback	XmAnyCallbackStruct
	XmNmodifyVerifyCallback	XmTextVerifyCallbackStruct
	XmNmotionVerifyCallback	XmTextVerifyCallbackStruct

Bibliography

Asente, P., "Simplicity and Productivity," *Unix Review*, vol. 6, No. 9, pp. 57–63.

Jones, O., *Introduction to the X Window System*, Prentice Hall, 1989.

Kerningham, B. W. and R. Pike, *The Unix Programming Environment*, Prentice Hall, 1978.

Kerningham, B. W. and D. M. Ritchie, *The C Programming Language*, Prentice Hall, 1985.

Lemke, D. and S. H. Rosenthall, "Visualizing X11 Clients," Proceedings of the Summer 1988 USENIX Conference, pp. 125–138.

McCormack, J. and P. Asente, "Using the X Toolkit or How to Write a Widget," in Proceedings of the Summer 1988 USENIX Conference, pp. 1–13.

_ "An Overview of the X Toolkit," in Proceedings of the October 1988 ACM SIGGRAPH Symposium on User Interface Software, pp. 46–55.

Nye, A., *The Xlib Programming Manual*, O'Reilly and Associates, 1988.

O'Reilly, T., "The Toolkits (and Politics) of X Windows," *UNIX World*, vol. 6, No. 2, pp. 66–73, February, 1989.

OSF, *OSF/Motif Programmer's Guide*, Prentice Hall, 1990.

Rochkind, M., *Advanced Unix Programming*, Prentice Hall, 1985.

Rosenthal, D. S., "A Simple X.11 Client Program, or, How Hard Can It Really Be to Write 'Hello World'?" in Proceedings of the Winter 1988 USENIX Conference, pp. 229–235.

Schaufler, R. W., and J. Gettys, "The X Window System," *ACM Transaction on Graphics,* vol. 5, No. 2, pp. 79–109, April 1986.

Stroustrup, B., *The C++ Programming Language*, Addison-Wesley, 1986.

Swich, R. R., and M. S. Akerman, "The X Toolkit: More Bricks for Building User Interfaces," in Proceedings of the Winter 1988 USENIX Conference, pp. 221–223.

Young, D., *The X Window System: Programming and Applications with Xt*, Prentice Hall, 1989.

Index

G

H

I

K

L

M

N

O

P

R